JESUS,
Revolutionary of the Poor

JESUS,
Revolutionary of the Poor

Matthew's Subversive Messiah

Mark Bredin

With a foreword by
Willard M. Swartley

CASCADE *Books* • Eugene, Oregon

JESUS, REVOLUTIONARY OF THE POOR
Matthew's Subversive Messiah

Cascade Books
An Imprint of Wipf and Stock Publishers
199 W. 8th Ave., Suite 3
Eugene, OR 97401

www.wipfandstock.com

PAPERBACK ISBN: 978-1-62564-137-3
HARDCOVER ISBN: 978-1-4982-8508-7
EBOOK ISBN: 978-1-5326-4254-8

Cataloguing-in-Publication data:

Names: Bredin, Mark. | Swartley, Willard M., foreword writer.

Title: Jesus, revolutionary of the poor : Matthew's subversive messiah / Mark Bredin, with a foreword by Willard M. Swartley.

Description: Eugene, OR: Cascade Books, 2017 | Includes bibliographical references and index.

Identifiers: ISBN 978-1-62564-137-3 (paperback) | ISBN 978-1-4982-8508-7 (hardcover) | ISBN 978-1-5326-4254-8 (ebook)

Subjects: LCSH: Bible. Matthew—Criticism, interpretation, etc. | Poverty in the Bible | Jesus Christ—Political and social views | Social justice—Biblical teaching | Christianity and politics—Biblical teaching

Classification: BS2575.52 B74 2017 (paperback) | BS2575.52 (ebook)

Manufactured in the U.S.A. 10/20/17

Dedicated to my beautiful granddaughter, Maddie (born 2016).
May she grow up to nurture and care for all around her and
experience the joy of doing so.

O Lord, take full possession of my heart, raise there your throne and command there as you command in heaven. Being created by you, let me live to you. Being created for you, let me always act for your glory. Being redeemed by you, let me return to you what is yours, and let my spirit ever cling to you alone; for your name's sake.

—John Wesley

Contents

Foreword

Every chapter of this book draws us into the loving care of our Creator God manifest supremely in Jesus, the God who made all things good for humans to enjoy. It also takes seriously the "have nots" that suffer for lack of the good things God desires for human *shalom*. It is a book of radical ethics, depth, Scripture study, and conversation-partners (John Woolman, Dorothy Day, Gandhi, numerous widely recognized Matthean scholars, and still many more), guided by the goal of enabling readers to achieve God's creation intent for humans to flourish and live *shalom*.

Under this canopy of the Creator God's desire for humans—abundance, *shalom*, dignity and more—Mark Bredin makes a distinctive, virtually unique, contribution to the study of Matthew's Gospel. How is this so, since Bredin is a PhD graduate from St. Andrews University, Scotland, with his dissertation supervised by Richard Bauckham,[1] whose wisdom influenced Bredin and shines through in this book, though Bredin's GPS at times takes him a different route? How and why does Bredin bring such diverse cultural eyes to this study? Once you read this book, you will never see Matthew in the same light of traditional interpretation. From whence do Bredin's eyes see and appreciate cultural diversity in textual meaning?

These days, intercultural reading of biblical texts is prominent, from the early work of Ernesto Cardenal's Solentiname to the more recent plethora of publications: R. S. Sugirtharajah to Musa Dube to Elsa Tamez to Hans de Wit, Daniel Schipani, et al. But Bredin's contribution doesn't fit this mold either. Yet there are similarities because Bredin's Quaker's eyes have been opened by multi-cultural experiences, of which three merit mention: working with the severely disabled,[2] teaching in Tanzania and Zimbabwe, and serving now as a prison chaplain. Each of these life experiences shape

1. Bredin, *Jesus, Revolutionary of Peace.*

2. Bredin, *True Beauty.*

his perception. But even more keenly, his passion for creation care,[3] being rooted and grounded in the soil for his own produce with love for God's generosity in the beauty and diversity of creation, shapes what he sees and how he reads and interprets Matthew. Add to this his dissertation on Revelation, which explores the comparison between Jesus and Gandhi on how to confront and transform systemic evil. In short, Bredin reads the text with multiple cultural eyes and perceptions.

From what "poor in spirit" means, to "care for the despised," to *shalom* justice,—Bredin makes us ponder who we are socially, economically, and politically, and why our readings of Scripture are unconsciously reflective of bourgeoisie/elitist culture.

How does a severely disabled person think about God? What in Matthew connects to prisoners? Why do Tanzanian Christians see truth in Scripture that eludes the western mind? Bredin's work on Matthew is a specific "showcase" of why and how biblical interpretation is profoundly influenced by diverse cultural, psychological, and even physiological realities.

In Bredin's work the Beatitudes shine brightly through different sun-rays. Creation care empowered by God's generosity pervades Matthew's narrative in ways most eyes have never seen nor ears heard. Torah justice and *shalom* righteousness mean hearing and responding to the poorest of the poor, and not piously attributing a special piety to them. His book's chapters are inspired by selections from almost all of Matthew's gospel.

Take the book, read, and eat the words. It will be sweet as honey but give heart-burn to those of us who blind our vision and harden our hearts to the cries of the poor, disabled, and helpless. Too often we read the Word with dimmed eyes and wax-filled ears. Jesus puts it more sharply when He speaks to His disciples as to why He speaks in parables (Matt 13:10–17).

In response to my email query, why this book? Bredin writes, "It has been a book that has taken shape for many years especially in my contexts of working in Africa, care homes, and prisons. I have worked in Tanzania, with people with learning difficulties, and now those in prison. I believe Jesus is concerned not only to empower the poor but to do something about their situation. My concern is for the voiceless who never will be able to help themselves unless someone helps them."

Indeed, Jesus' word about "the sheep and the goats" in Matthew 25:31–46 cuts to the nerve, and readers will "ouch" more than once. To taste Bredin's work, I quote his summary to Chapter 11 on Jesus as Wisdom, which on the surface would be the one least likely to reflect his emphasis on

3. Bredin, *The Ecology of the New Testament*.

God's good creation, generosity, justice, hope, and peace to all for human flourishing:

> Mercy, Torah, and wisdom are related. They each express aspects of God's righteousness and goodness which are the foundation of creation. God's creation is ordered to encourage and direct each of its parts to be merciful. This is God's will, when *shalom* is established. Torah is one aspect that emerges from creation teaching that the way of righteousness is to live for others. Jesus as Wisdom is presented as one who is in harmony with God; this harmony is expressed in Jesus being described as humble and gentle in heart. 'Humble' and 'gentle' do not describe a submissive figure, but one whose will is that of God. 'Humble' and 'gentle' are attributes of one who is God's child, one who lives for others. To live for others is to live according to the way of mercy in line with the law. To live in harmony with God is to live at odds with the competitive world that encourages greed and selfishness. When Jesus describes His way as easy, He refers to the way that God intended for His creation. God's creation is made for *shalom* and established through the teaching about living according to God's love.

Or, from the beginning of Chapter 8, as prelude to Bredin's view of "poor in spirit" in Matthew:

> It is my contention that Matthew has a particular sensitivity to God as a Creator who intended creation to be an expression of His homely self-giving love. The existence of the poorest of the poor is, therefore, inexcusable to such a God particularly made palpable in God's warning of condemnation to those who don't repent.

The book's title, *Jesus, Revolutionary of the Poor: Matthew's Subversive Messiah* is to be read in the context of God's creation-*shalom* that God wills for all people, including especially the poorest of the poor, the severely disabled, and prisoners regarded by other prisoners as most despised. The genius of this book links together God's *shalom*-creation and care for the poorest of the poor so they too may sit at Jesus' banquet table, a trope rarely heard. Each chapter ends with a "Summary," "Food for Thought," and Mark's own composed prayer. Thanks to Mark Bredin, we are moved to care with generosity for God's good earth and all humans that live thereon.

—*Willard M. Swartley*

Acknowledgments

Professor Willard Swartley deserves my grateful thanks for inspiring me to write this book. He has been a part of this project for the last five years. His concern to engage with the world through the lenses of Scripture has long been an inspiration to me. My wife and I were privileged to receive the generous hospitality of Willard and his wife Mary in Elkhart and there we were able to discuss the message of the Bible and its relevance to our contemporary world. He has given up much of his time in helping me to think carefully. He also organized a very warm and stimulating lunch-time seminar at Elkhart Anabaptist Seminary where staff and students alike engaged with my ideas about Matthew. I feel privileged to have Professor Swartley write his kind Foreword to this book.

I have also greatly benefitted from the time Graham Leverton (MA Student at London School of Theology) has given to me over the last few years through reading and commenting critically and helpfully. He has encouraged me both by his enthusiasm and his commitment to theology and biblical study while engaged in front-line mission work among the excluded and vulnerable.

Philip Vine has also read early editions of this book and am particularly grateful for his advice on points of presentation.

In the writing of this book I have held, over the years, ad hoc Saturday study mornings on Matthew. I am grateful to all those who attended and discussed with me particularly the teaching of Jesus as found in Matthew 5–7. I remember our breakfasts and strong coffee with fondness. In this group study I was forced by thoughtful and perceptive people with no formal training in biblical exegesis to make my thinking understandable.

I am as ever thankful for Fran, my wife, who has sustained me in my commitment to the message of Matthew and its relevance to the horror of extreme inequality and exclusion in our world. She also helped in proof reading. I continue to be inspired by her example of caregiving.

I am also thankful to my two daughters Hannah, and Charis, who have read different aspects of this work and undergone a lifetime of my preaching about inequality. Thanks to Alek and Gert who helped with computer stuff and discussions.

This book began at St Philip's Anglican Theological College, in Kongwa, Tanzania. Here I learned so much about living the Gospel amidst extreme poverty. I am thankful to the Madinda family and Janet Allen who made my teaching time there so wonderful. I am of course grateful to all my students there who heard various early reflections on Matthew that appear in this book and all the staff, teaching and non-teaching, that made me feel so welcome.

I would also like to thank the Area Meeting of Religious Society of Friends for Norfolk and Waverly who nominated me to work as Quaker Prison Chaplain. This appointment allowed me to enter into the world of several prisons. I am also very grateful to many prisoners, chaplains, and other prison staff, through whom I have learned more than I can measure. I am particularly grateful to those prisoners who join me every Saturday morning in the prison chapel for silent worship and fellowship.

Finally, I would like to thank my editors, Sallie Vandagrift and Robin Parry, for their support and help.

I wish to make clear that all errors and mistakes in this book are totally my own.

Introduction

A semi-starved nation can have neither religion nor art nor organization.[1] *—Gandhi*

Poverty and powerlessness are bound up with each other. Poverty leads to powerlessness, and powerlessness leads to poverty. —QF&P[2] 23.22

The only way to tackle poverty is to let people have money. More money for some inevitably means less for others. Are we willing to press for this? —QF&P 23.50

Poverty is an evil, a scandalous condition . . .[3] *—Gustavo Gutiérrez*

God gives so that we can help others exist and flourish as well. God's gifts aim at making us into generous givers.[4] *—Miroslav Volf*

IN A NUTSHELL

Henri Nouwen, theologian, prophet, Caregiver, and writer, states: "Jesus shows a distinct preference for those who are marginal in society—the poor, the sick, and the sinners—but I am certainly not marginal. The painful question that arises for me out of the Gospel is: 'Have I already had my reward?'"[5] Nouwen's typical honesty is a refreshing and important small

1. Jesudasan, *Gandhian Theology of Liberation*, 121.

2. *QF&P* is an abbreviation for *Quaker, Faith and Practice*. This is the book of Christian Discipline of the Yearly Meeting of the Religious Society of Friends (Quakers) in Britain. I refer to the Fifth edition. The full text is available on www.quaker.org.uk/qfp.

3. Gutiérrez, *Theology of Liberation*, 251.

4. Volf, *Free of Charge*, 47.

5. Nouwen, *Return of the Prodigal Son*, 79.

voice among Christian theologians in the West who avoid the unquestionable truth that Jesus has a preference for the poorest of the poor. My affirmation of Nouwen's understanding of Jesus is the dominant thesis throughout this study of Matthew's Gospel.

MATTHEW: AN OVERVIEW

Only in Matthew does Jesus teach that those who don't give generously from their hearts will have no reward from God (6:1–2, cf. vv. 5–16). In Matthew Jesus explains that on Judgment Day a person's eternal destiny is conditional on whether he or she was ready to give until it hurt to the poorest of the poor (5:10; 25:31–46). Of the Synoptic Gospels, only in Matthew does Jesus emphasize how a person will be accountable for their every action and word (12:36–37; 16:27). Moreover, in Matthew, Jesus recounts the parable of the workers in the vineyard (19:30—20:16) revealing how a person must put others before herself.

Volf observes that God gives so we can flourish, but it is necessary for us to give so others can also flourish. This leads me to state my book's thesis: *In Matthew, those who call themselves "disciples" of Christ must measure their claim in terms of the extent to which they live and give unconditionally and sacrificially.*

INTERPRETATIVE ASSUMPTIONS

Matthew does not organize his material to address a select audience with specific issues. Rather, he wrote to give the best account he could of the life of Jesus. Further, I see nothing in Matthew to suggest that Jesus had in mind the Roman Imperial setting.[6] Instead, Matthew arranges his Gospel in the light of the Old Testament, Jewish rabbinic material circulating orally and in writing, as well as Mark's Gospel and his own distinct eyewitness accounts of Jesus.

In short, much of the language of Matthew should be located within Matthew's cultural linguistic context and not the Roman Imperial setting. *Matthew's Gospel is ancient historiography presenting Jesus as He was remembered by actual eyewitnesses.*

6. This is in contrast to the book of Revelation that is fully aware of Rome and its Imperial Cult.

However, in examining Matthew, my discussion also engages with knowledge of the ancient world of the Middle East during Roman occupation at some point in the latter half of the first century.[7]

My analysis of Matthew occurs in the context of my own biography. I am greatly drawn to Wink's observations: "No scholar can construct a picture of Jesus beyond the level of spiritual awareness that they have attained. No reconstruction outstrips its reconstructor. We cannot present insights that we have not yet grasped. Our picture of Jesus reflects not only Jesus, but the person portraying Jesus."[8] Wink sees in the scholarly and non-scholarly writings about Jesus material information about the writer and what he or she has experienced and done as a human being.[9]

Part of my biography is my engagement with many Western biblical scholars, in whom I was formally trained. I believe, with few exceptions, Matthean scholars reach unsatisfactory conclusions relating to Matthew when they put a spiritual spin on Jesus, too conveniently to my liking, making Jesus more palatable to them. Because I am comfortably off, I am deeply suspicious of my biography which indeed leads me often to turn Jesus into a figure more in line with my culturally comfortable life.

The thought: "have I had my rewards through my material abundance?" makes me uncomfortable. Nouwen's claim that Jesus is a Revolutionary of the Poor makes the thought even more disturbing. However, if we through our clever exegesis conceal Nouwen's claim, we remove the troubling thought. My comforts surely lead me to avoid and shun Jesus the Revolutionary of the Poor.

I repeat to myself: "I am comfortably off." I am troubled by Nouwen's observations above. Because in Matthew, most prominent in Matthew, we are confronted by his message of fire and damnation against those who do not give from their hearts. Consequently, being troubled is a good thing opening us to God's revealing Word through Matthew. I am disturbed by

7. I agree with Carter, *Matthew and Empire*, 1: "It seems difficult to imagine that this world left no mark on the Gospel . . ." Similarly Weaver, "*Thus you will know them by their Fruits*," 107. While I agree, I am more cautious than Carter and Weaver and others of locating in Matthew precise Roman Imperial allusions. I am happy to do this in Revelation, see Bredin, *Jesus Revolutionary of Peace*, 23–24. But the language is not explicit enough in Matthew to warrant such imposition on the Gospel. I believe, further, with Bauckham, that Matthew is ancient historiography, see his *Jesus and the Eyewitnesses*. In Bredin, "Gentiles and the Davidic Tradition," I consider the women in Matthew's genealogy in the context of mission. I see no need to examine it in the context of Rome. I am cautious of over-extending what we know of the ancient world and reading this into the Gospel.

8. Wink, *Human Being*, 11.

9. Ibid., 12.

the parables of the workers in the vineyard and of the goats and sheep, and being accountable for every word and action. I cannot reconcile the message of these parables to being comfortably off. I am troubled and Matthew disturbs me.[10]

CREATION-CENTERED READING

Distinctive to my approach is to read Matthew and the whole Bible in the context that creation is an expression of God's goodness. Since my work on *The Ecology of the New Testament* I have become more sensitized to the importance of creation in terms of understanding the fall, and redemption. All are intimately linked. I have been particularly influenced by Fretheim's *God and World in the Old Testament*. In addition the works of Ellen Davies, Norman Wirzba, and Randy Woodley, who each in their distinctive ways examine Scripture in the light of an agrarian reading. In *The Ecology of the New Testament* I stated:

> The people of the New Testament did not live in distinct communities separated from the soil, flora, and animals; they recognized their need for the land around them as well as their livestock. Such a worldview was also central to the Old Testament writers. The New Testament writers were so familiar with their environment they did not feel any urgency to spell out what was very obvious to them but what is not so obvious to us.[11]

Woodley notes well: "As global development and urbanization continue, humans continue to lose their contact with the earth and her creatures."[12] This has profound implications for our readings of the Bible as it increasingly separates us from the social setting of Jesus. Davies points out that our readings of the Bible are influenced by the fact that we are cut off from creation. In living apart from creation we miss much of what is found in the Bible for much of the Bible originates in an agrarian context. Davies observes that when she became more aware of cultures whose existence depended on land care, she started to read Scriptures in a different way. She insists: "agrarianism is the way of thinking predominant among the biblical writers

10. Richard Bauckham in conversation was rather struck by my being troubled by the judgmental and wrathful God. He saw this as being a product of much of my research being on the book of Revelation and Matthew. Two texts distinct in their juxtaposing of God's love with His wrath.

11. Bredin, *The Ecology of the New Testament*, 8.

12. Woodley, *Shalom*, 51.

. . ."[13] In her agrarian readings of the Bible she urges interpreters of the New Testament to be aware of the agrarian perspective that dominates the Old Testament.[14] In doing so, she states that her readings of the Bible become "more *material*." She comments: "I notice how carefully the biblical writers attend to the physical means of human existence, the chief of those being arable land."[15]

Therefore, Davies urges we read the Scriptures through the lens of agrarianism: "Agrarianism is the way of thinking predominant among the biblical writers, who very often do not represent the interests of the powerful."[16] Woodley, in assuming the agrarian background to the Scriptures, writes: "If we try to read the Scriptures through the worldview of the biblical authors, Euro-western categories may be inadequate in helping to understand humanity's relationships to creation. Modern Euro-western categories most often have human beings over and above the rest of creation."[17] Woodley's following words summarize the extent to which the gospels are dominated by the agrarian outlook:

> Jesus' birth, and his whole life, was connected to all aspects of creation, from the animals in the stable, to the wheat in the field, to the grapes and figs in the vineyard, to the marginalized people of society. His worldview was one that understood the earth to be sacred . . . the stories told by Jesus are primarily about creation. Jesus spoke primarily of birds, crops, fields, fruit, fish, water, light, trees, livestock, relationships, and so on.[18]

I believe that in order to understand Matthew we must read it in the context of God being the Creator of something good which He intends to be an expression of His goodness which includes among other things *material abundance*. This reading is significant to my enquiry into Jesus' attitude about poverty and the poorest of the poor.

Lohfink's following words are also central to my thesis that sees the existence of the poorest of the poor in the context of God's intentions for creation: "God is the creator. He has created an abundant fullness of reality. He wills a world of wealth and plenty, he wills the overflowing happiness of his creatures."[19] If God's intentions for human beings and all of creation is to

13. Davies, *Scripture*, 1.

14. Ibid., 7.

15. Ibid., 26.

16. Ibid., 1.

17. Woodley, *Shalom*, 50.

18. Ibid., 47.

19. Lohfink, *Option for the Poor*, 9.

flourish, it follows that poverty and the existence of the poorest of the poor is evil. This premise dominates every chapter of this book.

WHY MATTHEW?

Why do I choose Matthew? In comparison to Luke, Matthew is a much underused Gospel by advocates of a subversive Messiah in solidarity with the poorest of the poor. Those Christians whose concern is for the poorest usually draw from Luke. For various reasons this has not been my journey. Matthew has been my daily spiritual food that has led me to see the existence of the vulnerable in society as an unacceptable evil to God. Matthew has challenged me continually to be ashamed of myself for the existence of the poor. It has confronted me daily with fear of God's judgment, making me more accountable for my every action.

I hope this book may show that Matthew has much to offer those who seek to integrate Gospel study with fighting violence and greed through obedience to God's will.

My argument is not unprecedented. Oxford Professor of New Testament, Christopher Rowland, himself observes that "At the heart of Matthew's Christology is the deliberate identification of Immanuel: 'God with us'—with the powerless and weak, an identification which is maintained consistently throughout the gospel."[20] Similarly Luise Schottroff writes: "the Gospel of Matthew expresses hope for the oppressed people."[21] There are a number of other scholars who see Jesus in Matthew as a subversive Messiah; to mention but a few: Tilborg, Carter, Powell, Crosby, Rukundwa, Van Aarde, and more recently Myles and Wilson.[22] They are an encouraging corpus who have nurtured my own increasing belief that Matthew's Jesus is a subversive Messiah in solidarity with the poor.

THE POOREST OF THE POOR

I tend to see Matthew's Gospel's depicting Jesus as addressing the non-poor, inviting them to repent and care for the poorest of the poor. I believe Jesus is concerned for the voiceless who never will be able to help themselves. They

20. Rowland, "Apocalyptic," 517.

21. Schottroff, *Parables*, 215.

22. Tilborg, *Sermon on the Mount*; Powell, *God with Us*; Carter, *Matthew and the Margins;* Crosby, *House of Disciples;* Rukundwa, and Van Aarde, "Revisiting Justice in the First Four Beatitudes in Matthew (5:3–6);" Myles, *The Homeless Jesus*; Wilson, *For I was Hungry*.

have suffered because the non-poor exclude them from fellowship and sharing. My own work with people with learning difficulties, those impoverished in Zimbabwe and East Africa, the homeless, and those suffering from severe mental health issues, has been significant to my belief that Jesus must be understood in the context of those who are so impoverished they have no voice or helper. The poorest of the poor to whom I claim Jesus refers may be for example: disabled, imprisoned, sick, hungry, thirsty, homeless, outcast, excluded, mentally sick, raped, abused and neglected as children, and so on, all in the context of an unstable and colonized Galilean setting. *They are not in any way pious because of their poverty.* They are the ones who have no helper or keeper. They are the victims of the non-poor.

In this book I show that Jesus not only teaches about God's preference for the poorest of the poor, but reveals the necessity of the non-poor becoming channels of God's goodness. Additionally, *failing to see the poor as anything but victims of the non-poor is irresponsible interpretation.*

Sakwa encourages biblical researchers to specify more precisely their conception of poverty that they are working with.[23] In biblical scholarship this conception is usually dominated by the elite who conceptualize poverty in terms of spirituality envisaging being poor vis-à-vis a quality of piety thinking a poor person is more open to God. Such a conception is held in spite of the horror of a billion people living on less that $1 per day, there being chronically hungry people who are also deprived of basic shelter, safe drinking water, sanitation, sufficient clothing, health care, and education. Anyone who has seen a sick, disabled, and hungry child lying helpless on the ground in pain with parents powerless to do anything, will realize that such a conception of poverty is foolish, negligent, and insulting.

God intends creation to be a place of abundance. God is for life, poverty is for death; life is abundance to the extent to which it is shared equitably as He intended. God does not wish for anyone to be in poverty as it thwarts His will for all. God orders creation to be a place of abundance so people can flourish. In order for people to be self-actualized they need food, water, warmth, shelter, sleep, companionship, acceptance, and employment. The very claim that the poor are more reliant on God when the statement is made by one who has all these basics makes me suspicious. *Only those who have wealth and comfort have the luxury of advocating that the poor are somehow through their needs open to God.*

I find helpful those who have worked and work among the poorest of the poor for an understanding of the conception of the poor which Jesus

23. Sakwa, *Bible and Poverty*, 108. For various approaches to poverty see Bryant Myers, *Walking with the Poor*, 107–31.

had. Dorothy Day (1897–1980), drawing upon her experience of material poverty, observed that the destitute could have "implacable hatred, or just cold loathing."[24] She asked regarding the poor: "is it to be expected that virtue and destitution should go together?" Her answer: "no ... they are the destitute in every way, destitute of this world's goods, destitute of honor, of gratitude, of love."[25] She further testifies to "the bitterness of the poor, who cheat each other, who despise each other as they are despised."

I reiterate that Jesus' message presupposes groups and individuals who are helpless and excluded from the fruits of creation. Matthew read in the light of this is illuminating. The poor are those who have very little means or capacity to legitimately live an abundant life. They will most certainly use illegitimate means to gain sufficient to survive.

I recall a lecture some years ago from a professor of theology rightly advocating the need for silent contemplation as necessary to being fully human. At the time I was supporting especially isolated single parents with young children with special needs. Many of those parents were in insecure situations both socially, economically, and physically. I asked the professor how she imagined a single parent with young children living in a high rise block of flats, in debt, with a partner serving prison time, would find the opportunity to satisfy the religious and spiritual needs the professor quite rightly had observed as necessary? Alas, her answer made no impression on me. I suspected she only knew the existence of her study overlooking the beautiful gardens of the college. My point in recalling this incident is to comment on the fact that many who romanticize poverty and simplicity in the Bible don't recognize or have become numb to the fact that more than two-thirds of the human population are unable to satisfy their basic needs such as food and water, or their social needs for security such as a place to live that keeps them warm, dry, and safe.

If my reader doubts my contention that we spiritualize poverty, I offer Kenneth Bailey's spiritualizing of Luke's parable of the rich man and Lazarus (Luke 16:19–31).[26] It is a superb example of both romanticizing and spiritualizing the hunger, sickness and poverty of a man. The parable's message is clear, the rich man is condemned for being rich and the poor man is exalted because he is starving. However, Bailey argues that the parable is about Lazarus' righteousness, comparing him to St Francis of Assisi; he writes: "In this parable, with the briefest of strokes, Jesus paints a clear

24. Day, *Selected Writings*, 175.

25. Ibid., 100.

26. A scholar from whom I have nonetheless gained much.

picture of Lazarus's gentle soul."[27] There is no depiction of Lazarus being a gentle soul who is a model of one who shows mercy to his enemies; Bailey writes: "Lazarus is quiet. The gentle, longsuffering man has no reservoir of anger . . . no score to settle and no vengeance to exact."[28] Baily's exegesis is an example of romanticizing and spiritualizing hunger and illness. There is nothing in this parable that depicts Lazarus as being a model of mercy. In short, Lazarus is a sick and poor man to whom God shows a preference while the rich man is condemned.

THE NON-POOR

The poor exist because the non-poor don't recognize that what they have depends on God. I, therefore, propose that those who have the means must act with generosity. Volf puts it: "we were created to be and to act like God. And so the flow of God's gifts shouldn't stop as soon as it reaches us . . . Indeed, in addition to making us flourish, giving to others is the very purpose for which God gave us the gifts. To pass them on, participating in God's gift giving, is the . . . thing to which God's gifts oblige us."[29]

WHY THIS BOOK?

This is not really a book written to scholars, although I use scholarship. It is a book I have written to keep myself in spiritual shape to do God's will in the same way I go to the gym to keep myself in good physical shape. Primarily it is written to myself. It originates from my time of devotional discipline when I seek to align myself with God so He might make me a better expression of His goodness. I seek to listen actively to the message Matthew proclaims. It has been a book that has been taking form for many years especially in my contexts of working in Africa, care homes, hostels, and prisons.

MATTHEAN COMMUNITY

Studies in the Synoptic Gospels have been for some time rooted in the assumption that the gospels are addressed to specific communities of the later first century. In fact this even results in full monographs on the history

27. Bailey, *Jesus Through Middle Eastern Eyes*, 386.

28. Ibid., 389.

29. Volf, *Free of Charge*, 49.

and social setting of the Matthean community.[30] In other words, the Gospels are not treated as historiographical documents recounting the life of Jesus. This is a view I don't hold to in the light of Richard Bauckham's award winning *Jesus and the Eyewitnesses.*

Bauckham has argued against the Gospels addressing specific social settings of the community or communities of the post-Easter church. R. T. France detects only general issues that were prevalent in the later church and nothing so specific to conclude the subject of the Gospels was not Jesus but the particular social setting of the church around when it is believed the Gospels were put together.[31]

However, it is hard to imagine any writer being totally untouched by what is happening around them. So we should assume Matthew is no different. Nevertheless, there is a difference between someone who, for example, states that he is addressing a particular set of problems and issues, such as Paul, and the author of the First Gospel, who does not. I envisage Matthew as being concerned to present the life of Jesus without reference to the specific and limited issues of his church. But I acknowledge at the same time that it is very difficult for an author to totally disentangle him or herself from his or her social setting. For this reason I found France's following words particularly relevant:

> It is generally true that the New Testament documents are occasional writings, so that it should in principle be possible to reconstruct something of the situation which caused the author to put pen to paper . . . even in the case of a gospel, whose framework is provided not by a particular set of problems, but by the life and teaching of Jesus, it may be possible with caution to suggest that an evangelist angles his presentation in a particular way because of certain tendencies in the church for which he is writing.[32]

While France is right when he says: "Few authors write *purely* from an abstract love of their subject,"[33] this means that particular settings and situations may indeed be hinted at in the writing. However, a reconstruction of the social issues is not easy, and conclusions are extremely tentative. They should not form the primary basis of exegesis.

30. Especially Sim, *The Gospel of Matthew and Christian Judaism.*

31. France, *Matthew. Evangelist and* Teacher, 113.

32. Ibid., 109.

33. Ibid., 109.

PRAYER

Teach us, good Lord, to serve you as you deserve, to give and not to count the cost, to fight and not to heed the wounds, to toil and not to seek for rest, to labor and not to ask for any reward, save that of knowing that we do thy will. —St. Ignatius Loyola

PART ONE

Introduction

Creation and Poverty

Creation's not about efficiency, it's about love. It's about shedding blood, sweat and tears to make the thing you care about come right.[1] *—Susan Howatch*

I believe that oppression and violence are to be understood in the context of a biblical doctrine of creation. Our failure to behold the goodness of God as generous and abundant leads to an understanding of goodness as mean, competitive, and self-empowering. Creation is not seen as abundant and overflowing with God's love, but a place of scarcity wherein each struggles to survive. Those who prosper are the "good" men and women in society's eyes who have manipulated situations to their own benefit neglectful of the suffering of others.

Ellen Davis argues that modern readings of the Bible in general don't fully appreciate God's goodness present in creation in the Bible. She writes: "if we who read the Bible, each in our own place, stretch our minds to reimagine the land we know as a home to be cherished, that effort will

1. Howatch, *The High Flyer*, 583.

make us better readers of Scripture."[2] To some extent this chapter draws upon the agrarian insights that put material readings at the heart of biblical interpretation.

This study also picks up on Lohfink's claim: "God is the creator. He created an abundant fullness of reality. He wills a world of wealth; he wills the overflowing happiness of his creatures."[3] When this happens God sees that creation is full of His goodness. When this does not happen God is angry and acts in favor of the poor.

Human beings' failure to see creation as belonging to God means seeing creation as ungenerous and limited. I show this premise leads to violence and oppression, permitting the powerful to pile up wealth that creates poverty. Such thinking has no place for the biblical idea that creation is designed to be a home fit for all its inhabitants as they each strive generously to serve the needs of others.

Therefore, the failure to perceive what is good in creation is the failure of humanity to experience God as Creator and God's goodness in it. Ellen Davis observes that in post-Enlightenment societies human cultures began to fail to perceive what is good.[4] However, such views I show are particularly evident also in the Bible which considerably pre-dates the Enlightenment. Davis draws our attention to the importance of the word and notion of "good/ness." This leads us to believe ourselves to be gods, and the goodness that there is, has no rootedness in God or biblical depictions of God's actions of liberating the poor. Biblical faith states that the goodness of God is in creation. God is goodness and His goodness is revealed in creation.

In Part One, I emphasize the extent to which God's goodness is fully present in creation when it is an abundant home wherein each cherishes the other. This biblical teaching is in contrast to seeing it as a place of scarcity wherein we must fight for survival. I observe that such teaching is often hammered out in polemic against the godless worldview that perceives goodness in terms of battle and competition. This ultimately leads to an oppressed and impoverished poverty class who have no voice, no skills, and no hopes. The existence of poverty reveals that we neither trust God nor believe His creation is a hospitable and generous home. Consequently, punishment and wrath, so strong in the Old Testament (especially the prophets) and Matthew, evince how God abhors poverty because His creation is not behaving as He intended.

2. Davis, *Scripture*, 27.

3. Lohfink, *Option for the Poor*, 9.

4. Davis, *Scripture*, 46.

1

The Goodness of God in Creation

Our gracious Creator cares and provides for all his creatures. His tender mercies are over all his works.[1] *—John Woolman*

The cause of the creation of the world was God's abundant goodness.[2] *—Sophrony*

As I see it, God is all that is good, He made all that is made, and loves all He has made.[3] *—Julian of Norwich*

Each person is unique and important, whatever their culture, religion, abilities or disabilities.[4] *—Jean Vanier*

God sees creation as *ṭob* (good, goodness) seven times in Genesis 1 (verses 4, 10, 12, 18, 21, 25, and 31). The Bible is rooted in the belief that *creation is an expression of God's goodness.* Goodness (Hebrew: *ṭôb)* describes God as merciful and showing limitless love (Psalm 69:16; 100:5a; 106.1; 109:5, 21; 118.1, 29; 136.1); the very name of God is *ṭôb* (Psalm 54:6); *ṭôb* is also the food and drink needed for humans to be satisfied (Genesis

1. Woolman, *The Journal and Major Essays*, 241
2. Sophrony, *The Monk of Mount Athos*, 98.
3. Julian of Norwich, *Enfolded in Love*, 9.
4. Vanier, *Drawn into the Mystery of Jesus*, 172.

3:6; Psalms 103:5; 107.1; 107:9c; Isaiah 1:19). In fact "good" can refer to food and drink with the word "goods" (Ecclesiastes 5:11 and others). According to Isaiah, to do "good" (*ṭôb*) is to rescue the oppressed and poor (1:17). Therefore, creation is good (*ṭôb*) to the extent that it corresponds to God's goodness which is consistent with the equitable distribution of creation's goods. I propose that the goodness of creation God sees refers to a harmonious beauty which inspires the beholder to give him or herself to others so they flourish.

According to Genesis 2:18, God says: "It is not good that man should be alone." This is in contrast to the seven occurrences of "good" in Genesis 1; good in creation is relational, harmonious, and dynamic. The goodness of God is vibrant and best understood in terms of creation-in-process of change and development. Central to this goodness is "togetherness." Creation is an expression and channel of God's goodness to the extent that each person works for the benefit of the other representing his or her Maker who is generous and self-giving.

Matthew, I believe, reinforces the Old Testament's teaching about the goodness of God in creation and sharing of its goods. Only in Matthew's parable of the hired workers is God described as good intentionally in contrast to those who are not merciful (20:15).[5] Matthew more than the other Synoptic Gospels depicts Jesus relating to God as Father. In short, goodness describes who God is and His will for all creation.

This biblical thinking is central to explaining why God has a preference for the poor, particularly those "who have no helper" (Psalm 72:6). When there are poor, the goodness of God is not evident in creation as He desired, and, therefore, that creation is not a fulfillment of God's will. Instead, it is a place of scarcity, battle, and exclusion.

Biblically the poor exist because humanity orders creation to exploit the worst aspects of human beings: greed, fear, hatred, and selfishness. Elsa Tamez comments that: "the poor in the Bible are the helpless, the indigent, the hungry, the oppressed, the needy, the humiliated. And it is not nature that has put them in this situation; they have been unjustly impoverished and despoiled by the powerful."[6] Poverty is not what God intended for His creation.

Human empires are depicted in the Bible (Egypt, Assyria, Babylon, Persia, Greece, and Rome) as organizing the world for competition based on an understanding that the earth is a place of limited resources and perceiving existence to be a battle. The earth is a battlefield where each is pitted

5. Greek is *agathos* and Syriac *ṭôb*.

6. Tamez, *Bible of the Oppressed*, 70.

against another in the fight for survival. The outcome is poverty on a global scale. Volf observes the world is rooted in "exclusion" whose purpose "is to exclude others from scarce foods, whether they are economic, social, or psychological."[7]

Such ordering militates against the goodness of God in creation, Tamez is unambiguous in stating that poverty is evil: "poverty is an unworthy state that must be changed. I repeat: poverty is not a virtue but an evil that reflects the socioeconomic conditions of inequality in which people live. Poverty is a challenge to God the Creator; because of the insufferable conditions under which the poor live, God is obligated to fight at their side."[8] The Bible, in contrast, sees creation as a place of goodness, generosity, love, and abundance. Consequently, biblically the world must be ordered for sharing and embracing. Herein lays the basis of Jesus' anger and resultant teaching which is found in Matthew.

BATTLE AND SCARCITY

It is fair to say from what we know of the powerful nations' expenditure on military power,[9] that Thomas Hobbes (1588–1679) was right to say that the world is a battlefield (*bellum omnium contra omnes*—the war of all against all). Mao (1893–1976) expresses surely the opinion of today's nation leaders that "Political power grows out of the barrel of a gun."[10] "Battle," "power," and "military might," are emblems of all that is thought good, normal, and worthy of worship in our divided and violent societies. Human beings rejoice more in power, battles, strength, weapons, and glorifying war, than in acts of generosity, care, and hospitality. Do we have stickers on the back of our cars honoring care-workers as heroes as we do for military veterans? I have not seen one yet! This is particularly visible in modern society with its ubiquitous media which exploits human beings' obsession with violence, greed, and killing. The world of Jesus was no different.

Underlying these views is the perception that creation is a place of scarcity; therefore, battle is an inescapable necessity for survival. If there is a God, He is not a generous loving God who we might call Father. Creation is a fatherless place and its inhabitants are orphans. The concept of creation as a battlefield originates, biblically speaking, from human beings rejecting the existence of a generous and loving God (i.e., the goodness of

7. Volf, *Exclusion & Embrace*, 87.

8. Tamez, *Bible of the Oppressed*, 74.

9. http://www.globalfirepower.com/defense-spending-budget.asp.

10. https://www.marxists.org/reference/archive/mao/works/red-book/ch05.htm.

God in creation). The cost is chillingly spelt out in Genesis 3:15–19 with its vision of battle and division; but these verses do not describe God's original creational intentions set out in Genesis 1–2. The psalmist observing the violence and the greed of human beings laments that "there is no one who does good" (53:1), while in Psalm 4 many cry out: "O that we might see some good" (v. 6). This is in contrast to God seeing that creation is good seven times in Genesis 1.

I consider several traditions that reveal how those depicted as godless reject the goodness of God in creation.

Psalm 10

Those who deny God's existence reject that creation is formed inwardly towards nonviolence and limitless love (10:4). They justify violence saying there is neither a loving God nor an order to creation other than violence which is in fact another word for *chaos*. The psalmist states that for such peoples God's judgments "are on high, out of their sight." In other words, there is neither a compassionate God nor judgment, only self-seeking rooted in violence. The godless live unfettered with no restraints believing only in their own right to grasp and subdue. They feed their insatiable greed (10:3) which leads them to steal from others causing others to have nothing (10:9). Poverty is the consequence of godless living.

Habakkuk

In the Old Testament we find the writings of the prophet Habakkuk. He too has something to say about those who deny God's existence. The prophet writes: "their own might is their god" (1:11b) and "their justice and dignity proceeds from themselves" (1:7). According to 1:3–4, the wicked are for destruction and violence and they are slack in the obedience of the Torah so that justice does not prevail. In other words, a people who are for themselves are godless. Their existence is rooted in controlling and threatening others. They have no belief in mercy or creation as an expression of God's limitless love.

Abel and Cain in Targumic Traditions

The Targums are Aramaic paraphrastic translations of the Bible that preserve some beliefs going back to the first century AD. In this corpus

Cain's murder of Abel is related to a debate about God and the goodness of creation. Cain says to Abel: "There is no judgment and there is no other world; and there is no giving of good reward to the just nor is retribution exacted of the wicked."[11] As a result of this belief Cain sees no reason to live according to any commandments given by God, as such did not exist, and so is enabled to murder without fear of recompense. Cain's reply to God's question "where is your brother?" that he is not his brother's keeper (Genesis 4:9) sums up a worldview the Old Testament denounces.[12]

Cain's inhospitable words reject God's creation as an expression of God's limitless love. In this Aramaic material Abel is righteous because he is acceptable to God as he lives according to the wishes of God while Cain doesn't. Cain's belief that he is not his brother's keeper is a key point by which to distinguish why one brother is righteous and the other wicked.

Wisdom of Solomon 1–3

According to Wisdom of Solomon 1–3, the sophistry about existence taught by the ungodly is summed up in the dark words "born by mere chance" (1.2) perceiving life as purposeless and time as "the passing of a shadow" (2:5). Birth is the consequence not of love between two people, but the result of labor and oppression. The godless deny there is order or love in creation; in doing so they mock those who call God "Father" (2:16). This explains their desire to plunder the resources of creation for their own benefits. In 2:10 they boast: "Let us oppress the righteous poor man; let us not spare the widow or regard the gray hairs of the aged."

In short, the rejection of the world as creation goes hand in hand with violence. The godless mock those who were known to call God "Father" suggesting that "Father" was understood as referring to the Creator Father of something that is ordered according to His goodness.

4 Esdras 7:23

The wicked are those who deny God's existence proposing "to themselves wicked frauds; they even declared that the Most High does not exist, and they ignored his ways." The consequences of this are denying the way of

11. McNamara, *New Testament and Palestinian Targum*, 159.

12. Wright, *Old Testament Ethics*, 152, comments that "'Am I my brother's keeper?' has become the selfish abdication of responsibility on a global scale."

God—particularly by scorning the laws—and denying that He ordered creation to be an expression of His limitless love (cf. 4 Esdras 1:28–30).

THE GOODNESS OF CREATION

God did not say to Adam and Eve: "Go, make a better job of creation; I can't do any better!" His creation is good in the sense that each lives for the other to flourish–that is what God sees when He calls what He made "good." Lohfink emphasizes that in biblical teaching "God is the creator. He created an abundant fullness of reality. He wills a world of wealth; he wills the overflowing happiness of his creatures."[13] The "good" God sees in creation describes the abundance of creation that happens when all are generous (i.e., when human beings live obediently to God). This can only happen when people allow others to flourish through generously giving. Quaker John Woolman writing in the eighteenth century observes: "Our gracious Creator cares and provides for all his creatures. His tender mercies are over all his works; and so far as his love influences our minds, so far as we become interested in his workmanship and feel a desire to take hold of every opportunity to lessen the distress of the afflicted and increase the happiness of the creation."[14]

The Bible's teaching about creation as a generous and non-violent place is illustrated by examining Genesis 1 as responding to and rebuking the violent Babylonian creation myth, the *Enuma Elish*. In this myth creation is formed from the blood of a murdered god in order to serve the gods. Wink writes:

> in the Babylonian myth, creation is an act of violence: Tiamat, 'mother of them all,' is murdered and dismembered; from her cadaver the world is formed. Order is established by means of disorder. Creation is a violent victory over an enemy older than creation. The origin of evil precedes the origin of things. Chaos (symbolized by Tiamat) is prior to order (represented by Marduk, god of Babylon). Evil is prior to good. Violence inheres in the godhead. Evil is an ineradicable constituent of ultimate reality, and possesses ontological priority over good.[15]

According to Genesis 1, in contrast to *Enuma Elish*, creation is good in the sense of being ordered according to non-violence and generosity, Wink observes: "A good God creates a good creation. Chaos does not resist order.

13. Lohfink, *Option for the Poor*, 9.
14. Woolman, *Journal and Major Essays*, 241.
15. Wink, *Engaging the Powers*, 14.

Good is ontologically prior to evil. Neither evil nor violence is a part of the creation, but both enter as a result of the first couple's sin and the machinations of the serpent. A basically good reality is thus corrupted by free decisions reached by creatures."[16]

Ellen Davis observes that the Bible uncharacteristically does not state: "God *said* that it is good." Instead, she notes, "God *saw* that it is good." "Seeing" rather than "saying" suggests that God experienced and felt its goodness.[17] Further, each aspect of creation is declared "good" independently of human beings, showing that God does not value one aspect of creation above another.

Creation is good to the extent that it is a place where relationships are based on care and being cared for. This is how God formed creation. One psalmist states: "How very good and pleasant it is when kindred live together in unity!" (Psalm 133:1). Son of Sirach calls humanity beautiful when there is agreement among brothers and sisters, friendship among neighbours, and a wife and husband live in harmony (Sirach 25:1). The Hebrew visions of creation are relational and show all creation living in harmony (Isaiah 11:6–9; 35; 65:25; Micah 3:4). God's purpose for humanity is caring relationships between each other and with the rest of creation. Proverbs laments that "The one who lives alone is self-indulgent" (18:1). Gillet, sums up well: "To cut oneself off, to become, or to remain, a stranger to the 'other,' goes against the whole meaning of the evolution of life."[18]

Wisdom of Solomon states of God: "For you love all things that exist, and detest none of the things you have made, for you would not have made anything if you had hated it" (11:24). The world is wholesome, and there is no destructive poison in it (1:14). Sirach states: "No one can say, 'This is not as good as that,' for everything proves good in its appointed time" (39:34). Each creature, each grain of sand, each entity is loved by God. Sirach writes: "for everything has been created for its own purpose" (39:21b). "Each creature is preserved to meet a particular need" (42:23); "each supplements the virtues of the other" (42:25).

God is Other than Creation

Creation, the heavens and the earth are distinct from God (Psalm 113:4; Job 38–42 are just a few examples). They are all created by God. In spite of the goodness of creation, it is only good to the extent that it is the fulfillment

16. Ibid., 14.

17. Davis, *Scripture*, 46–48.

18. Gillet, *In Thy Presence*, 44.

of God's will (i.e., God's goodness dwells in it). However, Isaiah emphasizes that creation is nothing compared to its Creator: "The heaven is my throne, and the earth is my footstool" (66:1).

Creation, *Shalom*, and Poverty

Brueggemann considers Genesis 1:2 to be a pre-creation vision *as being without shalom* from which He then establishes what is *shalom.*[19] He writes: "The biblical vision of *shalom* functions always as a firm rejection of values and lifestyles that seek security and well-being in manipulative ways at the expense of another part of creation, another part of the community, or a brother or sister. The vision of the biblical way affirms that communal well-being comes by living God's dream, not by idolatrous self-aggrandizement."[20] Brueggemann describes *shalom* as the *quality* of creation in contrast to chaos so that *shalom* designates abundance and health. By implication poverty means chaos. A world with *shalom* is one in which creation is an expression of God's loving generosity. His key text is Isaiah 11:6–7, (also see verse 9a):

> The wolf shall live with the lamb, the leopard shall lie down with the kid, the calf and the lion and the fatling together, and a little child shall lead them. The cow and the bear shall graze, their young shall lie down together; and the lion shall eat straw like the ox. They will not hurt or destroy on all my holy mountain.

Crosby writes of God's ordered work described in Genesis 1:

> God's work vis-à-vis the earth/land always involved delivering men and women from *whatever* chaos would create anomie in the form of meaninglessness and alienation, poverty and oppression, enslavement and disenfranchisement. Thus six hundred years after the Exodus, in the upheaval and darkness of the Exile, the Priestly writers described the beginning of the world not so much to express historical fact as much as to articulate God's perpetual plan for the ongoing liberation of creation accomplished in the Spirit. (Genesis 1:2a; cf. 2:7)[21]

So God's act of creating in Genesis 1–2 and His rescue of Israel from Egypt can be read in the context of creating order out of chaos. Egypt

19. Brueggemann, *Peace*, 15.

20. Ibid., 19.

21. Crosby, *House of Disciples*, 83.

represents a way of life that leads the land to be cursed as described in Genesis 3:18, but this is far from what God intends as set out in Genesis 1–2. God acts to rescue Israel and, consequently, all creation so that creation can be one community. Fretheim adds:

> Generally for Exodus, God's liberation of Israel is the primary but not the ultimate focus of the divine activity. The deliverance of Israel is ultimately for the sake of the entire creation. The issue for God finally is not that God's name be made known in Israel; the scope of the divine purpose is creation-wide; for all the earth is God's. To put this in different words: in order to accomplish God's mission in the world, God must have a world teeming with life.[22]

Gustavo Gutiérrez adds: ". . . the defense of the poor is the very meaning of the Jewish people's claim to nationhood. For this is a nation that, ever since the promise given to Abraham, has been called upon to enthrone justice and right."[23]

Creation of the Sabbath

The creation of the Sabbath (Genesis 2:2–3) tells us a lot about creation and God:

> And on the seventh day God finished (LXX: *synetelesen*) the work. And God blessed the seventh day and declared it holy. (2:3 NLT)

The Sabbath is said to be "finished." The *Peshitta* often translates the Greek *synetelesen* with *shalom* perhaps suggesting that creation was brought to a state of *shalom* on the seventh day. The Sabbath is "blessed" in the sense that it is as God desired it to be. Blessed is related to *shalom* where there is security, health, and abundance. It is when creation is *ṭôb* (good).

Sabbath for the ancient mind brings to mind that the world is creation and a place where *shalom* is the state God intended. The task of human beings is to worship God through serving creation. Disobedience to Sabbath laws shows human beings treating life and creation as a war zone in which human existence is rooted in restless striving to overcome others who are seen as a threat.

22. Fretheim, *God and World*, 119.

23. Gutiérrez, *God of Life*, 22.

GOD AS FATHER CREATOR IN MATTHEW

Abraham Heschel emphasizing the immanent God, writes that God is "the loving Father Who is intimately affected by what man does."[24] God is ultimately best understand as someone who has invested His goodness into forming creation and cares for it intimately. I think Heschel's description of God as "the loving Father" expresses well that creation is not a place of suffering and unloved orphans. Creation has a loving Father.

I consider Matthew's understanding of God as Creator to be rooted in the Old Testament teaching about the goodness of God in creation. God as Creator is depicted metaphorically as Father. Fretheim observes that "Biblical metaphors for God, with few if any exceptions, have relatedness at their very core . . . To characterize these metaphors generally, they are usually personal rather than impersonal . . . earthly rather than 'heavenly' . . . This earthy type of language used for God ties God closely to the creation and its everyday affairs."[25] In showing my reader that for Matthew creation is a place of goodness I am drawn to the fact that the First Gospel more than the other Synoptic Gospels depicts God as Father. This reveals that for Matthew God is intimately involved in creation and cares about the harm that is done to it.

Matthew prefers the term "Father" when he has Jesus referring to God often editing his sources to emphasize God as Father (cf. Mark 13:11 with Matthew 10:20).[26] Matthew's main source is Mark which has four occurrences of Father when referring to God (8:38; 11:25; 13:32; 14:36). There are thirty-one occurrences of Father for God unique to Matthew and forty-one overall. Matthew uses the phrase "Father in heaven" fourteen times presumably inspired by Mark 11:25. Further, Matthew refers to "son/s/children of God" considerably more times than Mark or Luke which correlates with Matthew's presentation of God as Father (2:15; 3:17; 4:3, 6; 8:29; 14:33; 16:16; 17:5; 26:54; 27:40, 43, 54).[27] More than any other Synoptic Gospel, Matthew uses brother/sister suggesting the connectedness and family relatedness of

24. Heschel, *Prophets*, 2:73.

25. Fretheim, *God and World*, 17.

26. God is Father three times in Mark, twenty-nine times in Luke and forty-two in Matthew. Among the Gospels, only Matthew uses plural pronouns (we, us, our) with Father (eight times); however, "our Father" significantly occurs in Isaiah 63:16 twice and once in 64:8. He uses "your Father" or "heavenly Father" thirty-three times: more than the other three gospels combined; "my Father" occurs thirteen times in Matthew.

27. Matthew preserves almost all Mark's references, takes over three from Luke, but adds six of his own.

all. Father is known to be used of God in nearly all the writings of the New Testament. But Matthew is distinct in terms of the Synoptic Gospels.

Matthew's liking for the term Father for God emphasizes my contention that creation is good in the sense of it being abundant. For Matthew, the goodness of God in creation is His limitless love that is expressed through the use of the term "Father."

Norbert Nguyen-Van-Khanh comments regarding Francis of Assisi: "God is Father because He is Creator. Francis saw an intimate connection between creation and the fatherhood of God. His vivid awareness that God Creator is also Father led him to recognize a bond of solidarity that links not just human beings but all creatures to one another."[28] Father is bound up with the belief in an ultimate begetter of the cosmos carrying with it the implication that the world had been created by a personal God. Similarly Gutiérrez writes that "The very name 'Father' evokes a profound everyday human experience and underscores the truth that God is the fount of life."[29] Desmond Tutu draws great significance from the fact that God is Father; he writes to his oppressed black brothers and sisters:

> We will grow in knowledge that they [white people] too are God's children, even though they may be our oppressors, though they may be our enemies. Paradoxically, and more truly, they are really our sisters and our brothers, because we dared, and have the privilege to call God 'Abba,' Our Father. Therefore, they belong together with us in the family of God, and their humanity is caught up in our humanity, as ours is caught up in theirs."[30]

In short, Fatherhood of God turns upside down notions of patriarchy and elitism instead urging that all creation is formed by one Father to be a cosmic unity in contrast to a cosmic battlefield. I will now pick out some particular texts referring to God as Father in Matthew to illustrate the connection between Father and creation. In other words, I argue that creation is not a fatherless creation that happened by chance. It is a creation formed to be an expression of God's goodness.

28. In Crosby, *Finding Francis*, 77; Vanier, *Drawn into the Mystery of Jesus*, 21–22 emphasizes Father in terms of Creator vis-à-vis John's Gospel.

29. Gutiérrez, *God of Life*, 1.

30. In Battle, *Ubuntu*, 31.

5:45–46

Jesus in the Sermon on the Mount teaches about loving and praying for one's enemies:

> so that you may be children of your Father in heaven; for he makes his sun rise on the evil and on the good, and sends rain on the righteous and on the unrighteous. For if you love those who love you, what reward do you have? Do not even the tax collectors do the same?

In a godless world love is only for those who will love you back. Elsewhere Jesus recalls that even an evil person can show generosity to his or her children (7:11). To the godless worldview, love is limited and constrained. When love is so constrained, it is clear that a person is selective in who they choose to love suggesting that they do not have a sense of creation as good and generous. Jesus' teaching is poles apart from the world's understanding of limited love and limitless hate.[31]

According to Matthew, God is distinctly the Father of all creation maintaining it through sending rain on the righteous and unrighteous (5:45) and the sun to rise on the good and bad (5:43). The rain and sun represent the fullness of God as the giver of life. "Father" is Matthew's preferred word to highlight God as a loving and self-giving Creator God who wishes nothing other than to allow for creation to flourish. Even amidst evil and hate God is still Father acting to enable love to flourish.

Matthew makes it clear that all creation is one, every creature in community with every other whoever they are, good or bad. Jesus teaches His disciples to be like the Father loving all as if all were brothers and sisters.

6:9–11

Jesus addresses God as "our Father" (cf. Mark 11:25). Does "our" refer to only those who follow Jesus? Or did the disciples understand "our" as more inclusive (i.e., referring to all creation)? Elsewhere in Matthew God is understood as one who cares for the grass and the birds (6:25–30; 10:29–30), He is by implication their Father too. Matthew's Jesus pronounces "our" to refer to God as the Creator of all creation including those who reject God.[32] Jesus was immersed in the Bible's teaching about creation and would have

31. Schnackenberg, *Matthew*, 62 states that Jesus' commandment of love here is unprecedented in Judaism of Jesus' time.

32. According to Carter, *Matthew and the Margins*, 164, Father refers to Creator of all and is used in contrast to those who declare their father to be Jupiter/Zeus.

uttered the last words of Psalm 150:6: "Let everything that breathes praise the LORD!"

However, only the disciples are taught to pray "our Father." Those who say "our Father in heaven" make a confession of faith declaring God is the Father of all. The disciples are those who will address God as "our Father" because they recognize that creation and all that is in it belongs to God and He cares for it. For Jesus, as was the case for Malachi, to call God "Father" must lead to the forming of true fellowships based on self-giving among those who profess together God is "our Father."[33] Sadly such confession does not always follow in action as was the experience of Malachi.

Bernard Häring laments at those Christians who supported Apartheid in South Africa singing: "the *Our Father* in their places of worship . . ." He further writes: "the ideology of apartheid and its terrible applications belie each of the words of 'Our Father.' Its meaning has been violated."[34] In fact the fatherhood of God is blasphemed and the unity and beauty of creation is denied.

Therefore, to confess "our Father" is to acknowledge one Father Creator of all and act as though all were brothers and sisters. Those who do not recognize God as "our Father" are loved by God who is their Father, but their failure to acknowledge God in this way is to live as though the world is a fatherless battlefield; they exclude themselves from God's love. Jesus tells the Pharisees that their Father is not the Creator of heaven and earth but one who murders (Matthew 23:31) because they acted as though they were the only sons of God; they are "children of murderers." In contrast the "*shalom*-makers" in 5:9 and 5:45 are children of God.

The subsequent petitions of the Lord's Prayer are rooted in God as "our" Father. Each reveals Jesus addressing God as both present in creation yet "other" in heaven. Still He cares for His creation desiring that it be abundant (His will be done on earth as in heaven). Jesus teaches people to look to God as one who gives what is necessary (bread in 6:11). To utter this petition is "an act of expectation that flies in the face of every ideology of scarcity."[35] Bread refers to that which sustains or redeems life, and for which humankind must count on God's providence. "The bread calls to mind . . . God's constant daily presence and care for people."[36] The flowers of the field and the birds of the air are all lauded by Jesus for trusting in God for their

33. Gutiérrez, *God of Life*, 137.

34. Häring, *Healing Power of Peace*, 52; Leech, *True Prayer*, 26.

35. Brueggemann, *Theology of the Old Testament*, 482.

36. Ringe, *Jesus, Liberation*, 82–83.

needs. For the flowers and birds God is Father acknowledged by their trust in their Father for their daily needs.

In the Lord's Prayer humans live to bring glory to God's name (6:9) through being expressions of His goodness. It is significant, to illustrate this, that the only aspect of the Lord's Prayer that involves human action is that of forgiving others their debts (6:12). In other words, in declaring God as "our Father" we know ourselves bound together as a community of creation with the sense of obligation to share all creation with one another.[37] In other words, showing mercy is to reveal that one experiences God as "Father."

6:25–30

Jesus may have in mind Job 12:7–8:

> But ask the animals, and they will teach you; the birds of the air, and they will tell you; ask the plants of the earth, and they will teach you; and the fish of the sea will declare to you.

God is the Father of both the birds and the grass of creation. The Father of human beings also feeds the birds of the air (6:26). Jesus sees creation as teaching humans how to trust in God for what is necessary.

6:25–30 must be read also in the context of Sabbath. We have seen that Sabbath marks the earth as creation that is ordered so that God's goodness is in the midst of it. Jesus teaches that in observing non-human creation the seer will perceive creation in terms of Sabbath. The Sabbath reaffirms and reiterates that creation is God's and it is abundant because of His generosity. Human cultures are dominated by anxiety and stress which reflects a distrust in God and a belief that life is a battle and competition for limited resources. Ellen Davis comments that "Sabbath is meant to enable Israel to see the world as God's creation . . . where every creature . . . can rest in the goodness of the whole."[38] Israel in its sojourn in the wilderness learned what it is to observe the Sabbath, it is to depend on God's abundant generosity.

Hoarding and worrying about items such as food and clothing seem to dominate those Jesus addresses. The community, Jesus teaches, must exhibit an alternative practice; not unlike what we observe in nature. It is to trust God's rule and provision demonstrated in the goodness of creation (Genesis 1; Psalm 24:1; Matthew 5:45).[39]

37. Battle, *Ubuntu*, 31.

38. Davies, *Scripture*, 78.

39. Carter, *Matthew and the Margins*, 176.

The goodness of creation is biblically evident in its abundance of food. Indeed, creation might be compared to a great food chain generously supplying all that every creature needs (Psalm 104:27–28; 145:15–16; Matthew 6:26).[40] Jesus' teaching about God the Father feeding birds recalls that "eating" should bring to mind that we live and have our being in the midst of a grace-filled world.[41] Eating brings to mind the extent to which we depend on hospitable and caring relationships so that food is plentiful. The way we eat is a reliable test to assess how obedient we are to the Father's creational intentions. If the world is a place where there is both starvation and excess, that world is not an expression of the Father's hospitable love. The way a person eats says a lot about the extent to which that person is an expression of God's limitless love.

In short, Matthew uses the concept of Father to subvert the hierarchical mentality of human beings who see themselves as more special than the rest of creation. The term Father describes one who cares deeply for all creation. The creation of which God is Father is a grace-filled world.

18:14

Only in Matthew Jesus teaches: "So it is not the will of your Father in heaven that one of these little ones should be brought to destruction." God the Father cares for that which does not appear to be fruitful. This may suggest a contrast with earthly fathers, perhaps even the rulers of Rome. God is described as the Father of orphans in Psalm 68; perhaps underlying this claim is the consensus understanding that God is the Father of the elite and successful. The elite saw orphans, widows, refugees, and prisoners as sinners punished by God. Their misfortunes were brought upon them by their own sinfulness. Particularly in this verse, Jesus, in calling God Father subverts the conventional use of Father through showing that God cares not just for what is successful in worldly terms; He is primarily concerned for the despised and neglected. God the Father's love is not limited to any one group, it is limitless.

40. Brueggemann, *Old Testament Theology*, 156 and 456; McConville, "The Old Testament and the Enjoyment of Wealth," 35 notes: "the unfolding story of Genesis has a good deal to do with food and drink . . . Blessing, indeed, often seems to be summed up in solid material and physical terms . . . And it is not only Genesis that holds out an Edenic ideal; it lies behind much of the Old Testament."

41. Wirzba, *Food and Faith*, 2.

23:8–9

Jesus teaches that we should not honor another person by calling him "Father." There is but one Father, and He is not like the powerful elite who claim to be Father. In so doing Jesus subverts hierarchy emphasizing that all share the same Father, Creator, and therefore all are equal (23:8).[42] In short, in these verses Jesus subverts the image of Father as patriarchal and oppressive replacing it with a loving Father who cares for all creation.

GOODNESS AS THE WILL OF GOD

Matthew uses *thelēma* (will) of God six times (6:10; 7:21; 12:50; 18:14; 21:31; 26:42). While Luke has Jesus teaching that "Your kingdom come" (Luke 11:2), Matthew has: "Your kingdom come, your will be done on earth as it is in heaven" (6:10). Matthew emphasizes "doing the will of God" which means being an expression of God's goodness in creation. It is to be a *shalom*-maker. Those who do the will of God are those who are channels of God's goodness. This is stressed in the exhortation to do to others what you would have them do to you. I believe that when we think of "will of God" we also should ponder on the phrase "goodness of God."

JOHN, JAMES, AND JUSTIN

I consider two other sources in the New Testament, and one second-century Christian writing, to support my claim for Matthew's use of "Father." Matthew does not invent his use of "Father" in isolation from other Christians in the first century.

Gospel of John

In John, Jesus is the Word made flesh (John 1:14). Father is a dominant metaphor for God in John's Gospel. He uses the metaphor more than any other writer in the New Testament. It is not possible here to do full justice to the many occurrences of "Father" in John. John's use of "Father" I propose is linked to this incarnation and John's strong teaching about the goodness of creation. The most obvious "Father" text is 1:18:

42. The NRSV plays down the language of equality by translating *adelphoi* "students."

> It is God the only Son, who is close to the Father's heart, who has made him known (NRSV)
>
> *Monogenēs theos ho ōn eis ton kolpon tou patros ekeinos exēgēsato* (Greek)

I propose the following translation:

> He who is the only son of God, He leads the way to the Father's embrace, care, and limitless love of the Father.

John writes of Jesus as born from God (1:13); *monogenēs* implies Jesus is birthed by God (cf. 1:14). NRSV translates *exēgēsato* "known." However, the dominant sense of this Greek verb is "to lead, show the way."[43] Vanier compares *kolpon* to the womb, but there is no occurrence of this word being used in such a way. Vanier is on firmer exegetical grounds, however, when he speaks of *kolpon* as the "innerness of the Father."[44] The "innerness of the Father" refers to God's very essence of being "limitless love" which is the ground of all being. *Kolpos* is used poignantly of the poor man's care (expression of limitless love) for his only sheep (2 Samuel 12:3; cf. 1 Kings 1:19). It is used of God carrying His people in His arms, in His bosom (*kolpon*) (Isaiah 40:11); hence my translation "embrace."

I have translated *ekeinos* as an emphatic pronoun (he) that refers to the only son of God. This fits with the dominant sense of Jesus as one who leads to the Father, He who is the creator of all. Vanier sums up well: "If Jesus speaks of God as 'Father,' it is because the Son flows from God. God is the source of all life. . . So when Jesus speaks of his 'Father,' he is speaking of the infinite Source of Life, from whom the very person of Jesus flows."

Epistle of James

It is possible that James and Matthew knew each other's work or similar traditions. I will consider James' reference to God as Father. I am particularly struck by "Father of Lights" (*tou patros tōn phōtōn*) (1:17; also 1:27 and 3:9). James 1:17 refers to God as the "Father of Lights" (cf. *Apoc. Mos.* 36.9). Father is used to refer to God as the one who creates. Lights (*phōtōn*) is plural denoting sun, moon, and stars.[45] In verse 18 James refers to Genesis 1:3, the word which God uttered at creation (cf. Psalm 33:6; 107:20; 147:15; Isaiah

43. Abbott-Smith, *Manual Greek Lexicon*, 160.

44. Vanier, *Drawn into the Mystery of Jesus*, 22.

45. Zerwick, *A Grammatical Analysis*, 692 refers to Father as Creator.

55:11; Wisdom of Solomon 18:15; Sirach 43:26). It is likely that James drew upon early Jesus traditions such as are found in Matthew combined with Job 38:28 in using Father to refer to creator of all.

Justin Martyr (165 AD)

Justin's use of Father refers to God as Creator. Justin was familiar with such use from Matthew and the New Testament in general. Justin quotes and affirms much of the teaching found in the Gospels (*First Apology* 13–17).[46]

Justin Martyr refers to God as "the Father and Creator of all" (*First Apology* 8, 15, 32, and 63). In his *Second Apology* 10 he speaks of God as "Father and Maker of All." However, Justin explicitly points out that Father is not a divine name, it refers to how human beings experience God's generosity sensed through His work of creation; Justin writes: "But these words Father, and God, and Creator, and LORD, and Master, are not names, but appellations derived from His good deeds and functions" (*Second Apology*, 6).

SUMMARY

- The world at odds with God sees itself as a place of battle for limited resources.
- In this world there is no belief in God's goodness nor of God as a generous Father figure.
- The Bible in contrast lays emphasis on creation being a generous and abundant place.
- God made creation to be a place where each creature lives and contributes to the welfare of others.
- The existence of poverty reveals that creation is not as God intended it to be.
- God works distinctly through Israel to reveal to all what it is to be good, what it is for creation to fulfill God's will.
- In Matthew God is predominantly Father.
- Father is depicted as one who cares and loves unconditionally all that He has formed.

46. Young, *Brokenness and Blessing*, 63.

- Father is used in other Christian texts as referring to God as merciful Creator.

FOOD FOR THOUGHT

Quaker writer Keith Helmuth wrote in 1990 words that still resonate today:

> As Christians . . . we are now required to critically assess the capital driven market economy and identify it as false religion, a fabulously productive but ultimately destructive system bringing closure on God's goodness in creation and bringing a creeping atheism to the soul. To look this system straight in the eye and call it to account is a critical test of Biblical faith.[47]

In writing this chapter I became more aware that the Bible's message of how to live is diametrically at odds with the way we live today. This is evident in our unbiblical economic ordering of the world towards market economics primarily focused on individual growth and choice, albeit believing that such will allow for the growth of all. When a nation spends more on weaponry than on its vulnerable, it is clear that the nation is at odds with God's intentions.

In adopting the biblical view, we must ultimately put God at the center of our thinking. In spite of all our great ingenuity and brilliance, we would do well to focus on the fact that God is ultimately depicted as one who loves limitlessly and cares unconditionally. Biblical faith regarding creation confronts me with an alternative way of seeing existence in terms of how we serve and care for what God has created. This must begin by measuring how we care for the victims of injustice, the children of abuse, the victims of rape, and those in prison, who are collateral damage on the way towards economic progress. Biblical faith puts them first. Helmuth writes: "Challenging market economics with a Biblical sense of the goodness of God in creation is to join a spiritual struggle. Faith in God, solidarity with the suffering poor and all others forms of life demands we take a stand and say, 'The destruction must stop.'"[48]

Overall, we would do well to meditate deeply on the fact that Matthew sees God as the cosmic Father of all. We are drawn to the idea that all creation is made up of brothers and sisters. If we experience God as Father of all creation, surely this experience leads us to cultivate ways of living

47. *QF&P,* 25:14.

48. Ibid.

without walls that divide one nation from another, and one religion from another, and one person from another.

PRAYER

Dear Father Creator, You have taught us to call you "our Father." Help us to respect your earth as an expression of Your goodness; make us act for Your glory through working towards the equal redistribution of its goods in the service of those who are without; to the glory of the Father, Son, and Holy Spirit. Amen.

2

God's Wrath and the Poor

God's love is inextricably interwoven with God's wrath.[1] *—Abraham Heschel*

God is described as handing us over to ourselves: this is the content of wrath.[2] *—James Alison*

To resist God was to run counter to the law of my own being.[3] *—Christopher Bryant*

God is a righteous judge, and a God who has indignation every day. If one does not repent, God will whet his sword; he has bent and strung his bow; he has prepared his deadly weapons, making his arrows fiery shafts . . . Their mischief returns upon their own heads, and on their own heads their violence descends. —Psalm 7:11–13, 16

His wrath is the clear shining of his light which of its nature burns up injustice and oppression.[4] *—Kenneth Leech*

I don't believe God's wrath can be understood without reference to material poverty. Psalm 147 sums up wrathful theology in the Old Testament:

1. In Shai Held, *Abraham Joshua Heschel*, 147.
2. Alison, *Living in the End Times*, 47.
3. Bryant, *Jung and the Christian Way*, 41.
4. Leech, *True Prayer*, 125.

"The LORD lifts up the downtrodden; he casts the wicked to the ground" (v. 6). Those who slay their brother by the sword, Amos comments, bring destruction upon their heads (Amos 1:9–11). According to Psalm 76 the purpose of God's wrathful judgment is to save the oppressed of the earth (v. 9). In this chapter I consider God's wrath and judgment vis-à-vis material poverty as a precursor to studying Matthew's presentation of Jesus as one warning of God's wrath.

According to J. P. Miranda, God's wrath must be seen in the light of His warring against injustice to establish justice.[5] He states that God's "bellicosity" is "at the service of compassion for the needy."[6] Ted Grimsrud points out that: "Justice is not soft on evil but rather seeks to destroy evil."[7] Perry Yoder similarly states: "Justice also shatters the power which enables oppressors to oppress."[8] W. M. Swartley hits the nail on the head commenting: "nothing stirs God's wrath against Israel more than failure to practice justice by caring for the needy."[9]

According to the Bible, poverty is an offence to God who has designed creation in such a way as to drive out from it all causes of poverty. My argument can be summed up: *poverty causes God to act in favor of the poorest of the poor and God's wrath is a tool to warn people to repent.* Those who deprive the alien, the orphan, and the widow of justice, will be cursed (Deuteronomy 27:19; cf. Ezekiel 22:29, 31). The biblical depiction of God's wrath gives strong evidence that poverty is the most heinous of crimes thwarting God's intentions for His creation. Andrew Lester expresses it well: "Scripture is clear that God becomes particularly angry in response to injustice against the helpless: widows, orphans, and other needy and oppressed persons. So when humans relate to other humans in ways that are abusive, oppressive, and painful, then God's fully invested and committed love is threatened, and God gets angry."[10]

GOD'S WRATH IN CREATION

The expressions of God's wrath especially stored up for the Day of Judgment are embarrassments to economically comfortable modern Christians. This is because such Christians have separated God's wrath from creation

5. Miranda, *Marx*, 121.
6. Ibid., 119.
7. Grimsrud, "Healing Justice," 79.
8. Yoder, *Shalom*, 33.
9. Swartley, *Health, Healing*, 130.
10. Lester, *The Angry Christian*, 244; cf. Stassen, *Living the Sermon*, 69.

along with the goodness of God that is at the heart of creation. In other words, technologically developed modern urban-dwellers struggle with the ancient agrarian mind-set that sees God as one who cares about the material well-being of all His creation. The urbanites, like those who built the tower of Babel (Genesis 11:1–9), are hell-bent on removing notions of God from creation. This modern response to God's personal wrath, moreover, is similar to the early Gnostics who distanced themselves from a God who directly raged against the powerful. Consequently they separated God from the material creation, which they saw to be the product of lesser divine beings called *aeons*.[11]

Writing in the early twentieth-century Rabbi Abraham Heschel significantly contributes to our understanding of God's wrath in the Hebrew Prophets. Heschel emphasizes that God takes personally the suffering of His creation pointing out that the Prophets disclose "a *divine pathos.*" The prophetic writings are filled with echoes of divine love and disappointment, mercy and indignation."[12] In Genesis the flood God sends to punish the world is introduced by a grieving God (6:6–7) and later, in prophet texts, God will lament over what has happened to His people (Jeremiah 9:17–18).[13] According to Heschel, God's wrath must be understood in the context of God's love or *pathos*. The wrath of God emerges from the very heart of His love.[14] Heschel writes: "Man is rebellious and full of iniquity, and yet so cherished is he that God, the Creator of heaven and earth, is saddened when forsaken by him. Profound and intimate is God's love for man, and . . . [therefore] harsh and dreadful can be His wrath."[15]

In short, God's *pathos* is the key to understanding God's wrath; God is "the loving Father Who is intimately affected by what man does."[16] The wrathful and judgmental language of the prophets for Heschel correctly reveals that God makes personal what happens to His creation. The sufferings of the poor and the oppressed "are not forgotten, that the unspeakable pain they endure does not go unnoticed. Indeed, although anger may be 'reprehensible when associated with malice,' it can be a blessing as well—'morally necessary as resistance to malice.'"[17]

11. Marcion taught that the creator-lawgiver archon or demiurge who had created this world was a far lesser power than the true God. See article by Herbert Christian Merillat, *Marcion and the Stranger God* in http://gnosis.org/thomasbook/ch9.html.

12. In Davis, *Scripture*, 15.

13. Fretheim, *God and World*, 20–22.

14. Held, *Abraham Joshua* Heschel, 147 and footnote 74 on pages 279–280.

15. Heschel, *Prophets*, I, 5–6.

16. Heschel, *Prophets*, II, 73.

17. Held, *Abraham Joshua Heschel*, 149.

Therefore, Heschel does not see wrath as irrational and impulsive. He understands wrath in the context of love. God's wrath is "an instrument rather than a force . . . a means of achieving 'the intents of [God's] mind.'"[18] God's intents are His creational purposes for creation to be an expression of His goodness. Creation matters to God. Kenneth Leech sums up succinctly: "God's wrath is not incompatible with His love, they are aspects of the same character. His wrath is the clear shining of His light which of its nature burns up injustice and oppression. The opposite of wrath is not love but neutrality: wrath and love are essentially one. The wrath of God is the Bible's expression for his essential hostility to all evil."[19]

We see this, for example, with Egypt who suffers God's wrath due to its wickedness and refusal to heed His warnings spoken by Moses. Central to this punishment is not just the warning of suffering and destruction of the unrepentant Egypt, but *it is a warning so that Israel knows that God condemns.* This is a threat and warning to the newly liberated Israel. Israel knows it is not to oppress because it has experienced God as one who frees the oppressed by bringing judgment on the oppressor. If Israel oppresses it should expect judgment. Exodus makes the consequences of Israel becoming like Egypt clear:

> You shall not wrong or oppress a resident alien, for you were aliens in the land of Egypt. You shall not abuse any widow or orphan. If you do abuse them, when they cry out to me, I will surely heed their cry; my wrath will burn, and I will kill you with the sword, and your wives shall become widows and your children orphans. (Exodus 22:21–24)

INSTILLING THE FEAR OF GOD

For some ancient Jewish writers the instilling fear of God's future condemnation is essential to achieving *shalom*. God warns Ezekiel, for example, of the grave responsibility he must bear in warning the wicked to repent:

> If I say to the wicked, "You shall surely die," and you give them no warning, or speak to warn the wicked from their wicked way, in order to save their life, those wicked persons shall die for their iniquity; but their blood I will require at your hand. But if you warn the wicked, and they do not turn from their wickedness, or

18. Heschel, *Prophets*, II, 62, 69.

19. Leech, *True Prayer*, 125.

> from their wicked way, they shall die for their iniquity; but you will have saved your life. (3:18–19)

According to Ezekiel, God has "no pleasure in the death of the wicked, but that the wicked turn from their ways and live" (33:11). Ezekiel makes it clear to perpetrators of injustice that "You shall be a mockery and a horror, to the nations around you, when I execute judgments on you in anger . . ." (5:15). In view of this I reiterate that the *warning of God's condemnation is a tool for shalom.*

God formed human beings to know how "they should live, and what they should observe to avoid punishment" (4 Ezra 7:21); such a way is to "Guard the rights of the widow, secure justice for the ward, give to the needy, defend the orphan, clothe the naked, care for the injured and the weak, do not ridicule the lame, protect the maimed . . ." (5 Ezra 2:20–21). It is because Israel did not keep these laws that they were scattered among the nations (5 Ezra 2:7). So God's judgment of the unrepentant is self-inflicted. Human free will comes with accountability, human beings can chose to disobey God but then suffer the consequences. Ultimately, however, warning of God's coming wrath is a tool of *shalom* informing all that there are consequences for abusing the free will that is given by God.

In short, it is God's will that those who are not from the poorest of the poor see that the existence of poverty should call them to repent. Repentance means to realize that the poorest are not poor because they are evil or lazy. They are poor because of the way our world is ordered for war and preparation for war in order to protect and acquire our greed driven possessions. Dorothy Day pointed out in 1953: "We are all guilty of concupiscence." She discerned that our cultures are ordered to "deliberately stimulate our desires, the satisfaction of which so often means the degradation of the family." Day remarked that "If the comfort one has gained has resulted in the deaths of thousands in Korea and other parts of the world, then that comfort will have to be atoned for."[20]

SELF-CONDEMNATION IS GOD'S CONDEMNATION

In the Hebrew mind God builds into His creation a means of rejecting that which goes against the Father's creational purposes. Those who condemn will be condemned in the same way they condemned others: "and on their own heads their violence descends" (Matthew 7:16 and 26:52; cf. Obadiah 15b–16; Psalm 9:16a; 28:4–5; there are many more examples of this).

20. Day, *Selected Writings*, 110–11.

Wisdom 5:17 states that God "will arm all creation to repel his enemies" (cf. 5:20). There is no contradiction between God's wrath against sinners being personal and impersonal. Fretheim puts it well: "Judgment is not something that God introduces into the sinful situation, such as imposing a penalty specified in the law; rather, God mediates the consequences that are intrinsic to the wickedness itself. God thereby sees to the moral order—a reality that God has built into the very structures of creation."[21] Genesis 3:17–19 describes the effects of disobedience on creation. Fretheim concludes: "human sin has had a deeply negative effect upon all creatures . . . has resulted in the degradation of the environment."[22] Life will be hard, the earth will be full of thorns and thistles. There will be enmity and hierarchy in creation. These verses are not a justification for seeing creation and life as a battlefield in a place of scarcity. These verses describe what happens when human beings don't trust God.

I am struck by the extent to which the godless reject a theology of condemnation of any kind (self-inflicted or God-inflicted). This fits with their refusal to believe that creation is ordered according to God's goodness. Volf puts it well: "Not to repent is to reject the condemnation. Unrepentant offenders implicitly say: It's wrong for you to forgive me; I've done you no wrong. Or more brazenly they say: I don't care if you forgive me or not, because I don't care whether I've wronged you or not."[23] We find, however, in the great prayer of repentance (Psalm 51) that the repentant person states of God: "you are justified in your sentence and blameless when you pass judgment" (v. 4).

MATTHEW

The two most wrathful (both impersonal and personal) texts in the New Testament are the Gospel of Matthew and the book of Revelation. I believe that wrath in both is best understood in terms of poverty which, according to both, is caused through the wickedness of human beings.

In studies relating to Matthew, the wrathful scenes are something of a scholarly conundrum to modern readers seeking to harmonize Jesus' teaching about loving the enemy with visions of God cutting them into pieces (cf. Matthew 24:51). Beare is strong in his criticism of the vicious imagery and punishment against sinners in Matthew which he points out is found nowhere in the other Synoptic Gospels or John; he comments that Matthew

21. Fretheim, *God and World*, 165.

22. Ibid., 194.

23. Volf, *Free of Charge*, 183.

has a morbid fascination with the destruction of sinners and evil.[24] Beare, I believe, misinterprets the vicious imagery failing to read it in its context of how justice is established. The language that Beare finds morbid actually reveals Jesus as one who was outraged at poverty and the way the poor were treated.

My explanation of Matthew begins by seeing it as being full of revolutionary zeal and hope for God's goodness to fill creation. I argued in the previous chapter that for Matthew creation is an expression of God's goodness. Because the First Gospel is true to the Bible's teaching regarding God's goodness in creation, God acts both with passion and zeal on behalf of those who suffer from lack of creation's abundance and, at the same time, removes the causes of suffering.

Matthew's heightening of condemnatory language demonstrates Matthew to be perceptive of Jesus' message of judgment and wrath in terms of good news to the poor and oppressed. The language of judgment originates in sinful humanity and Jesus seeks to free humanity from such sin.[25]

3:10–12

Intimately linked to God's wrath is the call to repentance (see Psalm 7:11–13 quoted above). Matthew alone has John the Baptist declare: "Repent, for the kingdom of heaven is at hand" (3:2; intentionally paralleled in Jesus preaching "repent" in 4:17). I suggest that Matthew's emphasis on repentance and wrath illustrates that real economic poverty is at the forefront of his portrayal of Jesus as He was remembered by eyewitnesses: repent because the time of judgment is coming.[26] Repentance is closely linked to economics. In other words, those who have means and power must change and live according to God's will and goodness. The consequences of not repenting are the same as in the Old Testament.

John the Baptist states that Jesus is one who smites the unrepentant (3:12). John's message is intended to bring sinners to repent. It is a far cry from rejoicing in destruction. John's message is clear: those who don't repent will be condemned and Jesus is the one who will condemn them.

Moreover, John the Baptist teaches that Jesus baptizes in fire (3:11; cf. Luke 3:16) while Mark has only "baptizes you with the Holy Spirit."[27]

24. Beare, *Matthew*, 149.

25. Carter, "Construction of Violence," 102.

26. Hagner, *Matthew 1–13*, 47 picks this up emphasizing that the anticipation of God's reign "involves judgment."

27. Unusually Matthew and Luke agree against Mark.

Matthew's fire imagery reinforces the nature of Jesus' baptism as judgment meaning destruction.[28] It explains and reinforces the nature of the Holy Spirit as one who blows away the chaff. It is a judgmental image that Matthew is partial to.

However, I see the imagery of Holy Spirit and Fire as representing ultimately "blessing." The Holy Spirit is the one who brings light out of darkness alluding to the Spirit of God hovering over the darkness in Genesis 1:2. The destructive aspects of the fire complement the Holy Spirit. In order for there to be life and blessing, evil must be destroyed. There is no contradiction between wrath and love. Fire in tradition refines and cleanses (Zechariah 13:9; Malachi 3:1–13; 1QS 4:21). Matthew's distinct "baptism with water for repentance" links the blessing and curse aspects of the Holy Spirit and Fire. People are called to repent; those who don't accept the truth of Jesus' teachings, will be destroyed.

In sum, Matthew emphasizes that John's baptism was related to repentance. Matthew states that John "baptizes with water for repentance" while Mark 1:8 and Luke 3:16 agree in stating John baptizes only "with water." For Matthew, John's baptism is related to the confession of sins (i.e., those who sought John's baptism must recognize their culpability in the suffering and injustices around them).

Gehenna (5:22; 5:30; 18:9)

Only in 5:21–26 Jesus teaches that those who kill are liable to be judged. He further teaches that those who call a brother or sister "a fool" are liable to hell (*Gehenna*). The language of murder in 5:21 is elucidated by reading Sirach 34:25 where murder is the same as depriving the poor of bread. Therefore, we should read 5:22 as Jesus condemning a person who insults the poor and sick calling them *Rakka* or *Mōre* (this is the word from which we get the pejorative term "Moron"). This word is used insultingly of a person with mild mental learning disability. The term is now considered offensive as it was for Jesus. Jesus rebukes those who not only take the life of another, but who insult the vulnerable.

According to 5:27–30 (cf. 18:6–9), only in Matthew does Jesus teach about adultery. Regarding looking on a woman to degrade her Jesus teaches that it is better to lose one of your member parts and to enter eternal life without them than to be thrown into *gehenna*. Adultery particularly in small agrarian communities violates God's will and social harmony. Those who do not cultivate habits that care for the welfare of others will bring

28. See Davies and Allison, *Matthew 1–7*, 316.

upon themselves God's wrath. Jesus emphasizes greatly the horror of oppression and that a person should go to extreme measures to avoid degrading another.

In 18:9 we hear again of those being thrown into *gehenna* because they despise the poor (18:10). We must envisage Jesus challenging His disciples for their elitist attitudes (15:21–28).[29] *Gehenna* is for those who think themselves above others (His disciples appear to do so in 18:1–5), and those who instead of helping the poor, make their situation worse through compromising with the exclusionary practices of society.

6:19–21 (cf. Luke 12:33–34)

Matthew has Jesus warning against laying up treasures on earth (6:19). These treasures are equated with the heart in 6:21. It follows that if your heart is focused on earthly treasures, then the rust and moths that consume such treasure will also consume your heart (cf. James 5:3).

7:1 (cf. James 4:11–12)

Jesus says: "Do not condemn, so that *you may not be condemned*" (Matthew 7:1; my translation). Jesus warns that if a person condemns another person, they will bring judgment down upon their own heads. France points out that *krinō* is about disparaging others with no sense of one's own failings.[30] His interpretation is supported by the Epistle of James which uses the word *kataleleite* (to speak evil of) synonymously with *krinō* (4:11–12; cf. James 5:9).

Warning of forthcoming condemnation of those who cause injustice against the poorest of the poor is prominent in Matthew. Therefore, I suggest 7:1 be read in the same light. I interpret the text as warning those who look down upon the poorest of the poor; they are to repent otherwise they will be condemned.[31]

29. In 20:29–34 the crowds set themselves against Jesus associating with two blind men. The disciples in this case are not the culprits.

30. France, *Gospel according to Matthew*, 142.

31. Jesus condemns the Gentiles for caring more about their own needs than the needs of others (6:2, 5, 7, and 32). Therefore, 7:1 refers to Jesus rebuking one who insults another by treating them as one not worthy of being called a child of God.

7:13–14, 21–23

God's kingdom was only for the remnant. Jesus teaches that "the gate is wide and the road is easy that leads to destruction, and there are many who take it" (7:13). Even being a disciple of Jesus will count for nothing if the disciple fails to live by Jesus' example (7:21–23; cf. 22:14; 25:31–48). The powerful and elite are not the only ones who will be condemned.[32]

This depressing language of limited salvation reinforces my argument that Matthew's Gospel is best interpreted in the context of God's wrath at the disparity that exists in creation between the poor and the non-poor. Jesus shows favor to the poorest of the poor, those who are right at the bottom of the social pile, those insulted even by the ordinary people who are barely above being impoverished themselves.

8:5–13

Jesus describes the centurion as having great faith. Such faith is evident in the centurion's concern for his suffering servant. In contrast, those called the children of the kingdom (i.e., the elders) are "thrown into the outer darkness, where there will be weeping and gnashing of teeth" (8:12). Matthew is striking in calling the religious leaders "children of the kingdom;" in doing so *Jesus recognizes them as God's children even in their condemnation.*

Vanier observes that God's preference for the poor "does not mean that those who are strong, clever, or well adapted to society are not precious and chosen by God." Vanier, however, states that such people need to repent through recognizing their own need for God.[33] They are called to be like Abraham and execute justice. They remove themselves from God by not practicing justice.

In Luke's account (7:1–10) the elders are presented in a positive light telling Jesus that the centurion is a good man. However, Matthew's account heightens the distance between the Jewish leaders and the centurion which allows Matthew to emphasize that there is condemnation against the Jewish people because they don't care for others. I suggest that the verses be read in the context of exhortatory warning to repent.

32. Carter, *Matthew and the Margins*, 462–463. I disagree with Carter when he argues that condemnation only relates to the powerful and elites.

33. Vanier, *Drawn into the Mystery of Jesus*, 173.

10:15 (cf. 11:20–24)

Matthew's theology of wrath comes through loud and clear: "Truly I tell you, it will be more tolerable for the land of Sodom and Gomorrah on the Day of Judgment than for that town." Matthew 10:15, in contrast to Luke, emphasizes that the towns and homes of Galilee that show no hospitality to Jesus' disciples are worse off than Sodom and Gomorrah (cf. Luke 10:12–15). The reference to Sodom would bring to mind Sodom's inhabitants' desire to rape the guests of Lot; it is a place from whence the cry of the oppressed originated.[34]

12:36

People will pay back to God the harm they cause through their careless and lazy words: "I tell you, on the day of judgment you will pay back for every careless word you utter; I tell you, on the day of judgment you will have to give an account for every careless word you utter (my translation)." Verse 37 states that "paying back" is punishment. Again the emphasis is on condemnation of the unrepentant. The language is judicial and the Day of Judgment is the day of reckoning. Some will be justified and others condemned.

13:11

Jesus says: "To them it has not been given to know the secrets of the kingdom of heaven." I believe this refers to those who reject Jesus' message of good news to the poor through not repenting with good fruits.[35] In other words Jesus' good news to the poor causes the hearts of the non-poor to be hardened. The non-poor live to profit by sacrificing the poor even if they don't know it. Jesus' good news to the poor is explained by God's will that the non-poor live for the other.

The parables, according to 13:34–35, point to Jesus' message of good news to the poor as uncovering God's intentions for human beings: their lives be lived for others. In 13:34–35 we read:

34. Matthew elevates his theology of wrath by: (1) truly; (2) Luke has "in that day" while Matthew has "in the Day of Condemnation;" (3) Luke has at the end of his verse "it will be more tolerable for" whereas Matthew has it at the front thus emphasizing the condemnation. (4) Matthew qualifies Sodom with "to the land;" (5) Matthew's "Gomorrah" brings to mind the great judgment in Genesis 19–20.

35. Hagner, *Matthew 1–13*, 373.

> Jesus told the crowds all these things in parables; without a parable He told them nothing. This was to fulfill what had been spoken through the prophet: "I will open my mouth to speak in parables; I will proclaim what has been hidden from the foundation of the world."

The parables reveal what has been hidden from the beginning of creation (13:35): greed, sin, blame, hate, and violence. The non-poor in 13:11 are blind to the will and goodness of God that is central at the beginning of creation but which has also become hidden because of human greed and sin. The parables expose the truth about a sinful world revealing its lies and aggressiveness. They also show ways to overcome them through love, mercy, and goodness.[36] The goodness of God challenges the *status quo* (rooted in sacrifice of the oppressed) causing many to close their ears and shut their eyes to him. In the same way Jesus' message of love would cause division and violence (Matthew 10:34–39). God, therefore, judges by giving the unrepentant over to the logic of their own wickedness.

Jesus faced opposition not only from the religious leaders but also the crowds: His own family, and people from His home town. This provides the setting for those who reject Jesus' message of a new kingdom based on justice and equality. In Matthew 13, the crowds are unable to hear or see Jesus' message. These are the crowds who, when stirred up by Jewish leaders, reject Jesus at His trial (26:18–23) and who reject the blind men in 20:29–34.

According to Mark 4:12 Jesus states that He spoke in parables "so that (*hina*) they may indeed see but not understand . . ." whereas Matthew alters *hina* to *hoti* (because); therefore Matthew has: Jesus spoke in parables *because* they may indeed see but not perceive, and hearing they do not listen, nor do they understand. Beare suggests correctly that Matthew emphasizes the failure to repent was not because God was a merciless despot; Beare argues that Matthew "affirms that this failure to understand was caused by their culpable hardness of heart and self-willed blindness, not by any intention of Jesus to leave them in their plight."[37]

Finally, Matthew 13:14–15 includes a quote close to LXX Isaiah 6:9–10 that helps us understand Matthew. The text warns that most people will not respond to Isaiah's message of God's judgment (only a tenth will remain). Those whose hearts are hard in LXX Isaiah 6:9–10 are those who stand to benefit from the *status quo*.

36. Girard, *Things Hidden*, 225: argues that the secret Jesus reveals is the secret of human violence in which human beings maintain stability by sacrificing others rather than by self-sacrifice; cf. Häring, *Healing Power of Peace*, 10.

37. Beare, *Matthew*, 294.

The tenth that are saved in Isaiah heed God's message and will be the basis of hope (a holy seed). What happened in Isaiah's day is happening in Jesus' day. The people are presented with clear indicators that repentance is needed, but the people refuse and in so doing bring upon themselves punishment. However, the language of chapter 13, while revealing the process of self-condemnation, puts God very much in charge and indicates that self-condemnation is linked to what God had ordered. It is ultimately God who condemns.

13:24–43

Jesus tells them a parable about a man who planted good seed in his field:

> He put before them another parable: "The kingdom of heaven may be compared to someone who sowed good seed in his field; but while everybody was asleep, an enemy came and sowed weeds among the wheat, and then went away. So when the plants came up and bore grain, then the weeds appeared as well. And the slaves of the householder came and said to him, 'Master, did you not sow good seed in your field? Where, then, did these weeds come from?' He answered, 'An enemy has done this.' The slaves said to him, 'Then do you want us to go and gather them?' But he replied, 'No; for in gathering the weeds you would uproot the wheat along with them. Let both of them grow together until the harvest; and at harvest time I will tell the reapers, Collect the weeds first and bind them in bundles to be burned, but gather the wheat into my barn.'" (13:24–30)

The parable of the weeds is found only in Matthew 13:24–30. The crowds and disciples hear the parable (13:1–2). Many who hear fail to understand or accept Jesus (13:10–15). Neither the scribes nor Pharisees are said to be present.

The following are key features in this parable: (1) the appearance of the weeds; (2) the work of the enemy (enemy occurs elsewhere in 5:43 where Jesus teaches that it is necessary to love the enemy); (3) the servants who want to pull the weeds up believing this is best for the good seeds; (4) the master forbids this because it would go against love of enemy; (5) the good and bad seeds must be allowed to grow together; (6) the weeds will be sorted out as the master sees fit. *The message is clear: destruction of the weeds is not the task of the servants.*

Many of those whom Jesus taught hated the tax-collectors, the Gentiles, the sick, poor, prisoners, migrants, and so on. His audience would have identified the weeds in the parable as representing those supposedly cursed by God (i.e., the Gentiles, the sick, and so on). Poverty was seen by many as a sign that the poor person was a sinner. In short, the weeds represented the weak, poor, and helpless.

The crowds who hear this parable are not those who went to hear John the Baptist and who repented confessing their sins. They refer to the fickle and easily influenced crowds that at one moment praise Him and at another moment mock Him (26:18–23).

I suggest Jesus' parable is an attack on the idea of hating, blaming and excluding warning that to follow such practices will result in God's wrath. Further, Jesus emphasizes that judgment belongs to God. The message Jesus gives is that His audience must co-exist with the things they don't like. In fact taken in conjunction with Jesus' teaching about loving your enemy, His audience would recall this and understand that Jesus is teaching about self-sacrifice for the gain of the other. In terms of the poor, this would mean caring for them and not excluding them. The emphasis in Jesus' teaching is on the inclusion of the sick and not the healthy (cf. 9:13b).

I now turn to the explanation Jesus gives of His parable. It is striking that it is given only to the disciples. Again punishment is at the heart of the parable. I quote verses 37–40:

> The one who sows the good seed is the Son of Man; the field is the world, and the good seed are the children of the kingdom; the weeds are the children of the evil one, and the enemy who sowed them is the devil; the harvest is the end of the age, and the reapers are angels. Just as the weeds are collected and burned up with fire, so will it be at the end of the age.

Jesus left the crowds and went into the house (v. 36a). The disciples alone are given the explanation of the parable by Jesus. They, like the crowds, are still immersed in their prejudices and dislikes, for example: the Canaanite woman (15:21ff); their reaction to those who brought little children (I again believe this refers to the excluded) to Jesus so that He may lay His hand upon them to pray (19:13–15); also the crowds that appear to be indignant at the two blind men coming to Jesus (20:31).

The good seeds are the children of the kingdom (13:38; cf. 8:12). The weeds are the children of the evil one (13:38). Jesus teaches that the weeds are all who cause stumbling and practice lawlessness (13:41 my translation). "Children of the kingdom" appears nowhere in the Bible except in Matthew 8:12 and 13:38. The phrase is another way of saying "children of God" who are identical to the peacemakers in 5:9. In 5:45 Jesus emphasizes that those who claim to be children of their heavenly Father are known through the love they show to their enemies. *It is assumed that disciples of Jesus would not exclude others.* The children of the kingdom are to be seen as the children of God.[38] They are those who bring glory to God through their good works (5:14–16) through living subversively in solidarity with the poorest of the poor.

Furthermore, I suggest the children of the kingdom in 13:38 are also the poorest of the poor. For example, in Matthew 18:1 (only in Matthew) the disciples ask: who is the greatest in the kingdom of heaven? Jesus sets a child in the midst of them. "Child" refers to the vulnerable and excluded. Jesus in putting the child in the midst of His disciples teaches that the greatest in the kingdom were considered weeds by decent folk. Jesus in His parable turns the whole idea of the kingdom of heaven upside down by having present in it those who are considered cursed (i.e., the poor and weak). Therefore, according to Jesus, these good seeds are the weakest and most vulnerable whom decent folk look down upon. In fact Jesus warns: "Take care that you do not despise one of these little ones" (18:10). Jesus surely in this context refers in 13:41 to stumbling as something others cause the vulnerable by looking down on them and misleading them.[39]

The parable of the goats and the sheep refers to those (the goats) who did not feed the hungry or thirsty, welcome the migrant, clothe the naked, visit the sick and prisoners. The king says: "Truly I tell you, just as you did not do it to one of the least of these, you did not do it to me." It is clear that these despised and excluded groups are specially related to Jesus. *They are the good seeds, the children of the kingdom* not because they are pious, but because they are excluded from the goodness of creation. Therefore, the weeds represent those who cause others to stumble through their disobedience to Torah (13:41). The scribes and Pharisees in Matthew cause others to stumble through their disobedience to Torah.

Jesus' explanation challenges the disciples to see that they too at times were slow in picking up Jesus' upside-down message that the last will be first, and the first will be last (19:30 and 20:16), the humiliated will be exalted, and the exalted will be humiliated. The disciples with their current hard-heartedness are also the weeds.

In short: (1) Peacemakers are good seeds who practice love of the enemy. It follows also that they don't look down on others. (2) The good seeds also refer to those who are despised: the poorest of the poor who have no

38. However, the children of the kingdom in 8:12 are those who are cast out of the kingdom.

39. I have thought about this in the context of those prisoners I visit in my capacity as Prison Chaplain and who often committed their crimes because they were easily lead astray. Many of them have low IQs.

help. (3) Those who hear the parable considered these poorest of the poor as the weeds of society. (4) The disciples themselves were being challenged to see themselves as the weeds who must repent of their excluding practices. (5) Those who do not repent will be thrown into the furnace of fire, where there will be weeping and gnashing of teeth.

15:14

Jesus is forthright in attacking both the elite and those who collude with them: "they are blind guides of the blind. And if one blind person guides another, both will fall into a pit." This verse exemplifies Matthew's understanding of creation as ordered to bring down punishment on those who reject God's will.

16:27

Jesus teaches: "For the Son of Man is to come with his angels in the glory of his Father, and then He will repay everyone for what has been done." In anticipation of the arrival of Jesus to condemn, Matthew has: "and then *he will repay* everyone for what has been done" (cf. Revelation 2:23; 18:6; 20:12–13; 22:12; there is no Synoptic parallel). This verse in Matthew echoes 24:45–50 and 25:31–46 which emphasize that a person will be judged according to how they have executed justice in favor of the poor.

22:1–14

In the parable of the wedding banquet Matthew states that both good and bad are present (v. 10) adding that few from among them will be chosen (v. 14). The good and bad refers to the non-poor. The good are the respectable and decent ordinary folk working hard to make enough to live. The bad are the tax-collectors, sex-workers, adulterers, and so on.

A similar parable is found in Luke, with differences. The poor, maimed, blind and lame are invited (14:21). Further, Luke, unlike Matthew, neither recounts the rejection of the servant (cf. Matthew 22:11–12) nor Jesus' teaching that many are invited and few are chosen (cf. Matthew 22:14). Luke leaves out the punishment theme we find in Matthew stating only that the poor are at the banquet. The banquet in Luke is the place where God's goodness is fully present and the poor are there regardless of whether they are good or bad.

Matthew, however, does not have the poor at the banquet because the banquet scene is a foil for condemnation and judgment. According to Matthew, the parable warns about condemnation of those who are not from among the poor (i.e., the good and the bad). In the First Gospel's account the poor are chosen while the non-poor are rejected because they have not born fruits of repentance.

In conclusion, Matthew does not have the poor at the banquet, unlike Luke, because the parable scene is about condemnation. The poor are not in danger of condemnation therefore they are not at the banquet.

23:29–36

Jesus warns the Scribes and Pharisees that the blood of their victims will be their downfall (vv. 35–36). This refers to the cry of the innocent victims for God to bring violence upon the heads of their oppressor (cf. Isaiah 40:2; Deuteronomy 32:43). In these verses Abel is a righteous person who is a murder victim of Cain. The Pharisees are compared to Cain, they are the children of Cain for they, too, are murderers (cf. 1 John 3:12). However, warning of condemnation is done with mercy and hope of repentance. They are warned and given every opportunity to turn from their violence (v. 34). Alas they fail and murder those who teach them God's will. Abel appears to be the type of one of those sent to teach the way of righteousness. It seems likely that Matthew's listeners would know of the traditions relating to Abel and Cain and how Cain is motivated to murder because he does not fear condemnation or hope for rewards for good works. The refusal to heed the words of the righteous results in the blood of the righteous being poured upon them; in other words, they have lived by violence and now they will die in the same way.

24:28–31 (Mark 13:24–27)

I suggest these verses in Matthew describe a scene of adverse judgment. Matthew has additions to Mark 13 that support this. In 24:28, for example, we read: "Wherever the corpse is, there the vultures will gather." I understand this to be a reference to the defeat of the ruling elites. In 24:30 we hear that: "all the tribes of the earth will mourn . . ." This refers to the despair of the wicked (cf. 1 Enoch 62:5 and Zechariah 12:10). In short these additions show Matthew understands judgment as something that will overtake the enemies of the son of man. Douglass comments: "In a lightning insight, whose implications are still far beyond us, Jesus sensed the connections between the violence done to the poor, the outcast, and the rebellious in a colonized first-century Judea and a violent end of the world—his world and any world in which the logic of violence is followed."[40] In short, Matthew describes a global catastrophe related to the existence of violence and poverty.

Walter Wink, similarly to Douglass, sees described in these verses what happens if the vision of a new and peaceable reality is rejected: "The Reign of God is not the climax of a long evolution toward goodness, but the radical negation of an inhumane, colossal, and entrenched system. Despite all attempts to change for the better, if that system simply proliferates blindly, heedless of the human or environmental costs, social collapse is predictable."[41]

I think this also relates to our reading of Matthew 24:28 (cf. Luke 17:37): "Wherever the corpse is, there the vultures will gather." The NRSV translates 'corpse' (*ptōma*; Luke has *sōma*) for both Matthew and Luke rather than 'body.' *Ptōma* specifically refers to a fallen body, a carcass, a corpse.[42] Luke's *sōma,* however, is not so strong. The most natural application of this proverb for Matthew is judgment. Jesus' arrival after His death is compared to the bird of prey that will consume the bodies of the wicked.[43]

24:48–51

Jesus warns the unrepentant that "(God) will cut them in pieces and put them with the hypocrites, where there will be weeping and gnashing of teeth."[44] The context is of mistreating slaves by use of violence. The language of judgment is violent imitating aspects of the very world Jesus resists.[45] Those who treat badly their slaves will bring upon themselves what they have inflicted on others. In short, I reiterate: condemnation belongs to God.

25:31–46

This parable found only in Matthew will be a feature of discussion in later chapters. It looks to the Day of Judgment when those who care for the poorest of the poor will be separated from those who ignore them. Those who

40. Douglass, *Nonviolent Coming of God*, 15.
41. Wink, *Human Being*, 168.
42. Abbott-Smith, *Manual Greek Lexicon*, 393.
43. Hagner, *Matthew 24–28*, 707.
44. Luke 12:46 has "cutting in pieces" but Matthew adds "gnashing of teeth."
45. Carter, *Matthew and the Margins*, 482.

feed and care for the poor are blessed by inheriting the kingdom prepared by God (v. 34) which is eternal life (v. 46). However, those who ignore the poor are accursed and destined to eternal fire prepared by God for the devil and His angels (v. 41). In verse 46 this place of fire is "eternal punishment."

There is debate as to whether the list of poor and suffering people refers to those disciples suffering through giving their witness or whether it points to the poorest of the poor in general. In a later chapter I argue for the latter. Miranda has demonstrated to me convincingly that Judgment Day is when justice is executed in favor of the poorest of the poor.[46] This in itself pushes me in the direction of seeing 25:31–46 as a judgment scene in favor of the poorest and not as the disciples suffering due to the testimony they give.

26:52

Only in Matthew Jesus teaches that those who live by the sword, will die by it (Matthew 26:52). The sword in this verse represents the way of the world signifying violence, greed, and oppression that causes poverty and great suffering. Jesus makes clear that violence perpetuates more violence which results in poverty and decay. Jesus warns: "Put your sword back into its place; for all who take the sword will *perish by the sword*." Here Matthew envisages punishment of those who live by the sword. Their condemnation is what they bring down upon themselves.

JAMES 5:1–3

In James 5:1–3 we see strong judgmental teaching: "Come now, you rich people, weep and wail for the miseries that are coming to you. Your riches have rotted, and your clothes are moth-eaten. Your gold and silver have rusted, and their rust will be evidence against you, and it will eat your flesh like fire. You have laid up treasure for the last days." Bauckham comments that these verses resemble the traditions of the sayings of Jesus.[47] As Jesus' sayings about judgment are most prominent in Matthew, a relationship of some kind can be envisaged between Matthew and James. These verses make explicit the link between judgment day and justice for the poor.[48] Such

46. Miranda, *Marx*, 111–137, especially 116–118. On page 137 he concludes: "There is an *ultimatum* in human history, and this *ultimatum* is defined and characterized . . . by the complete realization of justice on earth."

47. Bauckham, *James*, 57.

48. Tamez, *Scandalous Message of James*, 41.

traditions are to be found strongly in Jesus' parable of judgment days in Matthew 25:31–46 where those who care for the poorest of the poor are blessed and those who don't are accursed.

James 5:2–3 echoes also Matthew 6:19–21.[49] In 5:2–3 riches have rotted, clothes are moth-eaten, and gold and silver are rusted. James emphasizes that this rust will consume the wealthy like fire. In Matthew 6:19 Jesus warns against relying on wealth where moth and rust can consume. This is the rust that will also consume the heart rooted in wealth (Matthew 6:21).

In short, I consider James 5:1–3 to illustrate the line of tradition that sees judgment as involving execution of justice in favor of the poor and those who care for them.

SUMMARY

- God's judgment is best understood in the context of Jesus warning about condemnation for the purpose of *shalom*. This is particularly emphatic in Matthew.
- Our modern liberal sensibilities, so offended by ideas of condemnation, should be compared to the ancient godless idea that there was no such thing as reward or condemnation.
- God's compassion is emphatic not just in acts of forgiveness, but in the scenes of destruction that human sin brings upon itself.
- Matthew favors those who are on the wrong side of injustice. God's preference for them has nothing to do with piety. *Matthew's God does not respond only to the poor who cry to Him, He hears the cry of all who cry out in pain and hopelessness from oppression.*
- God has the divine perspective and has ordered creation accordingly to protect creation. Matthew makes it clear that condemnation is what God enacts through creation spitting out that which harms it.
- James 5:1–3 illustrates the line of tradition that sees judgment as involving execution of justice in favor of the poor and those who care for them.

49. Ibid., 73 notes this parallel.

FOOD FOR THOUGHT

Häring urges: "The rich and overprivileged must be freed from their blindness, individual and collective selfishness, superiority complex, refusal to share the power of decision and rewards of common work. The poor must be freed from their fatalism and passivity, freed to discover their own inner resources and the power of solidarity."[50] These words fit the call for repentance resulting in responding to the poor. However, Häring has in mind a different group of poor people from those I believe Jesus addresses in Matthew. Jesus, as we will see in part 3, does indeed free the sick and disabled. Häring's words risk making culpable the poor in their plight through their passivity. There is nothing to suggest this in Matthew. God accepts the poor whatever their moral status. The non-poor are to blame and unless they repent they bring God's wrath upon themselves.

Matthew's presentation of Jesus as one who preaches hell and damnation directs us to see God as being on the side of the powerless and oppressed. Jesus' teaching about punishment targets the powerful and those who accept the regime of the powerful. Jesus teaches that the suffering of the oppressed is coming to an end through Jesus' work, and that the powerful and their cronies will, ultimately, feel the suffering they have inflicted turned upon themselves.

I find the texts of wrath in Matthew an incentive and motivation challenging me to look at my life and ask whether I am feeding the hungry, giving drink to the thirsty, welcoming the migrant, clothing the naked, caring for the sick, and visiting the prisoner. I find myself wondering how I can make my church a place where people with disabilities of any kind can feel welcome.

Our society is very different from Matthew's. But the issues are still about violence and greed. In my own life I have found the poorest of the poor to be especially people with learning difficulties and many who are in prison. There are many who we look down upon in society.

In the light of this chapter's findings related to God's wrath, I am drawn to assess all aspects of my life in terms of how it might cause others to be excluded from the bounty of creation. I recall as a child hearing a preacher of hell and damnation. I heard people muttering and laughing at him. But when I was at school on Monday I gave the ten pence my mother had given me to buy a loaf of bread on the way home to a boy in my class called Tommy because he wore rags to school. Perhaps that mad preacher was proclaiming God's word after all!

50. Häring, *Healing Power of Peace and Nonviolence*, 15.

In our modern Western world we see, hear and know of the increasing sense of depression, guilt, and anxiety, people feel even though they have more than they need materially. I have come to know many people who have given up well-paid work to go and work in unpaid or poorly paid forms of care giving. Christopher Bryant observes that God's judgment works through a kind of in-built psychic mechanism. Guilt, depression, and anxiety, he believes are forms of punishment. I see many people overcoming their sense of existential crisis through acknowledging, consciously or unconsciously, they are hard-wired to care. This insight is being made more known by those working in the area of Neuroplasticity that shows human beings are only truly happy when they care.[51]

In short, God's wrath evident in its many guises calls human beings to change and care.

PRAYER

Dear Father, show us how we cause the other anguish, make us uneasy at our complacency and ease, broaden our vision about ourselves, that we might see how at odds with Your goodness we are, may we stop shutting our ears and eyes to the truth that we cause much anguish, call us to deep repentance and confession of sins. Lead us each morning to remember that our actions always have consequences. Amen.

51. McFague, *Blessed are the Consumers*, 122–24: "some scientific experiments in brain plasticity are supporting the significant idea that we may be hard-wired for altruism. . ." Alastair Mordey in http://www.intervene.org.uk/addiction-disease-doesnt-reduce-treatment-medical-model/ writes of addiction and insights from neuroplasticity, mindfulness and CBT: "Gaining interconnectedness with others (fellowship) has meaning. Service work with others (Step 12) has meaning. The altruism involved in service gives recovering addicts a sense of purpose and cuts right to the heart of our intrinsic nature as social animals."

PART TWO

Introduction

The Inner-Order of Creation

To cut oneself off, to become, or to remain, a stranger to the 'other', goes against the whole meaning of the evolution of life.[1] —*Gillet*

Mercy is a work which springs from the goodness of God.[2]
—*Julian of Norwich*

Chapters 3–6 consider the goodness of God as the internal "order of creation." This is best understood in terms of relationships rooted in living for others. Walter Brueggemann sees generous relationships as central: "it is evident that Israel's most characteristic and theologically intentional practice is to attend to the needs of those too weak to protect themselves (cf. Deuteronomy 14:29; 16:11, 14; 24:19–21; 26:12–15; Isaiah 1:17; Jeremiah 7:6; 22:3; Zechariah 7:10)."[3]

Central to those working in the area of biblical theology is the insight that life is bound together in such a way as to be an expression of God's self-giving love. This means we are ordered to live sacrificially, mercifully, according to righteousness, and lawfully. Such words as covenant, mercy, righteousness, law, and mercy, in some way describe the inner-order that is the infrastructure of creation. If creation is the outward expression of

1. Gillet, *In Thy Presence*, 44.
2. Julian of Norwich, *Enfolded in Love*, 16.
3. Brueggemann, *Theology of the Old Testament*, 422.

God's love and self-giving, then God's creational intentions of mercy and righteousness refer to creation inwardly. God has made creation to function covenantally.

In short, creation is inwardly ordered and such order is represented in words such as covenant, steadfast love, mercy, goodness, righteousness, law and justice. This order will be considered in chapter 3–6.

In part 1, I emphasized the goodness of creation. By this I understand God to have created what He intends to be an expression of His goodness. The meaning of good in terms of Genesis 1 is to be extrapolated from God's creating actions which reveal a God who is generous, selfless and defined by His forming of a home where all flourish. This goodness can now be further explored in terms of covenant, mercy, love, sacrifice, righteousness, law, and *shalom*.

3

Covenant

To live we must daily break the body and shed the blood of creation. When we do this knowingly, lovingly, skillfully and reverently it is a sacrament.[1] *—Wendell Berry*

We must be concerned . . . to "live answerable to the design of our creation."[2] *—John Woolman*

The central idea underpinning this chapter is that, for Matthew, Christians are to live covenantally meaning that they are to be ready to pour themselves out so others can flourish. And this must be done lovingly, skillfully, and reverently. Why? Because creation is ordered and conditioned to function like this by God who Himself poured out His whole Being in forming His creation. The goodness of creation that God sees is the goodness of God.

Covenant is the inner condition (essence), or order, of creation. Creation itself is an outward expression of God's goodness.[3] Terrence Fretheim is quite right to distance himself from a generation of biblical theologians who argue that covenant is distinct from creation. I agree with him in

1. http://www.goodreads.com/quotes/322669-to-live-we-must-daily-break-the-body-and-shed.

2. In *QF&P* 20.34 Michael Lee, 1976.

3. This relates also to Barth's insights that creation and covenant are complementary articulations, external and internal, of the same reality in *Church Dogmatics*, 3.1, 42–329. See also Gwyn, *Covenant Crucified*, 3.

referring to covenant as creation's basic infrastructure;[4] John Woolman similarly appears to see covenant as "the design of our creation." Covenant is therefore linked to the goodness of God which is seen in creation. The extent to which people live covenantally is the extent to which they act as expressions of God's goodness.

Matthew is the only Gospel that states explicitly that covenant is about selflessness even unto death so others can flourish (26:28).[5] Covenant describes how creation is designed for self-sacrifice. The goodness of creation that God sees in creation is good to the extent that it functions harmoniously. Agrarian writer Wendell Berry (at the beginning of this chapter) expresses this life as a self-giving. God formed creation ordering it so that all aspects of it live covenantally (i.e., in harmony with God's goodness). God made a community of creation promising that if human beings live according to that covenant, then all will flourish. *Covenantal living is based on living generously with no purpose other than to see others flourish.*

COVENANT WITH DEATH

John Woolman observes that one who grows rich at the expense of others "acts contrary to the gracious design of him who is the true owner of the earth."[6] The existence of poverty reveals the extent to which humans live by hatred and greed. Isaiah 28:15 and v. 18 state that such people have made a "covenant with death." People estranged from God's goodness are dead in their affluence consuming themselves into oblivion. Only in Isaiah 28:15 and v. 18 is found the phrase "covenant with death." It refers to those who are "bloated with rich food, of those overcome with wine" (Isaiah 28:1, 4). Dorothy Day gets to the heart of this when she writes: "The bread you retain belongs to the hungry, the dress you lock up is the property of the naked;" "What is superfluous for one's need is to be regarded as plunder if one retains it for one's self."[7]

4. Fretheim, *God and World*, 86: "Covenant is a means to that divine end for creation."

5. Compare Hebrews 12:24 which describes Jesus as the mediator of a new covenant sprinkled with blood.

6. Woolman, *The Journal and Major Essays*, 239–40.

7. Day, *Selected Writings*, 99.

MARRIAGE AND COVENANT

Francis Young observes that "you could tell the story of God's covenant with Israel in terms of a bridegroom with his bride."[8] Jeremiah 31:32 describes God as the husband of Israel in the context of covenant. It is helpful to think of marriage as an outer condition of love while love is the inner condition.

Two commandments are central to understanding what it is to be in a covenantal relationship with God. It is to love God (Deuteronomy 6:5) and your neighbor (Leviticus 19:18). Love is central to living obediently to God. Doug Gwyn states that "Love" evokes covenant.[9] Therefore the essence of marriage is covenantally rooted in love and unconditional service for others.

Marriage, for example, is a covenant relationship in which man and woman are bound together in a covenant of caring for each other.[10] Marriage embraces responsibility to husband and wife in areas of sexuality, economics, religion, and personal integrity. Marriage is like creation, it is to be bound by limitless and self-giving love. In short, marriage is an outward expression of love; love is the inner condition or order of marriage.

CREATION, COVENANT, AND ECONOMICS

Christopher Wright comments: "covenant-based economics called for economic relationships to be based on love and mutual support."[11] Covenant-based economics are an expression of how God intended creation to be ordered and ones that dominate the very fabric of Israel's story.

Brueggemann adds that "creation is covenantally ordered: that is, formed for continuing interactions of gift and gratitude, of governance and obedience."[12] He points out that covenant relates to sharing your bread with the hungry; bringing the homeless poor in your house; clothing the naked.[13] He argues that generosity is central to creation. Generosity is a covenant word and humans are "commanded to live on Yahweh's terms. When those terms are violated, trouble comes."[14]

8. Young similarly emphasizes covenant as a marriage-bond (*Brokenness*, 107). Young adds that "this is exactly what we find in the *Targum on the Song of Songs*."

9. Gwyn, *Covenant Crucified*, 3.

10. The Bible did not envisage same sex marriage, but I would include it as relevant today in discussing covenant.

11. Wright, *Old Testament Ethics*, 157.

12. Brueggemann, *Old Testament Theology*, 157–58.

13. Ibid., 464.

14. Ibid., 491. See also Brueggemann, *Peace*, 100.

Psalm 74:20–21 sees covenant as central for creation to be good and generous. Without regard for covenant (v. 20a) creation will be a dark place and the haunt of violence (v. 20b).[15] I suggest verse 21a be read in the context of v. 20a (i.e., people must "have regard for the covenant"); therefore, central to obedience to the covenant is not letting the downtrodden be put to shame. Verse 21b states: "let the poor and needy praise your name." This is the goal of the covenant that all praise God for His mercy. In other words, the poor and needy cannot exist where the covenant is not regarded. The poor cannot praise God because their lives are not as God intended for them.

MATTHEW

I now look to Matthew's understanding of covenant. I consider only a few texts briefly. In the following chapters of part 2 it is clear through the occurrences of mercy, steadfast love, Torah, and peace, that covenant is central to Matthew. In this chapter I chose a selection of texts that lend themselves to a covenant understanding of Matthew.

5:13

The phrase "salt of the earth" refers to the "salt of the covenant" (see Numbers 18:19; Leviticus 2:13; cf. 2 Chronicles 13:5; Jubilees 21:11; 11QTemp 20:13; *Sipra* on Numbers 18:19).[16] When the disciple is as salt he or she is someone who lives self-sacrificially (i.e., covenantally), giving to others.

5:14–16

Only in Matthew Jesus tells His disciples that they are the "light of the world." In Isaiah 42:6 covenant is in synonymous parallel with light. Further, love and generosity are associated with covenant, and the light here is linked to all. Jesus teaches that His disciples must be a light to the world, this means that they become expressions of God's goodness: it is an expressions of God's love shining over creation and overcoming the darkness (cf. John 1:5).

15. Perhaps echoing pre-creation vision of Genesis 1:2.

16. Davies and Allison, *Matthew 1–7*, 472; Schweizer, *Matthew*, 101.

In Isaiah 51:4 justice is compared to light. The servant is the light. Jesus' disciples are taught in 5:14–16 that they must shine in the midst of the darkness of violence and greed, and execute justice.

20:28 (see also 26:28)

Matthew states that Jesus came not to be served, but to serve others and to give His life as a sacrifice for the benefit of all. The idea of expressing love through suffering for others is not easy in our society. I find the following extract from James Douglass helpful:

> The logic of non-violence is the logic of crucifixion and leads the man of non-violence into the heart of the suffering Christ. The purpose of non-violence is to move the oppressors to perceive as human beings those whom they are oppressing. Non-violent resistance seeks to persuade the aggressor to recognize in his victims the humanity they have in common, which when recognized fully makes violence impossible.[17]

I read 20:28 in the context of the poor and oppressed. It is Jesus' identification and solidarity with the poor that leads to His suffering and death. When Jesus teaches about bearing the cross it is a political and revolutionary act that challenges the forces of domination and exclusion to see the horror of what such exclusionary politics results in. Ryne puts it well:

> Following Christ by taking up our cross does not refer to any and all suffering but to that suffering that results from acting as Jesus did, identifying with the poor and oppressed, laboring to relieve their suffering, and standing up to the powers that be. That is the kind of behavior that will bring a cross. Human suffering is not a good in itself . . . unless it is experienced as a consequence of the good cause that Jesus leads—nonviolent resistance to evil.[18]

26:28 (cf. 20:28)

In 26:28 Jesus says: "for this is my blood of the covenant which is poured out for many for the forgiveness of sins." Matthew adds to Mark "for the forgiveness of sins."

17. Douglass, *Non-Violent Cross*, 70; also Jesudasan, *A Gandhian Theology*, 116.

18. Ryne, *Gandhi and Jesus*, 161.

It is safe to say that *the covenant is about sacrifice rooted in self-giving.* Life can only flourish when love is the cement that binds all things together. The people of the covenant are to commit themselves to bringing about God's goodness through living selflessly for others. Michael Gorman emphasizes that the covenant is not:

> reducible to forgiveness of sins in some narrow (i.e., 'vertical' only) sense. Rather, receiving God's forgiveness is part of existence as a community of salt and light (5:13–16) that is called and empowered to forgiveness (5:21–24; 18:15–20) and its associated virtues, such as deeds of mercy and compassion (9:13 and 12:7, citing Hosea 6:6) like those of their Master (9:36; 14:14; 15:32; 18:33; 20:34).[19]

SUMMARY

- Covenant refers to the way creation is designed inwardly.
- Creation is a place of abundance and goodness.
- Covenant is the infrastructure, life-force, of creation.
- Covenant is about nurturing life through self-offering.
- Covenant is the binding force that enables all things to function as God desires.

FOOD FOR THOUGHT

I have argued that creation and covenant must go together. Creation is creation because it is formed for all to flourish in relationships of self-giving. It is like an altar where creatures metaphorically and sometimes literally offer their blood for others.

The marriage ceremony challenges me to understand creation as the outward expression of God's limitless love ordered inwardly for covenant understood as founded in love. A marriage is good to the extent that each partner lives selflessly.

In our world today as in Jesus' time, the gap between rich and poor demonstrates the extent to which humanity lives at enmity with God and the rest of creation. The very example of Jesus' life is to actively remove poverty. To live covenantally is to live hospitably sharing all things.

19. Gorman, *Death of the Messiah*, 36.

The sensitizing of ourselves to the nature of covenant and its presence in Jesus' teaching orientates us to seeing the importance of radical changes which Jesus calls forth from His contemporaries. He saw that the existence of poverty called for revolution. Quaker writer Gwyn puts it well:

> The locus of true revolutionary practice is in covenantal relations, in the integrity of communities—religious communities, racial and ethnic communities, economic communities, even ecological communities of the natural world. The internal coherence *within* covenant communities, concatenated by covenantal linkages *among* them, can re-build the web of life, the *shalom* of God.[20]

PRAYER

You Father are in heaven, but You are the active, creative love at work throughout all creation. Teach us to understand that to be bound to You is to give ourselves in love for others through becoming less that others can grow. Amen.

20. Gwyn, *Covenant Crucified*, 16.

4

Righteousness and Justice

Wealth is attended with power, by which bargains and proceedings contrary to universal righteousness are supported; and here oppression, carried on with worldly policy and order, clothes itself with the name of justice and becomes like a seed of discord in the soil.[1] *—John Woolman*

"Righteousness" (Hebrew: *ṣedeqā*; Greek: *dikaiosynē*), often translated "justice," appears in Matthew more than any other gospel (3:15; 5:6; 5:10; 5:20; 6:1, 33; 21:32).[2] Jesus teaches that righteousness is to be sought with the same passion and commitment as if pursuing the "kingdom of God" (6:33). So strong is this theme that Joseph Grassi calls Matthew "The Gospel of Justice."[3] The word righteousness, I propose, to which Matthew refers, is the "universal righteousness" of which John Woolman writes above.

Righteousness in Hebrew thought is mostly a relational concept.[4] Glen Stassen helpfully contrasts the righteousness of the world with that of righteousness as depicted in the Bible: "In biblical culture, righteousness

1. Woolman, *Journal and Major Essays*, 255.

2. Only once in Luke and absent in Mark. There is also the related word *dikaios* appearing in 1:19, 10:41, 13:17, 13:43; 20:4; 23:28; 23:35; 25:37; 25:46. Its verbal form *dikaios* is found in 11:19; 12:37. Outside of Paul, righteousness is found in 1 John (2:29; 3:7, 10, 12.) in a way that bears comparison with Matthew.

3. Grassi, *Informing the Future*, 132.

4. Dunn, *Theology of Paul the Apostle*, 341.

meant 'delivering justice that restores community relationships.' But in our individualistic and possessive culture, most people think of righteousness as a virtue possessed by individuals. That is actually self-righteousness, which the Bible says we cannot have . . ."[5]

Hans Heinrich Schmid provides an important lens for understanding righteousness.[6] According to Schmid, biblical righteousness refers to the foundation of created order that leads to a mutually enriching society made visible in the equal distribution of creation's abundance. I argue that righteousness in Matthew directs the reader to the foundation order in creation that exists so that the goodness of God is fully present in all creation (i.e., loving and generous living).[7] Ultimately, for humans to live in accordance with God's righteousness they must work for the good of others and all creation. When this happens creation is *full of goodness*. God's goodness is the same as His righteousness and it is in His creation when all things live generously so that all may flourish. In this world when all live according to God's righteousness, creation will satisfy all with what is necessary for a fulfilled life (cf. Psalm 103:5).

RIGHTEOUSNESS AS STRUCTURE AND FABRIC OF CREATION

Schmid's contention that righteousness is the very structure and fabric of creation has influenced eminent Old Testament scholars such as Walter Brueggemann, Terence Fretheim, and Christopher Wright.[8] Fretheim helpfully summarizes Schmid's contribution:

> He [Schmidt] specifies that *sedeqah*, 'righteousness' . . . refers to harmonious world order built by God into the very infrastructure of creation. So, wherever righteousness is practiced by human beings in the socio-political spheres, that act is in tune with the creation, and it fosters the proper integration of social

5. Stassen, *Living the Sermon on the Mount*, 34.

6. Schmid, "Creation, Righteousness, and Salvation," 102–17.

7. Yoder Neufeld, "Righteousness and Peace will kiss," 157.

8. James Aall Ottesen Preus in a 2015 unpublished Master's Thesis *Righteousness in Matthew*, 365, concludes: "Based on the thorough research of Hans Heinrich Schmid this paper concluded that righteousness is the divinely established world order. In creation God established righteousness. Man was in a right relationship with God, because he was perfectly made according to God's intention, in God's image. The fall into sin distorted man and removed him from the status of righteous. This removal was both normative and relational. If man is to be brought back into the right relationship with God, right order must be established according to God's norm."

> and cosmic orders. When humans do not practice righteousness, adverse effects are felt across all created spheres. And so, for the Old Testament, matters such as justice, politics, and nature are interrelated as "aspects of one comprehensive order of creation."[9]

Fretheim compares righteousness to "a moral order—a reality that God has built into the very structures of creation."[10] Brueggemann follows Schmid writing: "*Ṣedāqāh* belongs to the very structure and fabric of creation and must not be violated."[11] R. Yoder Neufeld is particularly helpful when he writes that "God's righteousness informs the order of creation, the liberation and defense of God's people, the covenant with Israel, and its stipulations in Torah, and the realization of God's promises. Righteousness is thus intricately related to *shalom*, the Bible's word for salvation, justice, and peace."[12] I believe such an understanding conforms to righteousness in Matthew and will inform my discussion below.

RIGHTEOUSNESS AND THE POOR

Steven Bouma-Prediger writes: "Because the God of the Bible is righteous and just, those who follow this God must be righteous and just. Of particular concern are those most likely to be treated unjustly, namely, the voiceless, the powerless, the homeless."[13] Similarly, Swartley points out: "In the biblical view justice means tending to the needs of the poor, orphans and resident aliens."[14] Howard Zehr, in the same vein, remarks that: "biblical justice seeks to make things better, justice is not designed to maintain the status quo. Indeed its intent is to shake up the status quo, to improve, to move toward shalom."[15]

The psalmist expresses well a dominant biblical theme regarding righteousness: "The LORD creates righteousness and justice for the benefit of all who are oppressed" (Psalm 103:6).[16] Miranda on the basis of a huge range of Old Testament texts argues that justice/righteousness "consists in doing

9. Fretheim, *God and World*, xiii.

10. Ibid, 165.

11. Brueggemann, *Theology of the Old Testament*, 461, note 26.

12. Yoder Neufeld, "Righteousness and Peace will Kiss," 156.

13. Bouma-Prediger, *For the Beauty of the Earth*, 157.

14. Swartley, *Health, Healing*, 129.

15. Zehr, *Changing Lenses*, 140; Grimsrud, "Healing Justice," 80.

16. My own translation.

justice to the poor, neither more nor less."[17] The first significant occurrence of justice/righteousness is in Genesis 18:19: ". . . I have chosen him, that he may charge his children and his household after him to keep the way of the LORD by doing righteousness (LXX: *dikaiosynē*) and justice (*krisin*);[18] so that the LORD may bring about for Abraham what he has promised him." God chose Abraham and his people to establish a world where God's goodness may be fully present in creation both spiritually and materially. Abraham practices righteousness in order to establish God's kingdom on earth. Genesis 18:19 reiterates the promise made by God to Abraham in Genesis 12:3: "In you all the tribes of the earth will be blessed."[19] God requires Abraham to follow the way of righteousness so that all nations may adhere to his example and so experience the harmony/*shalom* that is God's goodness in creation.

It is also striking that "justice and righteousness" in Genesis 18:19 are intentionally set in opposition to the unrighteousness of Sodom and Gomorrah in Genesis 18:20–21 and narrated throughout Genesis 19 where the oppressed victims cry out that 'justice and righteousness" be done. The word "outcry" in 18:20 is almost a technical word for the cry of pain from those who are oppressed. This suggests that the "outcry" against Sodom was specifically "a cry for help."[20] Wright observes:

> Almost certainly there is an intentional contrast between the *ṣĕ-ʿāqâ* (outcry against justice) that God hears from Sodom, and the *ṣĕdaq* (righteousness/justice) that He wants from Abraham's community. The justice of God is the justice of the God who sees and hears the cry of the weak and oppressed, cares about them and takes action on their behalf. That is the essential meaning of *šāpaṭ*—to take action on behalf of the wronged and put things right.[21]

Similarly in Isaiah 5:7 we encounter the play on words between *ṣĕʿāqâ* (cry of the poor) and *ṣĕdâq* (justice) where God looked for "righteousness, but behold, a cry!" This occurs in the context of God's creation of Israel,

17. Miranda, *Marx*, 127.

18. There are thirty-one instances of this construction. It is a hendiadys in which two words are meant to signify only one thing. Miranda, *Marx*, 93–94 observes: "the Old Testament uses these two words twenty-three times in strict parallelism. We find the same parallelism eleven other times but with *sedek* instead of *sedaka*. In addition to these thirty-four synonymic parallelisms, the two roots *spht* and *sdk* appear paired together in thirty-two other instances."

19. Miranda, *Marx*, 95.

20. Wright, *Old Testament Ethics*, 259–60; Miranda, *Marx*, 89.

21. Wright, *Old Testament* Ethics, 260.

compared to a vineyard (parallel with creation).[22] God makes Israel as a vineyard to be a righteous home extending its fruits to all so everyone can prosper. However, in verse 8 we read: "Ah, you who join house to house, who add field to field, until there is room for no one but you, and you are left to live alone in the midst of the land!" Isaiah reflects on how economics is ruled by competition where the powerful gain at the expense of the vulnerable. Israel is like every other nation disobeying God's Torah and righteousness; to oppose Yahweh consists of the monopolizing of the houses and fields by the rich.[23] Israel has become a thief disobeying God's basic Torah of prohibition against theft.

The outcry in Genesis 18:20 is explained in the story of injustice that follows where we learn how the cities' inhabitants rape Lot's guests (19:4). Lot says to them: "do not act so wickedly" (19:7). The people of Sodom are the initial prototypes of civilizations following the path of unrighteousness. They are in direct line with Cain, the builder of cities, and those who build Babel.

The Hebrew of Isaiah 5:7 also reveals the extent to which justice is the antonym of bloodshed. Above we have seen that the author likes wordplays: *ṣĕʿāqâ* (outcry against justice) and *ṣĕdāqâ* (righteousness/justice). There is a further play on words in the v. 7: "he expected justice (*mišpoṭ*) but saw bloodshed (*mišpoḥ*)." The rich murder the poor instead of bringing justice.[24]

MATTHEW AND RIGHTEOUSNESS

As we see above, righteousness occurs predominantly in the Old Testament in the context of God's will and where this is carried out. Righteousness designates the order of behavior in harmony with the inward structure and fabric of creation so God's goodness may be in creation. Righteousness is seen especially in the context of actions in establishing justice in favor of the poor and oppressed. Now I will consider occurrence of righteousness in Matthew.

3:15

Psalm 72 may be helpful in considering Matthew 3:15. The king in the psalm is given righteousness and justice for the purpose of serving the poor (vv. 1,

22. Fretheim, *God and World*, 2.

23. Miranda, *Marx*, 164.

24. Malchow, *Social Justice*, 42.

7). He is the one who defends the poor and crushes the oppressor. The king is one who brings God's presence (i.e., His righteousness) upon creation. In v. 7 we read: "In his days may righteousness flourish, and peace abound . . ." Jesus fulfills the expectation of the king in Psalm 72 as God's presence among His people Israel.

In 3:15 Jesus says to John the Baptist that he must baptise Jesus to fulfill all justice (*pasan dikaiosynēn*). Neufeld observes that Jesus fulfills all justice by "announcing and enacting God's reign, summoning to repentance, meeting human needs . . ."[25] In Matthew 11:2–6 (par. Luke 7:22–23) John the Baptist sends his disciples to find out if Jesus is the Messiah who represents the way of righteousness, one who embodies God's goodness. Jesus replies that the blind see, the lame walk, lepers are cleansed, the deaf hear, the dead are raised, and good news is proclaimed to the poor. Jesus' reply tells John that through His deeds all righteousness is being fulfilled. In Matthew 15:31 when the crowd see that Jesus has healed the mute, the maimed, the lame, and the blind, "they praised the God of Israel." Such a text suggests that Jesus' actions fulfilled righteousness.

In short, Matthew's Jesus is fulfilling all righteousness with His healings in a way that was expected by many Jews, particularly in a kingly figure.

5:6a/10, and 5:5b

Gandhi rightly observed: "You cannot present the hungry and famished masses with God. Their God is their food."[26] Therefore, the idea of the poorest of the poor calling upon God is a God to execute righteousness for them so they may receive what God intended for them. I propose, therefore we read righteousness in 5:6a as food. Jesus teaches in 5:6a:

> *hoi peiōntes kai dipsōntes tēn dikaiosynē*—those hungering and thirsting [for][27] righteousness = food

Commentators, generally, take *hoi peiōntes* (hungering) and *dipsōntes* (thirsting) *tēn dikaiosynē* (righteousness) in 5:6a as referring to those seeking justice on behalf of the poor. I, however, propose that Matthew has in mind the daily vicissitudes of the oppressed who are literally hungry and thirsty for food.[28] If Matthew 5:6a refers to those who seek *dikaiosynē* for

25. Yoder Neufeld, "Righteousness and Peace will kiss," 159.

26. Ellsberg, *Gandhi on Christianity*, 38.

27. The preposition "for" is not in Greek but needed in English.

28. Wilson, *For I was Hungry*, 133, "food shortages were a problem for a sizeable number of people in the first-century Roman Empire." On pages 244 the author writes

others we would expect: "hungering and thirsting *on behalf* of justice for others." The Greek would be *heneken dikaiosynēs* (on account of righteousness) which it is not.

The fact that 5:6a does not have *heneken dikaiosynēs* is made strikingly visible in 5:10 where the verse contains this exact Greek phrase. In 5:10 Jesus speaks of those who are "persecuted *on account of* justice" (*hoi dediōgmenoi heneken dikaiosynēs*). *Heneken* (on account of) emphasizes that justice/righteousness is embodied in human actions on account of others.[29] Thus persecution relates to the actions of the faithful who were seen by the powers and authorities as subversives because of their work in challenging an oppressive system for its greed and violence.

In short, those in 5:10 strive for justice for the poor. In 5:6a those who seek righteousness are those who actually hunger and thirst for food and drink for themselves. In the first chapter I emphasized that "good/ness" refers to God's generosity, it follows that God intends all to be satisfied with what is good (see Psalm 103:5).

I interpret 5:10 as those seeking righteousness for those who are hungry. Elsewhere Jesus teaches the faithful to limit their appetites (see 6:1 and 6:16–18) as a way of seeking God's kingdom and His righteousness.

To support my argument relating to 5:6a I compare "righteousness" in 5:6a with righteousness/justice in Ezekiel 34:16. In Ezekiel we read: "I will feed them with justice" (LXX: *boskēsō auta meta krimatos* [Hebrew: *mišpaṭ*]). This justice refers to food—I will feed them with food. The New Jerusalem Bible (NJB) translates well 34:16: "I will be a true shepherd to them." NJB implicitly translates justice to be food as the shepherd is one who feeds his sheep.[30]

Septuagint Genesis 32:11 (English verse 10) preserves a clear example of *dikaiosynē,* meaning the basics needed for life:

> *hikanoutai moi pasēs dikaiosynēs*—Let there be to me a sufficiency (*hikanoō*) of all the justice (*dikaiosynēs*). (Translated by Brenton)

---

regarding 5:6: "in Matt 5:6 with its desires for righteousness, the promised satiation would not be abstract but real."

29. Carter, *Matthew and the Margins*, 136.

30. However, this line could also refer to the harsh judgment on the oppressor (Brueggemann, *Theology of the Old Testament*, 260). Brueggemann in *Theology of the Old Testament*, 461–62 argues that "feed them with justice" refers to "rehabilitative work." Fretheim, *God and the World*, 195 sees the line as referring to "food and water made readily available." In contrast, Horsley, *Jesus and the Spiral of Violence*, 206 argues that justice suggests future deliverance and hope which he interprets as among other things: food.

In this verse *dikaiosynēs* refers to basic needs with which God's people will be satisfied.[31]

Further, LXX Proverbs 3:9 has: "Fruits of righteousness (*dikaiosynē*)." But the Hebrew has: "fruits of all your produce (Hebrew: *tĕbu'ātā*)." This is a clear example of *dikaiosynē* relating to food or produce from the land (*tĕbû'ātā*).

Possession of the land, claims Lohfink, "is the highest salvation good, and thus faith and the economy are closely connected to each other."[32] The possession of the land by the landless is the hope of the hungry who may well previously have had to sell their land (cf. Psalm 37:11). They are vulnerable to food shortages. Humans are unable to obey God in preserving and serving the land unless they have land; they are unable to work (cf. Genesis 2:15; cf. Naboth's refusal to sell his vineyard in 1 Kings 21). Without land they are in a state of slavery (sin) and unable to glorify God (cf. Sirach 38:6) although they are still God's special concern.[33] They are also in the situation of having to disobey God's Torah for example by stealing because out of dire necessity they must do so to survive.

The closeness between "land" in 5:5b and "righteousness" in 5:6b also contributes to my argument. *Tēn gēn* (the land) in 5:5b explains the content of *tēn dikaiosynēn* in 5:6b which among many things indicates food. The primary symbol of need at all levels of existence is "food."[34]

> 5:5b *makarioi hoi praieis, hoti autoi klēronomēsousin tēn gēn* (Joyful are the dispossessed, for they will inherit the earth)
>
> 5:6a *makarioi hoi peinōntes kai dipsōntes tēn dikaiosynēn* (Joyful are those who hunger and thirst righteousness)

It is no mere coincidence that the end of each line finishes with a singular accusative *ēn* (pronounced "ayn").[35] The hope of *hoi praeis* (the dispossessed) in verse 5b is "land" (*tēn gēn*) that will enable inheritors to feed themselves and their households. In verse 6 those who hunger and thirst for righteousness are those who seek food and that means land, what the *hoi praeis* (the meek) are promised in 5:5b (i.e., land which will feed them). Food is the right of all humans according to God's created order. Sharon

31. The NRSV in verse 10 is different from the LXX and is based on the Hebrew.

32. Lohfink, "The Appeasement of the Messiah," 236–37.

33. Yoder, *Shalom*, 49 adds that "being in bondage was a detriment to the worship of God." In bondage they could not fulfill God's creational purposes.

34. McFague, *Blessed are the Consumers*, 171.

35. It perhaps also explains why Matthew places the only other singular accusative construction before the verb in verse 8.

Ringe helpfully recalls that in the Old Testament "the basic human need for food is paradigmatic of all the needs that are met in the human establishment of God's reign."[36]

Righteousness in 5:6b must also take into account 6:33 (see below). It suffices simply to say that righteousness in 6:33 is equated with the kingdom of God where God's will is done. Central to this is that there is abundance and joy for all. It is essential, therefore, that righteousness is not separated from material necessities.

In conclusion, *tēn dikaiosynēn* is *tēn gēn*. Righteousness refers to the basic rights God intends for all creation. How does this relate to my argument that righteousness refers to the foundations upon which creations is ordered? Righteousness refers to the goodness of creation. Creation is when God's goodness is present, therefore, when there are those who are so oppressed that they have no food or drink, the goodness of God is not present. 5:6b could equally be translated: "joyful are those who hunger and thirst for the goodness of God." Such goodness is food to the poorest of the poor.

5:20

Jesus teaches that the righteousness of the Pharisees must be exceeded. While they appeared to be faithful to Torah, they in fact disregarded justice and mercy (i.e., caring for the needs of the neglected), which are the basic principles underlying Torah (cf. Matthew 23:23). To practice righteousness was to show hospitality to the poor and oppressed. When Jesus teaches that Torah is to be kept, He meant that people show righteousness (Matthew 5:20); in other words, they work towards the redistribution of God's land so all can partake in God's creation.

6:1

Here Jesus warns His disciples against doing things for their own benefit. He teaches: "Beware of practicing *(poiein)* your piety (*dikaiosynēn*) before others in order to be seen by them; for then you have no reward from your Father in heaven." "Practicing your piety" is more literally "to do righteousness." These words have much in common with Isaiah when he observes how the powerful practiced righteousness (LXX 58:2: *dikaiosynēn pepoiē -kōs*). Jesus cautions that "doing righteousness" is not for self-glorification,

36. Ringe, *Jesus, Liberation*, 53.

but is to re-order society according to God's goodness and universal righteousness so that there is joyful abundance for all.

Doing righteousness echoes LXX Genesis 18:19 when it describes the "way of Yahweh" as doing righteousness and justice (*poiein dikaiosynēn*). The way of Yahweh is to care for those on the wrong side of injustice (i.e., the poor). It is to be the opposite of the inhospitable inhabitants in Sodom (Genesis 18–19).

We find a similar expression of doing righteousness in 1 John 2:29; 3:7; and 3:10. In particular 3:10 states that one who does not do righteousness (*ho mē poiōn dikaiosynēn*) does not love his brother or sister. In 1 John 3:17 if a disciple sees someone without material needs and does nothing, he does not do righteousness. James 2:15–16 similarly castigates those who tell a poor person to "go in peace; keep warm and eat your fill" without supplying their actual bodily needs.

My argument regarding doing righteousness in Matthew 6:1 is further supported by verses 2–18 where we find Jesus' teaching about almsgiving, praying, and fasting. These actions, claim W. D. Davies and Dale C. Allison, are primarily about addressing the existence of material poverty.[37] In short, "to do righteousness" in Matthew 6:1 is to live in accordance with God's goodness showing hospitable love to others.

6:2–4

Davies and Allison are probably correct in detecting a polemical barb at ostentatious giving (the opposite of letting your light shine before others) and the verses' call for silent and unostentatious giving.[38]

Only in Matthew Jesus teaches that to do righteousness is to give alms (*poiēs eleēmosynēn*). The Greek *eleēmosynēn* translated alms is related to "merciful" and "mercy." I suggest underlying this is limitless love that binds communities and individuals together. To do righteousness (6:1) is to show limitless love to others. *Poiēs eleēmosynēn* is about sharing; Carter puts it well: "Sharing resources provides an alternative socioeconomic practice to dominant societal practices which deny access to resources through greed and oppression."[39] The reward for those who show limitless love in giving of their resources is to receive the joy that comes from seeing others benefitting.

37. Davies and Allison, *Matthew 1–7*, 577.

38. Ibid., 579.

39. Carter, *Matthew and the Margins*, 159.

6:16–18

Jesus teaches about unostentatious conduct when fasting. Gutiérrez comments: "Authentic fasting consists in liberating the oppressed and breaking the yokes that hold them captive."[40] At the heart of creation is God's goodness that emphasizes generosity and love. Faithful living is about living with restraint as set out in Torah. Isaiah 58 relates doing righteousness to fasting. The prophet castigates fasting done for self-interest:

> Is it [i.e., fasting] not to share your bread with the hungry, and bring the homeless poor into your house; when you see the naked, to cover them, and not to hide yourself from your own kin? Then your light shall break forth like the dawn, and your healing shall spring up quickly; your vindicator shall go before you, the glory of the LORD shall be your rear guard. (Isaiah 58:7–8; cf. Jeremiah 14:12; Sirach 34:31)

Isaiah 58:7–8 reflects the period soon after the Babylonian exile. At this time scholars believe that the elite of Israel neglected the practice of showing true righteousness. Bruce Malchow observes: "They [elite of Israel] were fasting and saw no consistency in oppressing the poor at the same time. However, only the wealthy have the luxury of fasting since the needy are always hungry."[41]

In short, to do righteousness, therefore, is to serve others so that they may act in accordance to God's goodness through bringing justice to all. The reward is the joy that service brings.[42]

6:33

Jesus teaches people to seek God's kingdom and His righteousness. Gutiérrez rightly observes 6:33 is a particularly significant verse showing Matthew's concern for the poor: "When Jesus speaks in Matthew's Gospel of seeking the kingdom and righteousness of God, he is calling attention to the demand that the seeking implies."[43] This means that the disciple is one who,

40. Gutiérrez, *The God of Life*, 47.

41. Malchow, *Social Justice*, 44.

42. Again I am drawn to the insights of neuroplasticity and the idea that human brains are hard-wired towards caring.

43. Gutiérrez, *The God of Life*, 103.

according to Gutiérrez, "causes the blessing of the kingdom to bear fruit."[44] This demands working for the benefit of all.

It is likely in 6:33 that Jesus rebukes those who hoard while ignoring the effects this has on the poor (cf. Isaiah 23:18; 34:2; 41:2; Baruch 3:17). In 6:19–24 Jesus addresses those who were at risk of making money their priority leading them to neglect Torah and righteousness (i.e., caring for the poor). These listeners are those who are tempted to do righteousness in such a way that brings rewards to themselves and not to the poorest of the poor.

Instead, Jesus teaches in 6:25–34 that trusting in God through thinking of others before your own needs will bring abundance—worrying and hoarding food is the opposite of living according to righteousness. Hoarding is poor housekeeping! Jesus is probably alluding to Israel's time in the wilderness when its people's primary lesson was to learn to trust that God would provide for their needs. These verses perhaps echo Torah's Sabbath and jubilee requirement stating that Israel show its trust in God for its needs by resisting the temptation to work the land on the Sabbath.

21:32

John the Baptist came in the "way of righteousness."[45] This phrase appears once in the Old Testament (Proverbs 8:20) and twice in the New Testament (Matthew 21:32; 2 Peter 2:21). The "way of righteousness" appears in synonymous parallelism with "paths of justice" in Proverbs 8:20. The juxtaposition of "way" and "righteousness" in 21:32 echoes also the righteousness of Abraham in Genesis 18:19. The remainder of the verse describes the way of Yahweh as "doing righteousness and justice . . ." Jesus, in alluding to Genesis 18:19, considers righteousness as central to God's nature; the "way of righteousness" in other words is the "way of God" which is the same as God. Righteousness is God's goodness in creation.

John the Baptist deplored the Pharisees and Sadducees for claiming that Abraham was their Father (3:7) whilst they lived selfishly. Jesus in 21:32 recalls that Abraham was righteous and just and was the father of all nations (cf. Sirach 44:19; Romans 4:17–18); further, his household are his children to the extent that they are righteous (Genesis 18:19). John claims, therefore, that they (i.e. Pharisees and Sadducees) are not children of Abraham because they did not practice righteousness. Their destiny as children of Abraham was to care for the poor and this they failed to do.

44. Ibid., 104.

45. In this seventh and final occurrence of *dikaiosynē*, Matthew directs his readers to the first occurrence in 3:15 which relates to John the Baptist.

SUMMARY

- Righteousness is the "order" or "foundation" upon which creation is built.
- Righteousness refers to God's goodness.
- Righteousness is the order of creation designed to restore the "have-nots" to abundant life while challenging and encouraging the non-poor to a life devoted to service for others.
- Righteousness is about how human communities order their behavior according to God's goodness.
- God's righteousness is not present when some deprive others of basic necessities and the opportunity to serve and preserve creation.
- Righteousness is linked to Torah and both point towards God's limitless love and mercy for His creation.

FOOD FOR THOUGHT

Willard Swartley observes that "The meaning and fulfillment of 'life are found . . . in human *relationships*, and qualities of justice, respect, concern, compassion, and support that surround' those relationship and qualities. All these factors contribute to personal and corporate *shalom*."[46] In our present society the most selfish aspects of our being are fed constantly so we desire always to have and possess more. The righteousness of which the Bible and Matthew speak is about the quality of community defined in terms of respect and care.

Jesus teaches that we must seek righteousness in the same breath as the kingdom of heaven. The righteousness is intimately linked to our everyday life and how we interpret Torah to apply to such a life. The one thing we can be certain of biblically speaking: God is outraged at the lack of righteousness in our world where the rich grow fat on the sacrifices of the weak and powerless.

46. Swartley, *Health, Healing*, 124.

PRAYER

God of justice, open our eyes to behold how we create injustice seeking to maintain the status quo profitable for a few. God of justice open our eyes. Help us to be alert to Your presence in our lives. For Your name's sake.

5

Torah

Jesus lived and died in vain if He did not teach us to regulate the whole of life by the eternal law of love.[1] —*Thomas Merton*

Turn my heart to your decrees, and not to selfish gain. —Psalm 119:36

I came not to destroy Torah, but to fulfill it. —Matthew 5:17

But those who look into the perfect law, the law of liberty, and persevere, being not hearers who forget but doers who act—they will be blessed in their doing. —James 1:25

José Pallares concludes from his study of Mark's Gospel that the law in Jesus' teaching is about service to the poorest of the poor.[2] The Gospel of Matthew furthers Pallares' conclusion because, in Matthew particularly, Jesus is the fulfillment of Torah (5:17). Therefore, this distinct significance of Torah found in the First Gospel contributes to this chapter's argument that Torah is best understood in terms of God's abhorrence of poverty and His concern for the poorest of the poor.

There is a tradition, however, of viewing Jesus as anti-law. The use of the word "legalistic" has been used pejoratively by some Christians to describe those especially Jews, who believe obedience to law is the only way to

1. Merton, *Gandhi on Non-Violence*, 26.

2. Pallares, *A Poor Man Called Jesus*, 22; also Wink, *Human Being*, 73.

salvation. Such views need to be modified in the light of more recent studies on Torah in Jewish literature.

I like Richard Foster's description of the Old Testament law in terms of "controlling principles for the outward expression of simplicity."[3] *I too see Torah as laying out principles to permit human beings to be expressions of simplicity* (i.e., generosity and restraint). In this understanding, Torah is about the poor and protecting them from the greed of human laws that lead to division and poverty. *QF&P 20.27* defines simplicity in way that is at the heart of Torah:

> The heart of Quaker ethics is summed up in the word "simplicity." Simplicity is forgetfulness of self and remembrance of our humble status as waiting servants of God. Outwardly, simplicity is shunning superfluities of dress, speech, behavior, and possessions, which tend to obscure our vision of reality. Inwardly, simplicity is spiritual detachment from the things of this world as part of the effort to fulfill the first commandment: to love God with all of the heart and mind and strength.

This definition of "simplicity" is close in meaning to the goodness of God that He sees to be present in creation in Genesis 1. The order of creation is such that creation flourishes when humans live for others.

The poorest of the poor are unable themselves to be as God designed them to be because of the failure of the non-poor to live simply and generously. The poor are forced into lawlessness in order to survive. Their need for food and safety gives them no chance to praise God or keep Sabbath. The poor according to Palm 119:13 are unable to keep Torah because they are oppressed.

In short, I consider Torah to be for the equal redistribution of creation, consequently *Jesus is the fulfillment of that which brings abundance to all creation.*

TORAH AN EXPRESSION OF GOD'S GOODNESS

Torah is an expression of God's goodness present in creation. Miranda observes that the laws of the Old Testament were originally called *mišpaṭim* meaning justice and righteousness (see chapter 4). He observes that *mišpaṭ* is the defense of the weak, the liberation of the oppressed, doing justice to the poor."[4]

3. *QF&P* 25.09.
4. Miranda, *Marx*, 137.

Torah is God's gift to all so each might live harmoniously, willingly practicing habits of joyful restraint; through Torah obedience, creation is filled with God's goodness. Heschel observes that the law in creation makes the state of blessedness conditional on each person entering into relationship with others harmoniously. This is the law of nature.[5] Torah shows how to live in a way that brings blessedness. This blessedness is when creation is good.

In short, Torah is designed to guide people in relationships to be loving, selfless, merciful, peaceable, and righteous. To disobey Torah leads to God's wrath as humans live contrary to the way their Creator intended for them.

Gandhi's more battle-hardened understanding of law sees being ready to die for the benefit of the other to be the highest expression of obedience to God and law. This is at the heart of my understanding of Torah. Psalm 119:36 surely captures this in its words that the opposite of God's law is selfishness .

Fretheim emphasizes that Torah is the inner mechanism of creation.[6] I propose that to understand Jesus, we see this inner mechanism in the context of the existence of material poverty.[7] Only in Matthew Jesus is the fulfillment of Torah (5:17).[8] Matthew is also alone in having Jesus teach: "because of the increase of lawlessness, the love of many will grow cold" (24:12). Violence, betrayal, and loss of love for others, result from lawlessness (*anomia*: without Torah) (24:12). Jesus sees Torah as an equivalent to love. I suggest that when Jesus claims to fulfill Torah He is claiming to be good news to the victims of lawlessness (cf. 11:5); those who suffer the consequences of living without Torah are in poverty.

GOODNESS, TORAH AND *SHALOM*

Torah is intimately linked to the goodness of God and *shalom*. I am struck by Randy Woodley's statement that "As long as there are hungry people in a community that is well fed, there can be no shalom."[9] Swartley rightly observes that "God gives laws, the Ten Commandments, to enable humans to experience a goodness approximating the intention of creation, living

5. Heschel in Rothschild, *Between God and Man*, 94.

6. Fretheim, *God and World*, 144.

7. Wink, *The Human Being*, 73.

8. Compare Wink in *The Human Being*. As the fulfiller of Torah, Jesus is the complete and self-actualized human being.

9. Woodley, *Shalom*, 21.

together in *shalom*."[10] "Shalom is the metanarrative of Torah."[11] According to Jewish writings found in the Talmud, "The entire Torah is for the sake of the ways of shalom" (*Gittin* 59b). Elsewhere in Jewish literature we read: "Great is Shalom, as the whole Torah was given to promote shalom in the world as it is stated, 'Her ways are pleasant and all her paths are shalom'" (*Maimonides, Mishnah Torah, The Laws of Chanukah* 4:14).[12]

My understanding of Torah and peace is drawn from Randy Woodley's statements that (1) "God has designed us all to live in a world of shalom,"[13] and (2) "The Creator has ingeniously designed a world in which shalom is the foundational stuff that God uses to create proper order to the world."[14] Torah and *Shalom* are inextricably linked as Swartley suggests.

Brueggemann sees Genesis 1:2 as referring to chaos which is a pre-creation vision *as being without shalom* from which God then establishes *shalom*.[15] Therefore, Genesis 1:2 is about God's Spirit overcoming the darkness.[16] Creation to be in a state of *shalom* is to be blessed in the sense that all in it are prosperous and abundant through each working for the benefit of others.

Shalom denotes *ṭôb* (goodness) which describes the quality of creation measured in terms of harmony, self-giving love, and level of sharing between different peoples and communities. Therefore *shalom* predominantly in the Bible is the essence or quality of creation (i.e., that to which creation is formed, toward unity and service). It can be translated with many words including peace and prosperity. *Shalom* is both a creation word (i.e., an outward expression of being in a state of being blessed by God); it also describes a quality of God's goodness towards creation that is ordered inwardly.

10. Swartley, *Health, Healing*, 28; Berry, *The Great Work*, 60 observes the basic understanding of law in Western society as directed "toward personal human rights and toward the natural world as existing for human possession and use."

11. Woodley, *Shalom*, 11 note 6.

12. Ibid., 12.

13. Ibid., 20.

14. Ibid., 14.

15. Brueggemann, *Peace*, 15; elsewhere he describes *chaos* as representing the landless situation of exile and the hovering spirit which gives hope of recovery of land with all its blessing and well-being. See also Crosby, *House of Disciples*, 84.

16. See Isaiah 6:11–12 perhaps refers to a return to the disorder described in Genesis 1:2.

THE TWO GREAT COMMANDMENTS

Creation is good to the extent it is ordered for *shalom*. This explains the central status given to the two great commandments: (1) Deuteronomy 6:5—love the LORD your God; (2) Leviticus 19:18—love your neighbor as yourself. It is not possible to love God without loving what God has made. Love is at the heart of Torah. However, to love God and neighbor is dependent on the biblical teaching that God loves creation (cf. 1 John 4 makes this clear. But it is implicit throughout Matthew). Israel experienced God's love when He acted to free it from oppression in Egypt. Israel's experience of God led it to reflect on love as the binding force that bound God to Israel. It is clear from Leviticus 19:18 that to love God is to do justice to the poor for they are of especial concern to God.

TORAH AND SABBATH

A central commandment is the fourth and lengthiest of the Ten Commandments. It is to keep the Sabbath holy through rest (Exodus 20:8–11; Deuteronomy 5:12–15). Swartley comments: "The Sabbath underlines all the commands."[17] The rational for observing the Sabbath is two-fold: (1) commemoration of creation (Exodus 20:9–11); (2) commemoration of the exodus (Deuteronomy 5:15). Exodus and creation are inseparable. In fact, the book of Exodus implicitly likens the advent of Moses to a new creation.[18]

This commandment is significant to the poor. On the Sabbath day, by resting, people are to remember that the whole earth belongs to God (Exodus 19:5). In practice this means exercising self-restraint to recall that God is Creator. This is challenging to arrogant humans as it demands confidence that the world will continue to operate benevolently for a day without human labor.[19] It is on the Sabbath day Israel is directed to remember how God *freed* them from their slavery and provided for their needs amidst the wilderness (Deuteronomy 5:12–15). On the Sabbath humans are to recall that God *releases* the poor from their oppression which viewed from a perspective of creation understands God's act as re-creation where equity and abundance abound. Central to obedience to the Sabbath was that Israel recognized that what it had was not the result of its own goodness, but the result of God's mercy (Deuteronomy 9:4–5). Through Sabbath observance Israel recalls that "all they have" is because God gives (Deuteronomy 8:17).

17. Swartley, *Slavery*, 69.

18. Allison, *The New Moses*, 202.

19. Lowery, *Sabbath and Jubilee*, 93–94.

Sabbath year and Jubilee Laws are extensions of the Sabbath day laws. Wirzba observes of them: "The effect of many of the Jubilee stipulations was to promote a just economic order that enabled the liberty and redemption of peoples and creation. It promoted the conditions in which all of creation could legitimately claim the right to flourish and be freed from those unjust cultural conditions that would oppress or maim."[20] To understand these stipulations we must recall that Israel is shown mercy by God when it is brought out of oppression in Egypt. One account of Jubilee in Deuteronomy 15 states: "every year you shall grant a remission of debts" (v. 1). God assures Israel, however, that they should not fear scarcity of creation's abundance through observing this law for God will bless them (vv. 4–5) for their trusting in Him. The basis of the Jubilee Laws like the Sabbath day is found in Leviticus 25:23: "the land belongs to me [God]; for you are 'guests' and 'residents' with me."

Finally, Sabbath year and Jubilee Laws are about calling humans to know that their existence is due to God's goodness, mercy and love. According to these laws, humans are inclined to godlessness leading them to misuse creation through hoarding, fearing that one day they won't have anything. The Jubilee Laws are fully aware that hoarding causes others to suffer scarcity. *Jubilee is a reaction to this culture of hoarding.* In the seventh year Israel is "to give liberally . . . open your hand to the poor and needy neighbor in your land (15:11). Every seventh year an Israelite will free his slave showing great generosity (15:12–14).

In short, Sabbath year and Jubilee Laws are designed so that households order their lives according to God's will in order that there be abundance and freedom for all. The laws in general, especially both Sabbath day and year, as well as jubilee invited people—images of God the Creator—to share the world's resources in a manner that reflected God's original economic ordering (cf. Genesis 1:26–28).[21]

TORAH AND THE POOR

Brueggemann observes that Torah "is not to protect acquired advantage, but to call that advantage into question when it does not benefit the community."[22] Pallares similarly comments: "the law of Moses was originally intended for the benefit of an oppressed slave people."[23] I reiterate that

20. Wirzba, *Paradise of God*, 39.

21. See Crosby, *House of Disciples*, 173.

22. Brueggemann, *Theology of the Old Testament*, 423.

23. Pallares, *A Poor Man Called Jesus*, 22; Wink, *Human Being*, 73.

creation is ordered according to Torah by God for abundance. Poverty is unacceptable and God is on the side of the poor.

Torah articulates Israel's deep concern for the less advantaged (cf. Exodus 22:21).[24] Ancient Jewish writers, such as Sirach, equate Torah with caring for the poor: "Help the poor for the commandment's sake, and in their need do not send them away empty-handed" (Sirach 29:9; cf. 29:1). The psalmist sums up the whole purpose of Torah: "Turn my heart to your decrees, and not to selfish gain" (Psalm 119:36). *Torah directs human beings to live for others and not for selfish gain.* Brueggemann puts it well: "Torah turns the community from self to the neighbor."[25]

Israel is commanded to be faithful to God's Torah in the context of recalling how God generously brought it out of slavery in Egypt (Deuteronomy 24:18). Torah is understandable only in the context of a people who know the pain and agonies of living in a lawless and loveless society. Those who live with Torah in their hearts don't wish that anyone should suffer the experience of being oppressed; to live in harmony with Torah is the way of *shalom* that removes all oppression. Torah is given to it to fulfill its calling to be God's agent of blessing to all nations.

In short, Torah intends people to focus on the weighty matters of justice, mercy, and faith (cf. Matthew 23:23) which are the foundations upon which God created the heavens and the earth.

TORAH IN MATTHEW

Jesus taught that no part of Torah should be broken (5:17–20; cf. 23:2). He summed up Torah as treating others as you would have them treat you (7:12) insisting that loving God and neighbor sum up Torah (19:19; 20:37–40). At other times Jesus refers to the weighty aspects of Torah which are justice, mercy and faith (23:23). Elsewhere Torah is emphasized through living within the boundaries God has established avoiding murder, slander, adultery, fornication, divorce, and theft (19:16–20/Mark 10:17–31). Ultimately, to obey Torah is to be a channel of God's goodness. Where there are debts, they must be cancelled. Where there is hunger, the hungry should be fed. Where there are unloved people, they should be loved.

24. Fretheim, *God and World*, 134: "by neglecting these texts we lose so much grist . . ." Compare Davis, *Scripture*, 82. Also Gnuse, *You Shall Not Steal*, 9: "the prohibition of theft was designed to protect the property of the poor and preserve the economic equality of all for the maintenance of a healthy society."

25. Brueggemann, *Social Reading*, 48.

5:3

Ringe argues that Matthew's beatitudes be considered in the context of Jubilee.[26] In Luke, Jesus' first words are found in 4:18–19 where He reads a version of Isaiah 61:1–2 that envisages Jubilee. Luke makes explicit Jesus as God's anointed one who comes to release the oppressed. In Matthew Jesus proclaims "blessed are those who are poor to their very core."[27] I suggest that both Matthew and Luke in their related but different ways order their Gospels to present Jesus as proclaiming the good news as a blessing of Jubilee.

5:9

Woodley observes that Jesus' understanding of Torah is to live according to *shalom*,[28] therefore, the heart of keeping Torah is to be a *shalom*-maker (5:9). Barely six verses separate Jesus' teaching that He is the fulfillment of Torah in 5:17 and His words about "blessed are the *shalom*-makers."

5:17–20

In these verses Torah is fundamental to Jesus and keeping it is related to making peace. No point in Matthew does Jesus permit the breaking of Torah. Torah is rooted in love understood in the context of God's nature as generous and hospitable (5:43–48; 7:12; 22:34–40). Jesus in referring to Himself as one who fulfills Torah thereby describes Himself as exemplifying how God intended His creatures to be. Jesus' whole life and ministry testify to His actions on behalf of the afflicted and His call to others to repent and show love. In these verses we also see that keeping Torah is linked to practicing righteousness (v. 20).

However, it is observed that Jesus appears at times to be lax in observance of Torah. Yet I hold with the scholarly consensus that sees Jesus as debating the nature of the law. Matthew has, for example, Jesus attack the religious elite for creating laws that are not God's laws because they are not rooted in love (e.g., plucking grain on the Sabbath in 12:1–8; washing hands before eating in Matthew 15:1–20; cf. 23:4, 23). Jesus' teaching about the Sabbath is linked with the fact that Sabbath Law keeping should not block care for the poor and sick, but enable it.

26. Ringe, *Jesus, Liberation*, 51–54.

27. This is my paraphrase of "the poor in spirit" in Matthew 5:3. See chapter 8 for detailed discussion.

28. Woodley, *Shalom*, 18.

Jesus teaches that those who neither keep Torah nor teach it are the least in the kingdom of heaven while those who keep it and instruct others to keep it are called great. Does Jesus have in mind any particular group/s? Jesus is vociferous in His attack on the Jewish leaders for keeping only those laws that made them appear to be good while they neglected the weightier aspects such as showing justice to those on the wrong side of justice (23:23). It is likely Jesus has in mind the leaders particularly when He teaches that true disciples must practice a righteousness that is greater than the Scribes and Pharisees.

Does Jesus teach that Torah will pass away? The following verse is important:

> *Amēn gar legō hymin heōs an parelthē ho ouranos kai hē gē, iota hen ē mia keraia ou mē parelthē apo tou nomou heōs an panta genētai*
>
> For truly I tell you, until heaven and earth pass away, not one letter, not one stroke of a letter, will pass from Torah until all is accomplished. (Matthew 5:18)

The Greek *heōs an parelthē ho ouranos kai hē gē* (until heaven and earth pass away) means "never." In other words, Torah will *never* pass away. This means that *panta* (all) refers to Torah and "what Torah demands." Torah demands God's will.

Keeping Torah is what God intended for human beings enabling them to live according to the will of God serving others in a world where laws are human constructs rooted in selfishness that results in poverty. When Jesus states that He completes Torah, Jesus is Torah personified through His service to the poor.

In short, the presence of God's goodness is in creation where all live in harmony caring for the other to flourish. All human beings who keep Torah are *shalom-makers.*

5:21–24

I am struck by the end of verse 23: "you remember that your brother has something against you." Davies and Allison write: "It is not immediately clear whether it is the offender or the offended who is to make reconciliation." They opt for the offender.[29] I opt for Jesus challenging His listeners to face up to those they have offended.

29. Davies and Allison, *Matthew 1–7*, 517.

I propose we understand these verses in the context of Jesus addressing those who have insulted and mocked the poor in their words and actions (5:22). Jesus makes clear that such actions are on a level with murder. I reiterate, Jesus addresses those who may have insulted the poor and the powerless. He points out the hypocrisy of doing acts of piety while at the same time perpetrating injustices against the powerless and vulnerable. Murder is often seen as oppressing the poor (Jeremiah 22:17; Ezekiel 22:27, 29; Sirach 34:18–22). In Sirach 34:25 to deprive the poor of bread is murder; to call person *Raka* or *Mōre* is to look down on a person seeing them as having no value: it is to call someone: "useless." *Raka* or *Mōre* are associated with fool. Such a person is not one who is rich (Proverbs 30:22). In our modern society people with learning difficulties are often considered to be fools and useless. They are perceived to be unable to offer society anything valuable and are fit for nothing other than begging in the dust. In Matthew 18:10 Jesus warns against despising those who are not valued highly by society because they are precious to God and to such belongs the kingdom of heaven (18:3).

Jesus teaches that one who insults the poor can only offer His gift when reconciled with the offended person through obedience to Torah. This may mean paying the workers that have not been paid (compare James 5:4). The poor may have been insulted by not being paid. Torah obedience calls for the non-poor to see that their actions have insulted the poor and they must put this right by restoring to the poorest what is necessary for existence. To mistreat the poorest of the poor is at the heart of disobedience to Torah.

5:33–37

Of the Gospels it is found only in Matthew, but similarly in James 5:12. My interpretation is influenced by Quakerism.

Jesus reiterates the law about not swearing falsely but giving to the LORD your oath (v. 33; cf. Exodus 20:7; Leviticus 19:12; Numbers 30:3–15; Deuteronomy 23:21–23; Psalm 50:14; Zechariah 8:17; Wisdom 14:28). Jesus, however, teaches that a person should not swear at all (v. 34). Instead, a person's word should be "yes yes, or no no. More than this is from the evil one" (v. 37). Matthew has Jesus intensify Old Testament teaching about honesty and integrity. Hagner writes:

> The absolute reliability of one's word renders an oath superfluous. And indeed, because in the contemporary situation oaths so often suggested not commitment but untruthfulness by the creation of loopholes, Jesus strongly condemns anything

> beyond the simple, genuine yes or no as being . . . "from the evil one," the one associated pre-eminently with deception.[30]

These verses give us a helpful insight into Jesus' understanding of Torah and its significance to the poor. Stassen believes that Jesus challenges the custom of making an oath that sounds real and honest "but actually has a cross-your-fingers-behind-your-back secret limitation that you are not really committed to do what you promise to do."[31] Jesus faces up to one particular law that is misused for manipulative and self-aggrandizing purposes. I believe the following from QF&P 20.43 contributes to my reading of 5:37:

> Are you honest and truthful in word and deed? Do you maintain strict integrity in your business transaction and in your relations with individuals and organisations? Are you personally scrupulous and responsible in the use of money entrusted to you, and are you careful not to defraud the public revenue?

These words bring Jesus' teaching about oaths into the context of economic integrity. Without relationships of trust and integrity injustice occurs and people are cheated, become angry, and impoverished. James' epistle is, at times, an attack on the way the poor are treated. In James 5:12 the writer urges honesty and truthfulness in similar language found in Matthew 5:33–37. I believe it is also helpful to read James 5:12 in the context of James 5:4–5:

> Listen! The wages of the laborers who mowed your fields, which you kept back by fraud, cry out, and the cries of the harvesters have reached the ears of the LORD of hosts. You have lived on the earth in luxury and in pleasure; you have fattened your hearts in a day of laughter.

Those James addresses are similar to those addressed in Matthew 5. They were guilty of following customs that ultimately led to suffering through lack of honesty. Perhaps Jesus has in mind those who swore that they would pay what is right but with no intention of doing so. Some Christians are untrustworthy and Jesus addresses this. Holding-back paying wages is indeed acting with evil.

30. Hagner, *Matthew 1–13*, 128.

31. Stassen, *Living the Sermon on the Mount*, 85.

5:42b

Jesus specifically teaches: "Give to everyone who begs from you, and do not refuse anyone who wants to borrow from you" (parallel Luke 6:30b). Jesus' teaching draws on traditions relating to Jubilee (Exodus 22:25; Leviticus 25:36–37; Deuteronomy 15:1–3; 4 Maccabees 2:8) expressing concern for the welfare of the poorest in society. Jesus' words are spoken in the context of creating "a system intent not on securing wealth but on ensuring justice and economic equality by providing the opportunity for adequate support for all."[32]

The language suggests that the basis of showing mercy is rooted in the teaching that all things belong to God and that to hold back something someone needs is to defraud the person in need. The Greek translated "do not refuse" is *mē apostraphēs* which can mean perverting or misleading someone (Luke 23:14), or, alienating or causing someone to revolt.[33] Jesus here teaches that to live in harmony and create *shalom* (God's will) is to share one's resources knowing that such belong to God. Lack of mercy will mislead someone perhaps to revolt or steal.

6:12

Crucial to Sabbath year and Jubilee Laws is cancellation of debts. A crucial aspect of Jesus' teaching is that the mark of discipleship is whether His followers reordered their possessions toward the dispossessed (19:21 and parallels). Matthew's account of Jesus' prayer about forgiving sins echoes debt cancellation and Jubilee traditions.[34] In Matthew 6:12, disciples are instructed to forgive (*aphēkamen*) debts (Greek is *opheilēmata* in contrast to Luke 11:4a who has the more general word for sin "*hamartia*" but also *opheilēmata* (11:4b)). Nevertheless, too much weight should not be given to the word change, it is likely that both Luke and Matthew have in mind the cancellation of monetary debts and offences generally (cf. Luke 4:18–19).

However, in Matthew 6:14–15 (cf. Mark 11:25) Jesus teaches about forgiving sins more generally (*paraptōmata*) perhaps suggesting that Matthew uses *opheilēmata* in 6:12 intentionally to refer to actual economic debts.

Some scholars observe that *aphēkamen* (forgive or release) is a significant Jubilee word. The semantic range of the root verb is virtually identical with that of the Hebrew verb *shamat* (to loose, release, or set free) in the

32. Carter, *Matthew and the Margins*, 153.

33. Bauer, Arndt, and Gingrich, *A Greek-English Lexicon*, 99.

34. Ringe, *Jesus, Liberation*, 77–84.

seventh-year laws in Deuteronomy 15 and Exodus 23). However, as Ringe observes, the Greek word has a wider range of meaning and that "there is no distinctive Greek vocabulary associated with Jubilee traditions."[35]

In short, the importance of cancelling debts in the Lord's Prayer is an act of bringing glory to the Father in Matthew and Luke. The emphasis on economic debts may be emphasized in Matthew. John Howard Yoder sums up well the petition: "Jesus is not simply recommending vaguely that we might pardon those who have bothered us or made us trouble, but tells us purely and simply to erase debts of those who owe us money; which is to say, practice the jubilee."[36]

7:1

Jesus commands against judging or condemning (*krinō*) others. The Greek *krinō* is associated with governing, bringing to trial, and judging.[37]

In Matthew 5:40 *krinō* appears of someone who wishes to sue (*krithē -na*) a person in order to take their outer garment. I argue in a later chapter that 5:40 does not refer to the poorest of the poor being sued, but the experience of the ordinary citizen being humiliated by the powerful. I suggest that in 5:40, Matthew refers to the use of law to maintain the *status quo* that supported the powerful.

How is this relevant to 7:1? I propose that Jesus warns His audience about taking advantage of others who are worse off than them. Perhaps Jesus is addressing the unjust and unkindly conduct of blaming others for their misfortunes when they are injured, or if their harvest fails. In 7:3–4 Jesus addressed the attitude of the non-poor condemning and blaming those suffering from poverty; He teaches them to take a good look at their own lives to see how they cause suffering. In other words, He calls them to repent.

11:2–6

Matthew here responds to John the Baptist's inquiry about whether Jesus is the Messiah; he cites Isaiah 61:1–2 that relates to Jubilee Law (cf. Psalm 146) depicting God's anointed one proclaiming "good news to the poor" a phrase found in Matthew. Jesus emphasizes that He is the fulfiller of the Law in this case being one who acts to obey God's Jubilee commandments.

35. Ibid., 34.

36. Yoder, *The Politics of Jesus*, 66.

37. Abbott-Smith, *Manual Greek Lexicon*.

12:1–14

According to Matthew 12:7 quoting Hosea 6:6, Jesus teaches that central to the Sabbath is the need to show *ḥesed* (mercy, limitless love)*; ḥesed* is in contrast to the sacrifices that cause oppression and disfigurement to creation (12:7). Sacrifice is good when it involves a non-poor person giving generously. Jesus teaches "it is lawful to do good on the Sabbath" (12:12). The sacrifice which Hosea condemns is the oppression of the poorest of the poor.

Jesus in these verses reacts against the Sabbath being used to prevent hospitality. Instead, for Jesus, the Sabbath is about the oppressed and poor and the need to include them in table-fellowship. Sabbath should not exclude them. *The Sabbath law for Jesus underlines Torah; in showing mercy to the needy, the law and the prophets find their fulfillment.*[38] The purpose of the Sabbath, therefore, is to do good, heal the sick, and commit acts of mercy. This is exactly what Jesus does when He heals the man with the withered hand on the Sabbath (12:13).

Walter Wink makes striking comments on these verses albeit based on his distinct understanding of the phrase "son of man" (*huios tou anthrōpou*). He points out that the Sabbath is designed to enable human beings to act as God intended them to be, generous (i.e., as fulfilled Human Being which is how Wink expresses *huios tou anthrōpou*). Verse 14 states that "*huios tou anthrōpou*" is the Lord of the Sabbath. Wink takes *huios tou anthrōpou* to describe the Human Being who is at one with God. The Sabbath laws exist to enable human beings to be as God intended them to be: i.e., Human Beings (*huios tou anthrōpou*). He writes: "to operate out of consciousness of the Human Being, which by definition indicates *more* than personal need is involved, is to function out of the heart of the sabbath."[39] Therefore, Sabbath laws foster the human being to be compassionate and generous. According to Wink, verse 14 in stating that the human being is the son of man who is the Lord of the Sabbath means that the human being acts in harmony with God's creation intentions; he is *huios tou anthrōpou* (i.e., as God intended). Such a person has the law in his heart and is even able to break the law at one level. However, for Wink, he is not really able to break the law for in acting according to God's will, such as healing the sick, he is fulfilling the Law because he acts in love and mercy, which is what the Law intends.

38. Hagner, *Matthew 1–13*, 330; Keener, *Matthew*, 357; Carter, *Matthew and the Margins*, 266.

39. Wink, *Human Being*, 70.

15:1–8

The Pharisees question accusingly why Jesus' disciples don't wash their hands before eating. His response is best understood by His denunciation of the Pharisees breaking of the fifth commandment: honor your father and mother. Jesus' attack on them has in mind a specific act that is considered by Jesus dishonorable: that of holding back basic support for elderly parents. They had forgotten the true importance of the commandment and instead focused on developments of the law that had nothing to do with generosity and care for human beings. The Pharisees and scribes are described by Matthew as having hard hearts (15:8). To have a hard heart is to be far from God, it is to be one who has no sense of being obedient to God's Torah having forgotten God's mercy to oneself.

15:18–19

Jesus teaches that obedience to Torah is not about what one can and cannot eat. The law relates to the heart. The law which should be rooted in the heart relates to issues such as murder, adultery and so on. The list Matthew gives in 15:18–19 is based on the Ten Commandments.[40] Carter adds that the mention of heart emphasizes the extent to which one is committed to obeying the commandments. When Torah is in the heart, one does the will of God. When Torah is in the heart, the person knows God's mercy and desires to live by showing mercy.

22:37–40 (cf. Mark 12:28–31; James 4:11–12)

A Pharisee mischievously questions Jesus about His understanding of Torah. Jesus emphasizes that Torah is to love God and neighbor echoing Deuteronomy 6:5 and Leviticus 19:18. Matthew omits from his source Mark 12:29: "Hear, O Israel: the LORD our God, the LORD is one." In so doing he emphasizes that Torah is about loving God. The only way to love God is to live in harmony with God by caring and serving creation (cf. Genesis 2:15). Matthew claims this is the greatest of all the commandments in addition to it being the "first" (Mark presents it only as the first of the commandments (Mark 12:28).

Matthew presents another, second commandment, like Mark, but emphasizes that this second commandment is like the first. This is to love

40. Carter, *Matthew and the Margins*, 320.

your neighbor as yourself. It is to treat others as fellow children of the one Creator. Both commandments are alike as it is impossible to love God but show disrespect to God's creation.

The Epistle of James has a similar tradition to this where he states that those who condemn a brother also condemns Torah. James differs from Matthew in that he does not have "love of God" but this demonstrates nothing other than that James took for granted the commandment to love God as the basis of loving and serving the orphan and widows in their distress (James 1:27). Underlying this is the fact that God is Father and Creator of all (1:17).

23:23

Only in Matthew, Jesus spells out that Torah will be where justice, limitless love, and faith are the foci of human beings (23:23). This is the basis of the Mosaic Torah of which the scribes and Pharisees were supposed to be the custodians.

JAMES 2:8–12

I finish again by referring to James to reinforce my discussion on Matthew. James 2:8 speaks of fulfilling (*teleō*) the royal law. What is this law? "You shall love your neighbor as yourself." This teaching is found also in Matthew 22:39 as well as assumed in 5:43–44. In Matthew 5:17 Jesus is the fulfiller of the Law. Although the words translated "fulfill" are different Greek words, the similarities are close and can both be translated by the same Hebrew word. James calls upon his readers to fulfill the Law as Jesus did. How does this relate to the poor?

In 2:12 James discusses the Law in terms of mercy and judgment. These are key words in Matthew. Those who do not show mercy to the poor will bring judgment upon their own heads. But those who show mercy live in harmony with Torah and will be blessed.

Matthew also emphasizes that not one iota or jot of Torah must be broken (5:19). In James 2:10 the author reinforces that the whole law must be kept (cf. James 4:12). By the whole law, it means that all should act in harmony with God's will.

SUMMARY

- Torah is for the service of the poorest of the poor.
- Jesus in His actions of caring for the poorest of the poor is the fulfillment of Torah.
- Torah is both a creation and covenant term. It refers to the foundation of creation, how it is inwardly designed.
- Torah is equivalent to self-giving.
- Torah will never pass away.
- Torah is an expression of God's goodness that enables creation to be a place of *shalom*.
- Torah provides the principles by which human beings can become expressions of simplicity forgetting their own needs seeking the welfare of others.
- Keeping Torah is ultimately about loving God and His creation.

FOOD FOR THOUGHT

Matthew is fully in line with the Old Testament and Jewish writings in his portrayal of Jesus being the fulfillment of Torah. Torah designates that which fills creation. It is synonymous with *ḥesed*, covenant, and *shalom*. It is the order God formed into creation so that it would flourish. In a nutshell Torah directs human action away from greed and selfishness, but towards service. Torah exists in order to cultivate the human being to become the Human Being (*huios tou anthrōpou*). Jesus as the fulfillment of the Law is the same as saying Jesus stands out against poverty; His ministry challenges human beings to obey Torah by eradicating poverty.

Another insight I have gained in thinking about Torah in the Old Testament and in Matthew, is that Torah contains the essence of human living. God sees the full picture of creation, just like the police know the resulting pain and suffering that can occur on the roads through lawless driving. Like the road laws we must also accept that Torah is for the benefit of all even though it doesn't always seem so.

Quaker writer, Richard Foster, expresses in 1979 words that are worth hearing as relevant expressions of Torah:

> I want to list ten controlling principles for the outward expression of simplicity. They should not be viewed as laws but as one

attempt to flesh out the meaning of simplicity in twentieth-century life. First, buy things for their usefulness rather than their status. Second, reject anything that is producing an addiction in you. Third, develop a habit of giving things away. De-accumulate. Fourth, refuse to be propagandised by the custodians of modern gadgetry. Fifth, learn to enjoy things without owning them. Sixth, develop a deeper appreciation for the creation. Seventh, look with healthy scepticism at all "buy now, pay later" schemes. Eighth, obey Jesus' injunction about plain, honest speech. Ninth, reject anything that will breed the oppression of others. Tenth, shun whatever would distract you from you main goal. —*QF&P* 25.09

PRAYER

Lord Jesus, you have taught us that love is the fulfilling of the law. Teach us what love really is, how much it costs, how far it leads, how deep it digs into our selfish selves. Then give us the courage and generosity to accept what this means today and tomorrow in the whole future of our lives. —Michael Hollings

6

Goodness, Mercy, and Love

Loving care is not something that those sound in mind and body "do" for others but a process that binds us together. God made us loving and the imparting of love to another satisfies something deep within us. —QF&P 12.01

Love is the will to nurture life and growth in oneself and in another. —QF&P 22.42

The true felicity of man in this life, and that which is to come, is in being inwardly united to the fountain of universal love and bliss.[1] *—John Woolman*

The mystery of the universe is limitless Love, but Love which has sacrificed itself for us . . .[2] *—Gillet*

Everything is bound by a Love that is limitless.[3] *—Gillet*

Mercy is a work which springs from the goodness of God.[4]
—Julian of Norwich

1. Woolman, *Journal and Major Essays*, 249.
2. Gillett, *In Thy Presence*, 24.
3. Ibid., 25.
4. Julian of Norwich, *Enfolded in Love*, 16.

The psalmist says: "surely goodness and mercy will pursue me" (23:6a).[5] The Psalms often praise God's goodness in the same breath as they rejoice in His steadfast mercy and limitless love (100:5). For the psalmists, the goodness of God is the steadfast love of God. *Love is goodness, and goodness is God, and God is love.* All creation is good to the extent that love and mercy are the foundations of existence. As *QF&P* states, love is "a process that binds us together."

Where there is no love, God's goodness is not in creation. Where there is greed and competition, goodness is not present. In Matthew 24:12 Jesus observes that love is growing cold and with it an increase in hatred because people do not live according to the way God intended (i.e., for Jesus this was according to Torah). The world is at war with love in Matthew 24:12, and the consequence is hatred for one another. Hatred leads to poverty and to a place wherein God's goodness is rejected. Gillet writes: "A violent warfare is constantly being waged against Limitless Love."[6] Love and mercy are seen as weak in the world, but they point towards how God designed creation wherein His goodness is present.

Davies and Allison observe:

> Matthew's gospel has a great deal to say about mercy. It is a fundamental demand (cf. 9:13; 12:7; 23:23) which is fleshed out both by Jesus' words (5:43–8; 18:21–35; 25:31–46) and by his example (9:27–31; 15:21–28; 17:14–18; 20:29–34). In much of this there is strict continuity with the OT and Jewish tradition, for the disposition towards mercy—both an outward and an inward feeling—was of course acknowledged as a human virtue as well as a divine attribute . . . throughout Matthew (including 5:7) 'mercy' and its cognates imply that merciful action is the concrete expression of loyalty to God, and that what God demands is not so much activity directed Godward ('I desire mercy . . . not sacrifice') but loving kindness benefiting other people ('I desire mercy').[7]

In this chapter I consider this key theme as far as it reflects upon and elucidates my main argument that Matthew is a gospel for the poor.

5. My translation. The Hebrew word is strong in the sense of someone that pursues another.

6. Gillet, *Burning Bush*, 20.

7. Davies and Allison, *Matthew 1–7*, 454–55.

GOD'S GOODNESS EVIDENT IN MERCIFUL LIVING

Human beings were made and designed to live for others.[8] When Genesis 1 states seven times that God saw that creation is good, it is at the same time stating that human beings are good to the extent that they are generous and merciful like their Creator. Sallie McFague succinctly puts it: "self-fulfillment is achieved through a form of *self-sacrifice.*"[9] God created all things so that they would find happiness in loving and serving others. Happiness cannot denote a state separated from others.[10] Life is ordered that we each look to the interests of others (Matthew 20:28 and parallels; 26:28; cf. 1 Corinthians 13:5; Philippians 2:5–6). *The extent to which human beings serve themselves is the extent to which they are cut off from God.*[11]

In short, mercy represents the essence of goodness. Matthew 5:7 sums this up: "Blessed are the merciful" meaning that you will be joyful only when you bring joy to others. To show mercy, for example, to a person who has no food or drink involves giving them food and drink (cf. James 2:15–16).

Good is what God created. Good is the predicate of "limitless love" echoing *ḥesed* (steadfast love) as well as righteousness/justice, and Torah. I am struck by the relevance of Kallistos Ware's words: "'Mercy' denotes the bridging of the gulf between God's righteousness and the fallen creation."[12] I consider love and mercy as synonyms in the context of the way God inwardly orders creation. From the fall God immediately shows His mercy to human beings to bridge the gulf between Him and them. The more merciful and generous humans are the more they represent and express the goodness of God in creation.

I am also drawn to Gillet's words: "the mystery of the universe is limitless love." I have found Gillet's description of God's eternal love as "limitless" helpful. It is well attested biblically: in Psalm 100:5 we read: "because the LORD is good, His love is limitless" (my translation of the Hebrew: *kî -ṭôb*

8. See Bodkin's article on brain research that we are hard-wired to be merciful: http://www.telegraph.co.uk/science/2016/08/15/generosity-down-to-brains-wiring-new-research-suggests.

9. McFague, *Blessed are the Consumers*, 3.

10. Ibid., 126. On 122 McFague discusses the science that suggests the brain is hard-wired to generosity.

11. These insights are not just the thoughts of religious people, but psychologist, Martin Seligman, draws attention to three components necessary for happiness. In order to be happy a person needed to be engaged with friends and family, have a sense of meaning or purpose that involved being dedicated to a greater good. His third component, "pursuit of pleasure" could only be sought in the context of the two previous components. See Crosby, *Finding Francis*, 204.

12. Ware, *The Power of the Name*, 19.

yĕhwâ lĕ ʿôlom hasdô. The Hebrew *ʿôlom* indicates "limitless" suggesting eternal. The phrase *lĕʿ ôlom hasdô* (limitless love) is found over fifty times in the Hebrew Bible and on a number of occasions it occurs beside God being good (*kî-ṭôb*) (Psalms 106:1; 107:1; 118:1; 136:4: God is good and limitless love).

MERCY AND LOVE IN THE OLD TESTAMENT

Israel experienced God's limitless love active in His actions of liberating it from political and economic oppression.[13] We find in the Bible significant occurrences of *ḥesed* (often translated mercy and steadfast love) being interlinked with executing justice (liberation) to the victims of violence and greed. On the basis of Old Testament scholarship, and my assessment of some key texts, *ḥesed* denotes giving dignity to someone through making sure each has access to what God intended (goodness: *ṭôb*).

I fear that this connection between mercy and restoring justice has been lost; most significantly, its economic and material moorings are lost to today's readers who are materially and economically well off. This failure to take seriously *ḥesed* economically is linked with worldviews that see creation to be a place of dis-order, scarcity, and battle. Mercy has no place in a world of material scarcity.

The word *ḥesed* occurs numerous times in parallel with justice and righteousness (Jeremiah 9:23; Isaiah 16:5; Micah 6:8 and many others).[14] It is often paired off with nouns of mercy (*raḥum;* e.g., Psalm 103:4; Zechariah 7:9). It is known (but not normal) to see LXX translate *ḥesed* with *dikaiosynē* (Genesis 32:11; Proverbs 1:22). One scholar notes: "It [*ḥesed*] is a kind of love including mercy, *hannun*, when the object is in a pitiful state."[15] Miranda points out: "It [*ḥesed*] . . . always denotes a volitional attitude orientated to the concept of right."[16] In other words, *ḥesed* is intimately linked to economic activity. Miranda's "concept of right" is best understood as creation inwardly ordered towards a love dynamically anchored in a process of continuing creation, and through, and by which, we *either* live in harmony with God's goodness in creation by being expressions of His limitless love, *or* against God by living ungenerously. To put it simply: *God orders creation to live in order to dignify all creation in imitation of God's work as Creator.*

13. Brueggemann, *Theology of the Old Testament*, 599.

14. See Miranda, *Marx*, 47 for full list.

15. Harris, *Theological Wordbook*, vol. 1, 307.

16. Miranda, *Marx*, 120.

The earth is full of God's steadfast love (*ḥesed*) and it follows that to live on earth as God intends is to be an unblocked channel of God's goodness.

In Hosea 6:6 *ḥesed* denotes care and hospitality: "For I desire steadfast love (*ḥesed;* LXX: *eleos*) and not sacrifice, the knowledge of God rather than burnt offerings" (cf. Proverbs 21:3). Hosea uses *ḥesed* in the context of the prophet's denunciation of the elite members of Israel for their lack of compassion: they murder, rob, and shed blood.[17] In 6:6b "knowledge of God" is in parallel with *ḥesed* in 6:6a, thus to know Yahweh is to achieve justice for the poor.[18] "Knowledge" is not intellectual knowledge, but describes a person's sense of being at one with God evident in him or her showing mercy and love to others.

Hosea encourages *ḥesed* and not sacrifice. However, the prophet does not attack sacrifice *per se.* Instead, when he speaks of sacrifice he has oppression in mind.[19] Hosea does not condemn, for example, the validity of the Temple cult, but rather the separation of the sacrifice from Torah whose purpose is to protect the vulnerable. Sirach makes explicit what Hosea refers to as unjust sacrifice castigating those who sacrifice ill-gotten goods, he calls it "a blemished offering" (Sirach 34:21). In 34:24 an ill-gotten good is the "bread of the needy" (34:25), and not paying wages is like shedding blood (34:27). Ezekiel attacks Israel for failing to shepherd those entrusted to it; in contrast, it lived off the flesh of the sheep for whom it should have been caring (34:8). The elite of Israel sacrificed others but failed to give anything of themselves.

The Hebrew of Psalm 23:6 equates *ḥesed* with *ṭôb* as companions guiding the faithful through life. I suggest we see each as expressions of God's goodness depicted in creation. God is experienced as *ḥesed* and *ṭôb* and all that He formed are expressions of them. *Ḥesed* should be seen as relating back to the act of creation in which God gives of Himself pouring out His love and goodness; the result of that was an abundant creation.

MATTHEW: MERCY AND LOVE

Davies and Allison note that Matthew's gospel has a particular concern for mercy and love. I select several texts from Matthew to illustrate their observations.

17. Ibid., 46.

18. Ibid., 44; Brueggemann, *A Social Reading*, 66.

19. In Micah 6:6–8 God declares that burnt offerings are not what God requires. God needs people to do justice and to love *ḥesed* and to walk humbly before God (6:8).

In addition to mercy being a strong theme in Matthew, love also appears dominantly in Matthew.[20] Jesus particularly laments how love has grown cold evident in the escalation of violence and disobedience to Torah (24:12). He comments how love is corrupted through love of self (6:5; 6:24). Jesus emphasizes the importance of loving more than one's own kin, emphasizing love of enemy (5:43–48). In 19:19 Matthew particularly adds to Mark "love your neighbor as yourself" (cf. Mark 10:19).

1:19

Joseph is a righteous person (*dikaios*) for dignifying his future wife, Mary, who is on the verge of being humiliated. Joseph acted in a way that would not "expose her to public disgrace." While the words love or mercy are not mentioned in verse 19, Joseph's actions set a benchmark for love and mercy throughout Matthew; further, he is praised precisely for giving "dignity" to a person who was about to be humiliated and excluded.

5:7

Only Matthew has Jesus teach "blessed are the merciful, for they will be shown mercy." God gives dignity to someone if someone gives dignity to the poor. Giving dignity is the foundation of life in which God's goodness is in creation bringing spiritual and material abundance to others; it is not a way of life rooted in pitying and patronizing acts that prevent the recipient from flourishing as an equal.

5:42

Jesus instructs His disciples to give to those who ask and beg (cf. Luke 6:30). Jesus has in mind people who beg for food and shelter; they are the poorest of the poor. In 6:2, showing mercy (*poiēs eleēmosunēn*) involves fighting material poverty. One way of showing mercy to the poor is through fasting. This is recounted in Matthew 6:16–18 (see below) echoing Isaiah 58:6–9: "to loose the bonds of injustice," it is "to share your bread with the hungry and bring the homeless poor into your house."

20. More than the other Synoptic Gospels; *agapatē* only in 5:44; cf. 1 John 2:15; *agapē* only in 24:12.

5:48

Jesus teaches: "Be perfect, therefore, as your heavenly Father is *perfect* (*teleios*);" the same tradition, but with an interesting difference, is found in Luke: "Be merciful, therefore, as your Father is *merciful*" (Luke 6:36). This difference reveals the close similarity between "merciful" and "perfect."

This parallel also supports Grassi who argues that *teleios* "is used in regard to the distribution of possessions."[21] According to Matthew, God is Father who is *teleios* meaning one who is complete by the fact that He is self-giving so that others can flourish. God is the Father in the sense that He is one who gives of Himself.

6:2–4

Does Matthew imply that we act generously only in order to receive rewards? An affirmative answer would be contrary to the idea of showing unconditional mercy and love. However, those who give, do so not for the purpose of self-enhancement; rather, their reward will be to live in harmony with creation experiencing the joy that comes through seeing others flourish. Those who give to get the praise of others, will have the approbation of others as their reward, but it is not the reward of God.

6:12 (Luke 11:4)

Both Luke's and Matthew's accounts of the Lord's Prayer record Jesus teaching His disciples to ask God for mercy. The central aspect of this verse is that people forgive because God forgives. This is repeated in 6:14–15. God does not need human beings to ask for mercy, but Jesus teaches disciples to ask because in asking they acknowledge their need to live in harmony with God. In so doing they recognize that they must act towards others as they perceive God acting towards them. As God is generous, humans must be generous.

6:14–15

Jesus teaches that if we don't forgive others their sins, then God will not forgive our sins (Matthew 6:14–15; cf. Mark 11:25). When we see that the word sin, *opheilēmata*, in 6:12 refers to economic "debts" then we must

21. Grassi, *Informing the Future*, 156.

conclude that love, mercy and economics, are intimately linked. Matthew's *opheilēmata* is debt only used in regard to business matters.[22]

Here more than in the other gospels, Jesus teaches that if human beings don't forgive others their sins God will not forgive them.[23] Gardner clarifies: "The point of Jesus' saying is that there has to be reciprocity between the ways God responds to the misdeeds (trespasses) of others and the ways God responds to our own."[24] If human beings do not show mercy they disrupt God's ordering of creation according to goodness. These verses emphasize the necessity of doing God's will as being an expression of His limitless love. Jesus does not teach that a person must forgive to be forgiven. Matthew 18:23–35 and 26:28 show that God's forgiveness precedes and underlines our forgiveness of one another.

9:13 and 12:7

Only in Matthew Jesus teaches that God desires mercy and not sacrifice (9:13 and 12:7) through linking the call to discipleship with Hosea 6:6, translating *ḥesed* with *eleos* (9:13; 12:7). Jesus states that God desires that people dignify the poor and stop murdering and oppressing the vulnerable and powerless (cf. Ezekiel 34:2–4 for sacrifices rooted in violence against others).

In Matthew 9:13, Jesus' quote of Hosea occurs in the context of the Pharisees rebuking Jesus for eating and drinking with sinners and tax-collectors. The sinners and tax-collectors are not the poor. They, like the Pharisees, lived off the work/sacrifices of the poor. Jesus challenged sinners and tax-collectors to recognize that their privileges are rooted in the suffering and oppression of others. Jesus addresses tax-collectors, sinners, and the Pharisees in the same way Hosea challenges the oppressors of his time.

Repentant sinners and tax-collectors saw themselves as sinners (those who caused others to dwell in the sin of poverty and oppression) and were open to Jesus' teaching sensing their culpability in a regime of violence and oppression.[25] Matthew intends his listener to understand the tax-collectors as the same group who went out into the wilderness to be baptized by John confessing their sins; those who were receptive to His teaching and were ready to repent with fruits of repentance.

22. Grassi, *Informing the Future*, 160.

23. The closest to these words are found in Mark 11:25–26.

24. Gardner, *Matthew*, 121.

25. Sinners is often found in synonymous parallelism with the rich in the Old Testament (e.g., Isaiah 53:9a).

On the contrary, the Pharisees saw themselves as a "cut-above-the-rest" and, therefore, were not open to the truth of Jesus' teaching about God's *ḥesed*. They were the ones who opposed John the Baptist's teaching and his baptism.[26] Jesus' challenge to them is for them to see and understand that they live by violence and exclusion.

In 12:7, Hosea 6:6 occurs in the context of a conflict between Jesus and the Pharisees about proper Sabbath obedience. Jesus attacks the Pharisees for distorting the Sabbath turning it into an opportunity to assert domination and exclusion. Ellen Davis helpfully points out that the Sabbath: "is meant to enable Israel to see the world as God's creation."[27] This means recalling that creation is God's generous gift through abstaining from normal productive work activities. Sabbath obedience is to confess trust in God as Creator Father from whom all sustenance comes. In short, Jesus challenges the Pharisees to recognize that the Sabbath calls human beings to dignify each other through generously caring and loving.

9:27–31 (see also 20:29–34)

Two blind men cry out to Jesus: "dignify (*eleēson*) us, son of David" (9:27).[28] The phrase "son of David" echoes the son of David found in Psalm 72; he is one who defends the cause of the poor (Psalm 72:4).The imperative verb *eleēson* (have mercy, give dignity) occurs in the context of men who are economically vulnerable sustaining themselves by undignified begging.[29] They are reliant on the pity shown to them by others. Carter observes well that "Mercy means not Jesus' condescension or pity, not only a healing, but a transforming act which opens up a new way of life."[30]

12:36 and 16:27

Matthew alone has Jesus teach that everyone will pay for what he has done or said (12:36; 16:27), whether they have acted mercifully to others as God has acted towards them or contrary to God.

26. I translate the Greek preposition *epi* in Matthew 3:7 "against." The Pharisees and Sadducees went out *against* his baptism. See Abbott-Smith, *Manual Greek Lexicon*.

27. Davis, *Scriptures, Culture*, 78.

28. My translation.

29. Carter, *Matthew and the Margins*, 227.

30. Ibid.; Hill, *Matthew*, 180: "the cry of the men is not for pity or sympathy, but for that mercy which acts and helps."

15:22

A Canaanite woman cries out to Jesus, using the same language as the blind men in 9:27–31 (see above): "son of David." In the parallel account found in Mark 7:24–30, the woman does not ask Jesus to show her mercy. In Matthew she asks Jesus to give her dignity that has been taken from her because of the sickness of her daughter that has resulted in her being shunned.[31] This can only be done through the healing of her daughter. There is no mention of the daughter being present, but it is implied when Matthew recounts "her daughter was healed instantly" (v. 28) suggesting there was eyewitness evidence of her healing. It is equally likely that the woman had been divorced for it seems that men divorcing their wives for something small was possible in Jewish circles (Matthew 19:3).

I suggest, according to Matthew, the woman is deliberately portrayed to echo Israel crying out against its oppressor Egypt. I propose this on speculative grounds although I think Matthew's use of "Canaanite" is to contrast the woman to Jews while depicting her as the poorest of the poor as Israel once was. There is now a reversal, the hated Canaanite has become the new Israel.

18:21–35

Only here we find the parable of the servant who is shown limitless love by the king in cancelling a large financial sum. Alas, the servant is unable to extend such love to another who cries out to him for mercy (18:21–35).

The parable is to be understood in the context of the whole of Matthew 18. Jesus in this chapter teaches about how to create cultures of *shalom* and righteousness, as according to Torah. The poor and powerless are the greatest in the kingdom of heaven (18:1–6). Their poverty is particularly emphasized in Matthew stating they were unwelcomed and scorned (18:5): *those whom the world scorns God welcomes.* Those who receive them hospitably become channels of God's limitless love flowing into them. In 18:10–14 the disciples are taught to be expressions of God's in dignifying those treated with contempt.

The parable of the merciless servant therefore is best read in the context of all belonging to God depending on His mercy. Central to the message of the parable is that the disciple must acknowledge God as a Creator of limitless love and aspire to live by showing limitless love to all.

31. Also in economically developed countries mothers of disabled children are often left isolated with husbands walking out.

20:1–16

In this story the land owner shows great generosity paying one day's salary for one hour's work (20:1–16).[32] God is depicted as distinct in being good through contrasting him with servants who complain at his mercy.

23:23

Luke speaks of the "love of God" (11:42) whereas Matthew has *eleos* (mercy) (23:23). This shows clearly that no distinction exists between love and mercy. *Mercy and love* denote an inward sense of selflessness expressed outwardly in seeking the spiritual and material health and happiness of others. The love which proceeds from God is defined as *eleos*. The same cannot be said of love that looks only for selfish gain which is *not love*.

Jesus castigates the Pharisees for ignoring and despising the poorest of the poor. Even though they tithed, such actions were done for self-gain.[33] Tithing made them ostensibly kind so as to be thought highly of by others. But God saw that such tithing was not done as an act of giving dignity to those treated with contempt. They gave with an ulterior motive.

24:45–51

While mercy and love are not mentioned in these verses, they emphasize the importance of showing mercy and love to the poorest of the poor. Jesus instructs His disciples about the difference between a faithful and unfaithful servant. The faithful makes sure that he or she feeds those whom God has entrusted into his or her care (v. 45). In verses 48–51 the unfaithful is one who acts as though there is no loving God (i.e., absent landlord, v. 48); he beats people while eating and drinking with drunkards (v. 49). The lot of the wicked servant is judgment in which he will be cut in pieces and put where the hypocrites are, where there will be weeping and gnashing of teeth (vv. 50–51).

32. Herzog, *Parables*, 84, argues the master is an ungenerous and oppressive elite.

33. In comparing this with 5:21–24 the same phenomenon of doing actions that make a person look good in the eyes of respectable folk while at the same time their day to day actions fall short of God's standards as they despise others by not paying them their wages or verbally mocking them.

25:31–46

In Jesus' final teaching section in Matthew about judgment, we find that judgment is dependent, precisely, and only, on merciful actions evident in the unostentatious caring for and providing for the poor (25:31–46). While mercy or love are not referred to in this parable, it is the summary of Jesus' whole teaching about showing dignity and love to the pitiable. Jesus makes clear that judgment is dependent on the extent to which the way of mercy is followed. Those who are condemned showed no mercy (the goats) while those who showed mercy, particularly through feeding the hungry and showing hospitality to the poor, will enter the joy of their Creator.[34] *In short, mercy is a behavior required of the followers of Jesus.*

I also add that the theme of ostentatious giving is unmistakeable in this parable. The goats represent those who believe themselves to be righteous disciples who tithe, give alms, pray, and fast. Their question to the son of man in verse 44 is telling: "Lord, when was it that we saw you hungry . . .?" The question gives the impression that the goats represent those who are exclusivist and elitist and only give when it is expedient. We know from Matthew on several occasions that Jesus' disciples failed to recognize that the kingdom of heaven belonged to those who were scorned.

26:28

In Matthew alone is the idea of the renewal of the order of creation explicitly stated in terms of "forgiveness" when Jesus declares that the wine He gives is His blood poured out for the forgiveness of sins (26:28).[35] Jesus' pouring out of His blood (life) refers to His self-giving and generous act to free people both from the sin of being in poverty and oppression as well as the sin of causing poverty and oppression (26:28; cf. 1:21). In short, Jesus' life is one of life lived that others can live.

SUMMARY

- Creation is good to the extent that it is a place of love and mercy.

34. The goats in the parable who claim not to have seen Jesus also echo those in Matthew 7:21–23 where they claim to have knowledge of God but are condemned for not doing the will of the Father.

35. In contrast Mark and Luke talk of the baptism of repentance for the forgiveness of sin (Mark 1:4).

- Mercy is best understood in terms of self-sacrifice.
- Self-fulfillment (being blessed and joyful) comes through self-sacrifice.
- Mercy is a covenant word like Torah and righteousness. It is relationally rooted and it is the bond that binds all creation together so it flourishes.
- The existence of poverty and inequality suggests mercy and love are not at the center of how humans order their lives.

FOOD FOR THOUGHT

According to Gillett, love is the essential bond between all beings, between all things, and the Father of all creation who gives life.[36] Love is something "that binds us together." Love and mercy describe the way communities are ordered to allow all to act so that all have access to God's goodness in creation. The extent to which a person acts to do this is a measure of the degree to which he or she fulfilling God's will.

Human beings are creatures dependent on the mercy of others. Living by mercy and love is to live thankfully receiving care and giving care as God intended. God made us loving and the imparting of love to another satisfies something deep within us. To live contrary to this is to pollute creation.

I am struck by research in the area of neuroplasticity. I find that the brain is hard-wired for acting altruistically. Sallie McFague draws our attention to neuroplasticity in *Blessed are the Consumers*. Such work has also influenced the Dalai Lama in his work found in *Ethics for the New Millennium*. Henry Bodkin helpfully summarizes the new research that the brain is wired for generosity.[37]

I finish this chapter with a quote from John Woolman written in 1763 that expresses well what I have attempted to put forward in this chapter:

> Our gracious Creator cares and provides for all his creatures. His tender mercies are over all his works; and so far as his love influences our minds, so far we become interested in his workmanship and feel a desire to take hold of every opportunity to lessen the distress of the afflicted and increase the happiness of creation. Here we have a prospect of one common interest from

36. Gillet, *In Thy Presence*, 21.

37. Bodkin observes: "The subgenual anterior cingulate cortex (SACC) has been pinpointed as the area of grey matter that activates when we think of helping our fellow man or woman." http://www.telegraph.co.uk/science/2016/08/15/generosity-down-to-brains-wiring-new-research-suggests.

which our own is inseparable, that to turn all the treasures we possess into the channel of universal love becomes the business of our lives . . . —*QF&P* 23.14

PRAYER

Dear Lord Love, You have given each of us dignity. Show us our sins of robbing people of their dignity. Call us to repent that we may truly give of ourselves so all Your creation abounds in Your goodness. We pray Lord that Your goodness and mercy shall follow us. Amen

7

Shalom

The peace testimony [of Quakers] is not about being nice people and living so that everyone likes us. It will remain a stumbling block and will cause conflict and disagreement . . . We need to train to wage peace —*QF&P 24.11*

The virtues of mercy, non-violence, love and truth in any man can be truly tested only when they are pitted against the ruthlessness, violence, hate and untruth.[1] —*Gandhi*

The universe gives no peace to him who professes to separate any situation or person from total love.[2] —*Gillet*

The world's peace is the very peace that Jesus says He has not come to bring (Matthew 10:34–36). In the very same Gospel Jesus teaches: "Blessed are the peacemakers for they will be called children of God" (5:9). According to 5:44, to be a child of God is to love enemies and persecutors alike. Jesus' words are best read in the context of biblical peace-making in contrast to a world whose "peace" is sustained by violence, walls, and threat of coercion. The biblical peace of which Jesus speaks of is subversive to this world's peace.

My understanding of biblical peace in this chapter in part is drawn from Randy Woodley's statements: (1) "God has designed us all to live in

1. Merton, *Gandhi on Non-Violence*, 31.

2. Gillet, *In Thy Presence*, 25.

a world of *shalom*;"[3] (2) "The Creator has ingeniously designed a world in which *shalom* is the foundational stuff that God uses to create proper order to the world."[4] I add another point (3): *shalom* is the love that underpins creation which is God's limitless love, righteousness, and mercy.

It follows that inequality, violence, greed, and poverty are at odds with *shalom* that God intends for creation.

SHALOM, COVENANT AND CREATION

Orthodox monk and priest Father Gillet states that peace is the infrastructure of the universe, a person who does not live generously will not experience peace or generosity. In a related way, H. H. Schmid understands *shalom* to refer to the order that God established in creation. When creation runs according to this order, it is an expression of His goodness. *Shalom* order, therefore, is intimately linked to Torah, mercy, and righteousness. I agree with Schmid that biblical thought about *shalom* is embedded in the wider context of the Bible's understanding of creation and order.[5]

Similarly Brueggemann recognizes *shalom* in the Bible within the context of creation and covenant.[6] On three occasions in the Bible the phrase "covenant of peace" occurs (Ezekiel 34, 37, and Isaiah 54). But in these texts covenant is creation which is a place of *shalom*. *Shalom* is intrinsically linked to covenant in the same way that a married couple are formed covenantally to *shalom*. Marriage corresponds to creation, and *shalom* like love is the basis for the marriage to be bound together in a process leading all to flourish.

Brueggemann sees Genesis 1:2 as a pre-creation vision: "a formless void and darkness." He strikingly enunciates that 1:2 is *without shalom* arguing, therefore, that what is found in Genesis 1:3–2:4a is the creation of *shalom*.[7] God's Spirit is the *shalom*-maker who overcomes the formless void and darkness. In short, *shalom* is when creation is prosperous and abundant and all creation is ordered for the benefit of others.

I suggest it is helpful to see *shalom* as corresponding to the good/ness (*ṭôb*) that God sees seven times in Genesis 1. This goodness refers to the quality of creation measured in terms of harmony, self-giving love, and the level of sharing between different peoples and communities. Therefore *shalom* predominantly in the Bible is the essence or quality of creation. Quaker

3. Woodley, *Shalom*, 20.
4. Ibid., 14.
5. Schmid, "Creation, Righteousness, and Salvation," 102–17.
6. Brueggemann, *Peace*, 99–106; also Yoder, "Shalom Revisited," 9.
7. Brueggemann, *Peace*, 15.

writer Doug Gwyn states that *shalom* is the quality of community created by covenant that is lived out in *hesed*.[8]

It can be translated with many words including peace and prosperity. *Shalom* is both a creation word (i.e., an outward expression of being blessed by God); it is also a covenantal word suggesting creation is ordered inwardly towards *shalom*.

Gerhard von Rad notes that covenant is commonly designated by the word *shalom* (Genesis 26:30ff; 1 Kings 5:26; Isaiah 54:10; Job 5:23); he writes: "the making of a covenant is intended to secure a state in intactness, orderliness, and rightness between two parties, in order to make possible, on the basis of legal foundation, a relationship in matters affecting their common life."[9]

In Ezekiel 34:25 the "covenant of peace" is mentioned in which all will be blessed and live securely. The soil will be good (v. 27); there will be no slaves (vv. 27–28); there will be neither hunger nor violence (v. 28). Israel will no longer be insulted by the nations (v. 29). God's promise to Noah and all flesh never to abandon creation underpins especially Isaiah 54:9–10. Ezekiel 37:26 explicitly links the promise of the covenant of peace with Genesis 1:28 where the command to be fruitful and multiply becomes a promise: God *will* multiply them.

In short, covenant of peace is at the heart of creation and refers to how God intended creation to be when humans live mercifully and in harmony. *Shalom* is what God forms from "a formless void and darkness" (Genesis 1:2). Creation and covenant are intrinsically linked.

MEASURING THE PRESENCE OF *SHALOM*

Gutiérrez observes that "peace is the establishment of authentic justice and salvation . . ."[10] In other words, *shalom* is the consequence of justice and righteousness.[11] Therefore, *the quality and presence of shalom can be measured, I believe, only in terms of whether or not poverty exists.* I am struck by Woodley's statement that "As long as there are hungry people in a community that is well fed, there can be no *shalom*."[12] One who works for *shalom* refers to one who seeks, against the social grain, to redistribute God's gift of

8. Gwyn, *The Covenant Crucified*, 7.

9. von Rad, *Old Testament Theology* vol. 1, 130. Gwyn, *The Covenant Crucified*, 6–7.

10. Gutiérrez, *The God of Life*, 126.

11. Brueggemann, *Peace*, 18.

12. Woodley, *Shalom*, 21.

creation equally and partially to those who are deprived of it. This is important when considering Matthew's beatitude about the peacemakers (5:9).

Woodley further comments: "The Creator required us to reshape the world we know into the world God has intended."[13] That world is to be a place of *shalom* which is intimately linked to concern for the poorest of the poor. Woodley specifies that "A society concerned with *shalom* will care for the marginalized among them."[14] Therefore, there is no *shalom* if a society and communities are divided.[15] The existence of the poorest of the poor in our world testifies to how far the world is from being in a state of *shalom.*

SHALOM AND THE NON-POOR

Brueggemann emphasizes that *shalom*-making is the task and burden of the well-off and powerful. They are the ones held accountable for *shalom.*[16] *Shalom* is, therefore, inextricably linked to removing injustice against the poor and the sick. Isaiah's attack on the powerful and greedy for causing many to be in need (57:19) illustrates this point. God rebukes particularly those who are greedy observing how they profit but at the same time say "*shalom, shalom*" while not caring for their victims (Jeremiah 6:13–14).

SHALOM AND MATTHEW

I now examine texts in Matthew that relate to *shalom*-making and consider how these relate to my overall argument that Jesus is a subversive messiah, whose message is revolutionary.

5.9 and 5.45

Those called "children of God" are peacemakers (5:9). Isaiah 9:6 may provide helpful background understanding to this:

> For a child has been born for us, a son given to us; authority rests upon his shoulders; and he is named Wonderful Counselor, Mighty God, Everlasting Father, Prince of Peace.

13. Ibid., 14.
14. Ibid., 15.
15. Ibid., 19.
16. Brueggemann, *Peace*, 19.

Matthew 1:23 is the only gospel that draws upon the prophecy found in Isaiah 7:14 meaning "God is with us" (Emmanuel). Further, because Matthew is fond of terms such as "Father," "peace," "justice" and "righteousness," it is more than coincidental that these, too, are found in Isaiah 9:6–7. Also, Matthew's interest in the Davidic king, central to Isaiah 9, similarly makes it likely that Matthew is aware of Isaiah 9:6 .[17] In short, there are strong grounds to think that Matthew 5:9 and v. 45 had Isaiah 9:6 in mind.

However, the fact that Matthew does not refer to Jesus as "Prince of Peace" may argue against my contention. On the contrary, the Gospel states that Jesus is accused of being the "Prince of Demons," albeit by the Jewish leaders, in 12:24. I detect in this accusation reason to argue that Matthew is inspired by Isaiah 9:6–7. I suggest that the Pharisees' demonizing of Jesus is best understood in the context of their wish to counter those who claim him to be "Son of David," thereby: "Prince of Peace." The leaders allege He is not the prince of peace, but the "prince of demons." Jesus' followers, in opposition, argue that He is the prince of peace as prophesied in Isaiah 9:6–7.

This seems an acceptable argument in line with the context of Isaiah 9:6–7. It is plausible that Matthew reads the Hebrew to claim credibility for Jesus' work as alluding to the Prince of Peace. Such peaceable work is further validated by the Father's (God's) testimony to Him through His acts of healing.

Further, it is more than chance that Jesus, only in Matthew, is the figure of Emmanuel prophesied in Isaiah 7:14, it would seem best to understand that in Isaiah 9:6–7 we read the Father witnessing to the Prince of Peace in the sense that the Prince of Peace is at one with God, the Father.

Furthermore, in 5:9 "children of God" are called peace-makers (i.e., those who establish *shalom* from chaos as the Father Creator does in Genesis 1:2). In 5:45 Jesus teaches that loving your enemies is the sign of one who acts and claims that their Father is none other than the Creator of all. Jesus describes God as sending rain and sun to the good and bad revealing God as one who is involved in all creation and is the origin of all creation. All creation belongs to God even that which rejects His will.

8:23–27

Jesus, according to Matthew 8:26, "got up and rebuked the winds and the sea; and there was a dead calm." Mark 4:39 has: "He woke up and rebuked

17. Swartley, *Israel's Scripture*, 224. Also it is central to Swartley's thesis in his chapter on Matthew in *Covenant*, 59: "a distinctive portrait of Matthew's royal Christology, which deepens the peaceable portrait of King Jesus as Messiah and Son of God."

the wind, and said to the sea, "Peace! Be still!" Then the wind ceased, and there was a dead calm." Brueggemann believes that Mark's "peace" echoes the notion of *shalom*. He writes:

> The storm at sea represents all the same ominous, chaotic forces presented in Genesis 1:2. And the words of Jesus in Mark serve the same purpose as the hovering spirit of God in Genesis 1:2, namely, to bring fundamental disorder under God's rule—into harmony—so that light, life, and joy become possible. Creation in Genesis and by Jesus (see Colossians 1:17) is the establishment of *shalom* in a universe that apart from God's rule is disordered, unproductive, and unfulfilling.[18]

Brueggemann specifically focuses on Mark but his comments are more valid and appropriate for Matthew even though the First Gospel does not have the word "peace." There is some speculation as to why Matthew omits the "peace" found in Mark. I see no significance in Matthew's omission other than his tendency to abbreviate Mark.[19] Matthew, however, makes some significant changes to Mark's account of the calming of the storm which makes, I suggest, Brueggemann's comments more appropriate to the First Gospel.

Matthew places his account of the calming of the storm after Jesus teaches that following him is costly. He presents the story more as an allegory relating to the dangers that are involved in doing God's will. The boat, for example, portrays perhaps creation in the context of an evil world that threatens it (cf. Tertullian, *De Baptismo*, 12).[20] Matthew has the disciples follow Jesus onto the boat (8:23, whereas in Mark 4:36 they take Jesus with them). Thus Matthew puts his account in a situation requiring total discipleship where following Jesus is emphasized. Matthew uses the Greek word *seismos* (quake) which is associated with earthquakes. The scene perhaps assumes the ancient Near Eastern view of the sea as a threatening, chaotic force which God controls (Genesis 1:6–10; Job 38:8–11). The evil powers of chaos rebel against God's created order while God subdues them (Psalm 89:8–11; 107:23–30; 1QH 3:13–18).[21] *Seismos* also represents the hardship of discipleship before Jesus' return (Matthew 24:7; 27:54; 28:2). In short, the scene of the boat struggling in the storm depicts the threat of chaos against the *shalom*-order of creation.

18. Brueggemann, *Peace*, 16.

19. It is another example of Matthew abbreviating Mark.

20. In this context we should recall Jesus' allegory of the house built on firm foundations that is threatened by floods and a storm (7:24–27).

21. Carter, *Matthew and the Margins*, 209–10.

According to Matthew Jesus asks the disciples before He calms the storm: "Why are you afraid, you of little faith?" (Matthew 8:26). In Mark the question is asked after Jesus calms the storm. It can be concluded that Matthew puts the stress on giving the disciples a chance to grow in following and trusting Jesus. Hagner comments:

> The question comes in Matthew before the stilling of the sea . . . in keeping with the discipleship theme and thus heightening its impact. If the disciples respond to an absolute call to discipleship and hence leave all and risk their lives, they must also understand that the one who calls them will also preserve them in whatever circumstances they may find themselves.[22]

Overall, the allegorical nature of Matthew's account of the calming of the storm lends itself better to Brueggemann's creation versus chaos reading than does Mark's. While "peace" is not present in Matthew, it is implicit that Jesus is the peacemaker doing the will of the Father in His calming of the storm. Jesus through His trust in God in the midst of the chaos overcomes it. The chaos is symbolic of violence and greed, the values of the world rooted in an understanding of creation as a battlefield. Such forces destroy creation and are contrary to God's will.

10:13

Jesus tells His disciples that they are to find those who are worthy and to let their peace come upon their homes. Scholars agree in general that this peace refers to the arrival of the kingdom. This peace is a symbol of God's eschatological work of establishing reconciliation and *shalom*.[23] The peace is intimately linked to prosperity and harmony. Human communities are to be expressions of God's goodness.

10:34–36

The peace Jesus announces is not peace achieved through threat and coercion. The good news of peace which Jesus brings is for the poor. Its message is the promise of abundance that God intended for His creation. However, Jesus warns that the powerful will reject this message for it threatens the *status quo* that benefits them. Being a child of God who confesses "God is

22. Hagner, *Matthew 1–13*, 222.

23. Davies and Allison, *Matthew 1–7*, 176.

our Father" is to be a peacemaker and that means living in opposition to the peace of the world.

I find Proverbs 10:10 helpful in imagining what Jesus thought about the peacemaker: "Whoever winks the eye causes trouble, but the one who rebukes boldly makes peace (*eirēnopoiei*)." In short, to be a peacemaker, as Jesus understood it, is to oppose the peace of the world maintained by the threat of force.

12:18–20

In these verses Matthew portrays Jesus alluding to Isaiah 42:1–4. I find Brueggemann's comments on Isaiah 42 helpful in so far as they depict Israel as the servant of God. The servant's task is:

> to reorder social relations for the sake of the vulnerable . . . Israel itself is to practice vulnerability and to be attentive to others who are vulnerable, "bruised reeds and dim sticks." Israel's way of relationship is thus drastically contrasted with the way of Babylon (or any other worldly power), which is to break such reeds and snuff out such wicks. Israel is to pursue a different way in the world—to refuse the modes of power mostly taken for granted.[24]

In short, Matthew 12:18–20 refers to Jesus as the servant: (1) he will not wrangle or cry aloud; (2) he will not be heard in the streets; (3) he will not break a bruised reed or quench a smoldering wick. Each point reveals Jesus to be unlike the normal political agitators or rulers who sought popularity through words and signs.

Schnackenberg is right to observe that "Bringing justice to victory" in verse 20c is reminiscent of the promise of blessing to the poor.[25] Similarly Miranda sees the victory as referring back to the works of Christ done on behalf of the poor mentioned in 11:2–5.[26] Jesus is the new Israel through whom all nations will be blessed. Carter interestingly reads 12:18–20 in terms of *shalom* which he believes, like Brueggemann, refers to the original created order. Therefore, he argues that "each healing or exorcism is a victory of God's reign over that which opposes it (4:1–11; 12:24–28), and

24. Brueggemann, *Isaiah 40–66*, 42.

25. Schnackenberg, *Matthew*, 114.

26. Miranda, *Marx*, 129, 222.

anticipates the establishment of God's empire in full, in which wholeness, plenty, and justice will prevail (cf. 2 *Baruch* 73:1–2)."[27]

In sum, Jesus is depicted in the tradition of being a *shalom*-maker who acts to bring justice to the poor through ordering his or her life according to the covenant of *shalom*.

SUMMARY

- *Shalom* is one of a cluster of words that describes God's covenant.
- Poverty corresponds to "formless void and darkness" in Genesis 1:2. Poverty is the opposite of *shalom*.
- *Shalom* is inseparable from doing to others as you have them do to you, loving the loveless, and loving God through serving His creation.
- *Shalom* is inseparable from the Old Testament vision of a community of creation where all are ordered to participate in God's love and be expressions of His love.
- *Shalom* does not exist where there is inequality. Inequality is anti-creation.
- *Shalom* is measured vis-à-vis the economic spread of wealth and opportunities for human beings to care and preserve what they are entrusted with.
- Matthew has Jesus declare *shalom*-makers to be those who show love for the loveless; those who live in order that others may flourish.
- Matthew sets *shalom* at odds with peace that is rooted in violence and coercion.

FOOD FOR THOUGHT

I am drawn to the famous beatitude in which Jesus commands His disciples to be peacemakers. In the light of my discussion in this chapter I cannot but conclude that to be a peacemaker is not about being upwardly mobile, strong, independent, and a worldly success. It is about not looking to enhance one's own interests; it is about looking to the interests of others. In the midst of our creation perceived as a battlefield, peace is understood from the perspective of the powerful in which peace is linked to the

27. Carter, *Matthew and the Margins*, 270–71.

status quo. Creation as a place of abundance sees peace as harmony and joy through living in harmony with God's will of self-giving.

Being peacemakers for Jesus is, I suggest, best paraphrased more provocatively: "disturbers of the status quo." Peacemakers are the non-poor when they repent and bear the fruits of repentance through challenging the peace that sustains inequality, oppression, sickness, and hunger.

PRAYER

Lord, make me an instrument of your peace; where there is hatred let me sow love; where there is injury let me sow pardon, where there is doubt let me sow faith, where there is despair, let me give hope, where there is darkness let me give light, where there is sadness let me give joy. —St Francis of Assisi

PART THREE

Introduction

The Poorest of the Poor

God comes to us in the midst of human need, and the most pressing needs of our time demand community in response.
—QF&P 23.48

Creation is ordered according to God's designs to be an expression of His goodness. Where there is poverty creation is not an expression of His goodness but reveals, rather, human beings in rebellion against God's creative intentions.

Throughout the Bible God works through creation to enable it to be as He intended. The outward expression of God's goodness is seen in creation as a place of generosity and abundance. It is not a dark chaos where violence and battle dominate. When God's spirit hovers over the darkness it forms cultures of *shalom*.

In part 3 we discover in ancient Galilee that a mind-set existed that facilitated the exclusion and demonization of the poorest of the poor. Jesus' message is one of inclusivity through looking out for the interests of others.

Distinctive to my understanding of the poor is that they are those without helpers. They are the disabled, the physically weak, the mocked, those considered scum and sinners. We find instead that Jesus embraces those on the extreme margins of society as His brothers and sisters.

8

Matthew 5:3 and 25:31–46

The Poorest of the Poor

Poverty is the whole family of our relationships that are not all they can be.[1] —*Bryant Myers*

You cannot present the hungry and famished masses with God. Their God is their food.[2] —*Gandhi*

A certain amount of goods is necessary to lead the good life.[3] —*Dorothy Day*

It is my contention that Matthew has a particular sensitivity to God as a Creator who intended creation to be an expression of His hospitable self-giving love. The existence of the poorest of the poor is, therefore, inexcusable to such a God particularly made palpable in God's warning of condemnation to those who don't repent.

My overall argument in this book has been that poverty is evil and God wills to remove it so there are no poor. I have emphasized a reading of the Bible which affirms that creation is an expression of God's goodness in the material sense of it being abundant and generous. Therefore, God

1. Myers, *Walking with the Poor*, 15.
2. Ellsberg, *Gandhi on Christianity*, 38.
3. Day, *Selected Writings*, 110.

is outraged at the existence of scarcity, poverty, and exclusion in creation. Bryant Myers sums up my own position about the poorest of the poor:

> The poor are poor largely because they live in networks of relationships that do not work for their well-being. Their relationships with others are often oppressive and disempowering as a result of the non-poor "playing god" in the lives of the poor. Their relationship within themselves is diminished and debilitated as a result of the grind of poverty and the feeling of permanent powerlessness. Their relationship with those they call "other" is experienced as exclusion. Their relation with their environment is increasingly less productive because poverty leaves no room for caring for the environment. Their relationship with the God who created them and sustains their life is distorted by an inadequate knowledge of who God is and what God wishes for all humankind. Poverty is the whole family of our relationships that are not all they can be.[4]

Only in Matthew does "the poor in spirit" (*hoi ptōchoi tǭ pneumati*) occur. Further, in this Gospel, Jesus' first words of instruction are "blessed are the poor in spirit." I argue that *the poor in spirit* (5:3) refers to *the very poorest of the poor*; those who have no reason to hope.[5] I agree with Sjef van Tilborg that the poor in spirit are those who are poor to their very breath, those who are so poor that their actual life is in the balance.[6] I also concur with M. A. Powell: "They are people who have no reason for hope in this world, period. The presence or strength of their trust in God remains unaddressed in this beatitude . . ."[7] Such people are those who are often incapable of doing work because of their illnesses or disabilities, victims of colonial violence and abuse, those whose mental and physical conditions makes it difficult to survive unless supported. As a result, they are prevented from keeping Torah.

Only Matthew portrays Jesus' final words to His disciples in the parable of the goats and the sheep (25:31–46). The message of this parable reveals that to inherit the kingdom of heaven a person must feed the hungry, give water to the thirsty, clothe the naked, care for the sick, and visit the prisoners. I agree with Rowland in seeing this list as referring to the poorest

4. Myers, *Walking with the Poor*, 15.

5. Rukundwa and Van Aarde, "Revisiting Justice," 931. They argue specifically that the phrase refers to the powerless victims of the non-poor.

6. Tilborg, *The Sermon on the Mount*, 16.

7. Powell, *God with Us*, 124.

of the poor in general.[8] However, a good number of scholars argue the list of the suffering in 25:31–46 signifies missionaries afflicted for their witness to Christ. In other words, the list does not denote the poorest of the poor in general. In this chapter I argue that 5:3 corresponds well to the list of the poorest of the poor in the parable of the goats and sheep.

SPIRITUALIZING THE POOR

The *Living Translation* interprets poor in spirit as "those who are poor and realize their need for him (i.e., God)," likewise, the scholarly consensus understands *hoi ptōchoi tǭ pneumati* to denote an interior attitude of unattachment to the goods of this world. The poor, therefore, are those who are not attached to possessions—even if they possess them.[9] *In other words*, they are those who realize their need for God whether or not they are materially poor. Robert Ellsberg in his book *Blessed Among All Women* takes the phrase "Blessed are the Poor in Spirit" as a chapter heading referring to women saints as the spiritually poor. He comments that "those who are poor in spirit have an acute sense of their own limitations and of their reliance on grace."[10]

Why do so many spiritualize poor in spirit? Perhaps the Greek word *ptōchoi* translated as 'poor' is ambiguous: perhaps it could mean 'meek' or 'humble.' No. The word refers to helpless beggars. More precisely the poor who have no helpers (cf. Psalm 72:12).

Therefore, maybe "in spirit" (*tǭ pneumati*) changes the meaning of *ptōchoi*. This seems to be in my view the central basis for spiritualizing the *ptōchoi*. The poor become conveniently those who are generous and who are at one with God doing His will while remaining detached from material wealth. It is suitably easier for the non-poor to apply this reading of the verse to themselves when it is not seen to refer to the poorest of the poor. It is an example of conscience tranquilizing interpretation that removes the reader from the troubling presence of material poverty and their culpability in its existence. This interpretation removes the reader from being called to repent.

I believe no responsible biblical theology observing the goodness of God in creation can agree to the idea that poverty and the presence of the poor are what God wants. God may require people to enter voluntarily into poverty in order to eradicate it, but it is not a state to rejoice in; rather

8. Rowland, "Apocalyptic," 504–18.

9. Gutiérrez, *Theology of Liberation*, 255.

10. Ellsberg, *Blessed Among All Women*, 21.

something to repent over. While ideas of the poor being pious are present in the Bible, this is not a dominant concept. Romanticizing poverty is grossly demeaning to the poor. I suspect also that where the poor become the pious in the Bible, those particular sources are not written by those in extreme poverty but from those whose comforts lead them to spiritualize poverty as is done today.

BEING MATERIALLY POOR

According to Proverbs 30:9, poverty leads people to steal and in so doing profane the name of God. Quaker John Woolman (1720–72) notes that if poor men are eased of their oppression they would be able to lead a "well guided life." Woolman believed that being poor made it very difficult for a person to live the life God designed for him or her. He thus had no sense that being poor led a person to be holy or pious. Founder of the Catholic Workers, Dorothy Day (1897–1980), drawing upon her experience of poverty observed that the destitute could have "implacable hatred, or just cold loathing."[11] She asked regarding the poor: "is it to be expected that virtue and destitution should go together?" Her answer: "no . . . they are the destitute in every way, destitute of this world's goods, destitute of honor, of gratitude, of love."[12] She further testifies to "the bitterness of the poor, who cheat each other, who exploit each other even as they are exploited, who despise each other as they are despised."[13] Schottroff sees the poor in spirit to be people who "are so impoverished that their relationship to God is breaking."[14] In short, there is nothing blessed about being poor.

WHO HEARS THE SERMON ON THE MOUNT?

It is unlikely that the crowds who hear Jesus are the poorest of the poor, although His teaching relates to the conditions that cause and sustain extreme poverty.[15] The poorest of the poor, as in today's society, were people with severe learning difficulties, those with mental health conditions, the mothers of disfigured and disabled children, victims of physical and psychological

11. Day, *Selected Writings*, 175.

12. Ibid., 100.

13. Ibid., 99–100.

14. Schottroff, *The Parables*, 206.

15. Drawing on the poverty scale for the first-century set out by Scheidel and Friesen, "The Size of the Economy," 61–91; also Wilson, *For I was Hungry*, 90; I envisage groups PS^6 and PS^5.

violence, the starving and many others.[16] Galilee was colonized by brutal forces, where land could be seized by force, huge taxes imposed, women raped, and cultures decimated. This would result in a collapse of families and support networks that led to what we now call mental health issues. The victims were often left impoverished because they were unfit to work because of their illnesses and excluded status.[17]

In short, the poorest of the poor had neither the motivation, strength nor ability to hear and understand Jesus let alone respond to His teaching. Instead, I will show by observing key texts in the Sermon on the Mount that the audience were the non-poor, especially His disciples.

5:13–14

Those who hear the sermon are understood to be the salt of the earth (5:13) and the light of the world (5:14). They are not the poorest of the poor. Instead, they bring hope to the victims of lawlessness (i.e., the very poorest of the poor). They are sustenance and light to the hungry and those sitting in utter darkness.

5:19

It is hard to imagine the poorest of the poor being in mind when Jesus teaches that those who break the least of the commandments will be condemned. How can, for example, the unemployed and those who beg keep the Sabbath holy? They cannot. I think it is unlikely that Jesus taught obedience to Torah to people who were suffering pain as a result of poverty and illness. It seems more probable that Jesus taught those who had the means to keep and do Torah.

16. I have in mind Attachment Disorder, which is a broad term intended to refer to mood disorders arising from a failure to form normal relationship in early childhood. I am thankful to Graham Leverton MA student and foster care provider who brought my attention to this. I am particularly aware of this condition among prisoners in my work in prisons.

17. Many of those in prison today are such victims; they are unable to hold down jobs, have undeveloped IQs, and because of this act in ways seen by society to be dangerous. Such I believe must figure within how we imagine first-century Galilee.

5:23

This verse I believe refers to those who cause offense (i.e., take away the dignity of the poorest of the poor). Those who despise and insult the poor are some of those who hear Jesus. Not the poorest of the poor.

5:25–26

Jesus teaches:

> Come to terms (*eunoōn*) quickly with your accuser while you are on the way to court with him, or your accuser may hand you over to the judge, and the judge to the guard, and you will be thrown into prison. Truly I tell you, you will never get out until you have paid the last penny.

Does this verse imply some who were listening to Jesus were very poor? This seems unlikely. It points instead to one who has power and responsibilities who is being taken to court for actions considered unlawful. Jesus teaches that the accused should show good will to his enemy. The participle verb *eunoōn* placed first in the Greek New Testament emphasizes that the verses are about reconciliation. Jesus would not instruct the poorest of the poor to be conciliatory in this way to their oppressor. Schweizer writes: "admonition calls on the hearer to seize the chance for a fruitful encounter with his brother . . ."[18]

5:36–37

Jesus would hardly teach about honesty and integrity to people who had no food. Jesus addresses here those who would make oaths falsely, they are people who take advantage of others and in so doing cause harm.

5:38–41

Jesus teaches:

> You have heard that it was said, "An eye for an eye and a tooth for a tooth." But I say to you, "Do not resist an evildoer. But if anyone strikes you on the right cheek, turn the other also; and if anyone wants to sue you and take your coat, give your cloak as

18. Schweizer, *Matthew*, 129.

well; and if anyone forces you to go one mile, go also the second mile."

From these verses we can imagine people who would expect to have their right cheek slapped, be sued for their coat, and forced by a soldier to carry a load for a mile. Usual interpretations of these verses suggest that the people referred to here would be poor and oppressed.

In verse 39 Jesus teaches against physical retaliation. The one who strikes the right cheek is a superior, either Roman soldier or land owner. The right backhanded strike was used by a superior to an inferior. The person striking the face of another saw his victim as an inferior, a fool, one considered incapable of rational thought.[19] However, Jesus' teaching suggests that the one struck was in a position to respond rationally to the superior in a way that was restrained and showed dignity. This victim was not the very poorest of the poor, he was one who may have been tempted to use violence. It seems unlikely that a superior would slap, for example, a leper or a blind person. They would not want to humiliate themselves by striking someone who could not strike back.

In 5:40, a person who needed to pledge their coat was vulnerable. However, he had a coat to use as a pledge. Jesus' teaching about giving the oppressor not only the coat but your undergarment suggest that such examples were common. According to Matthew 25:36, Jesus teaches about clothing those who were actually naked (this is neither metaphorical nor hyperbolic). However, Jesus is not teaching the naked, but someone who is angry and is sufficiently strong and secure to consider rising against such a system with a gesture of protest. That person is not from the very poorest of the poor.

Verse 41 alludes to the practice of the elite making subjects carry their loads. For example, soldiers compel Simon of Cyrene to carry the cross (Matthew 27:32). There is no reason to think that Simon was from among the very poorest of the poor.

5:42

It is hard to imagine that the very poorest of the poor were Jesus' audience when He teaches that people must give money to the poor (5:42).

19. Carter, *Matthew and the Margins*, 152.

6:12

Jesus emphasizes the need to forgive others their debts and to be merciful and generous (6:12; cf. 18:23–35); Jesus would not teach this to people who had nothing.

6:16–18

Jesus would not condemn a hungry child from stealing from the wealthy in order to survive. He would not teach about fasting to those who have no food.[20]

6:22–23

Jesus also addresses those who felt anxious for their own well-being urging them to think of others and be prepared to be generous (6:22–23: the light of the body is a generous [*haplous*] eye).

6:25–34

Jesus warns against worrying about clothes and food; such teaching would be incomprehensible and cruel to those who had no food and clothing (cf. James 2:15–16).

7:9–11

Jesus instructs those in positions of responsibility for others (7:9–11) to care for them; perhaps He had in mind heads of households (cf. 20:1–16). The ordinary, too, are guilty of hoarding and not caring for the *ptōchoi*. Ezekiel 22:29, for example, writes of the wickedness of the ordinary: "Even common people oppress the poor, rob the needy, and deprive foreigners of justice" (New Living Translation).

PTŌCHOI (DESTITUTE)

As I have said, *ptōchoi refers to those suffering economic poverty; those whose basic needs are not met.* See LXX Exodus 23:11; Leviticus 19:10, 15; 23:22;

20. Malchow, *Social Justice*, 44.

Ruth 3:10; 1 Samuel 2:8; 2 Kings 24:14; 25:12; Esther 1:20; 9:22; Job 29:12; 34:28.

A crucial text for understanding Matthew's *ptōchoi* is Isaiah 61:1–2:

> The spirit of the LORD GOD is upon me, because the LORD has anointed me; he has sent me to bring good news to the oppressed (MT: ʿ*ănavim*; LXX: *ptōchoi*), to bind up the brokenhearted, to proclaim liberty to the captives, and release to the prisoners; to proclaim the year of the LORD's favor, and the day of vengeance of our God; to comfort all who mourn;

The NRSV's translation of the Hebrew ʿ*ănavim* and Septuagint's *ptōchoi* as "oppressed" is well-supported. The groups mentioned are the victims of lawlessness. The spirit-anointed servant brings healing to victims who are weak, powerless, and marginalized.[21]

According to Matthew 11:4–5, 19:21, and 26:9, Jesus refers to the *ptōchoi* as a social class to whom He and His disciples did not belong. The *ptōchoi*, in 11:4–5, 19:21 and 26:9 are the many unnumbered and unnamed individuals and groups who were, for Jesus, conspicuous by their neglected, excluded, and despised state. They were without friends and family and were the recipients of insults and anger.

Further, it is unlikely that Matthew sees the disciples as lowly and poor. In 18:4 Jesus speaks to the disciples as those who previously looked down on the poor and lowly. Jesus teaches that in order to enter the kingdom of heaven the disciples must lower (*tapeinōsei*) themselves to the level of the lowest in society. In other words, the disciples while not from the educated and elite classes (cf. Acts 3:13), were by no means the lowest in society.

However, in the Epistle of James, *ptōchoi* refers to those who are rich in faith (2:5). James writes: "Has not God chosen the poor (*ptōchoi*) in the world to be rich in faith and to be heirs of the kingdom that he has promised to those who love him? But you have dishonored the poor. Is it not the rich who oppress you? Is it not they who drag you into court?" (2:5–6). Bauckham comments that this verse "brilliantly encapsulates the Jewish tradition of regarding the pious poor as the paradigms of faith, since in their lack of resources of their own to rely on they exemplify the utter dependence on God which true faith is."[22]

Tamez, however, emphasizes that "the poor are the *ptōchoi*, those who have absolutely nothing, not even a job; they indeed depend on alms."[23] In contrast to Bauckham, she writes: "It is not true that James is here thinking

21. Brueggemann, *Isaiah 40–66*, 213.

22. Bauckham, *James*, 87.

23. Tamez, *Scandalous Message*, 36.

of the poor as the devout or pious, as certain late rabbinic literature would have it. Many of the commentaries also follow this interpretation . . . if we make the poor and pious synonymous then real economic oppression and God's concern for this very class of people are lost."[24] Tamez's points are well made.

J. S. Kloppenborg commends Tamez:

> Tamez's observations should alert us to the possibility that *Armenfrömmigkeit*[25]commended itself to modern North Atlantic interpreters precisely because it stressed values (morality and piety) as a key to the construction of Christian identity and suppressed other features (material poverty) that by the early-twentieth century had come to belong to other realms of cultural discourse and hence were supposed to be irrelevant or peripheral to genuinely religious' claims.[26]

James states that "God has chosen the poor," he does not write: "God has chosen the pious." It is demeaning and naïve to assume that the poorest and sickest people in the world have a special sense of God because of their poverty. On the contrary, pain, suffering, lack of security, fear of being raped or beaten up, do not give to them any sense of God. I have worked with people with profound learning difficulties, they can have fulfilled lives if they are cared for and protected. But Bauckham's notion that the poorest of the poor are more inclined to depend on God because of their poverty has little basis in the experiences of those of who have worked with the poorest of the poor. I believe that some non-poor biblical writers perceived the poorest of the poor to be pious as many non-poor Christians do today. However, these views are not in harmony with the whole Bible's teaching about creation and God's concern for the very poor. Further, such views are extremely patronizing and demeaning of the poorest of the poor. Poverty is evil and God's will is for His creation to be without poverty.

Tamez argues that the verses refer to the hope of God's reign. James addresses the non-poor asserting the Old Testament and Jesus' teaching that God has a preference for the poor and will bring blessings upon them. In addressing the non-poor He is challenging them to repent and change their way of life. They are to be expressions of God's goodness to the poorest of

24. Ibid., 36.

25. German meaning pious poor.

26. Kloppenborg, "Poverty and Piety in Matthew," 203. I would add to this that piety readings of the poverty and the poor is not just a phenomenon of modern Western society, but within the biblical corpus such exists as some writers of the Bible themselves wrote from the context of wealth and comfort.

the poor. When this occurs, the poor will be rich in faith. James, for example, calls upon the non-poor He addresses to see their treasures as rooted in injustice (5:3) pointing out how they refused to pay the wages of the laborers (5:4). When justice and generosity occurs all will be blessed.

"Rich in faith" refers to "being heirs of the kingdom." Tamez writes: "To be rich in faith cannot be relegated . . . to a spiritual plane, completely disconnected from their situation of poverty and suffering."[27] Those who love God refers to those who repent and serve creation working hard to redistribute creation's goodness to all through living in obedience to God's righteous covenant and Torah. Those who claim to love God will love their neighbors and work toward serving them. Poverty will have no place in God's reign when creation is full of God's goodness and abundance.

TO THE CORE/IN THE SPIRIT

Schottroff writes: "Poverty 'in spirit' in Matt 5:3 is wrongly interpreted as spiritual poverty that has nothing to do with material poverty."[28] I agree . I suggest *tǭ pneumati* (in spirit) be translated "to the core" suggesting *that those who are poor in spirit* are the *poor to their very core* or *the very poorest of the poor*.

Psalm 33:19 (In English Psalm 34)

> The LORD is near to the brokenhearted, and saves the crushed (*tapeinous*) in spirit (*tǭ pneumati*) (cf. Isaiah 66:2 stricken in spirit but Hebrew does not have "in spirit")

LXX Psalm 33:19 provides a close Greek parallel to Matthew 5:3. *Tǭ pneumati* does not change the primary meaning of *tapeinous* in LXX Psalm 33:19 which suggests crushed/humiliated/contrite. The English preposition "in" is not present in the Greek. Literally it means "to the spirit." The spirit refers to the *core* or *main substance* of a person. The phrase, therefore, emphasizes "badly humiliated" or "humiliated to a person's very being or core."

27. Tamez, *Scandalous Message*, 37.

28. Schottroff, *Parables*, 253, note 6.

Mark 2:8

> At once Jesus perceived in his spirit that they were discussing these questions among themselves (NRSV) (Greek: *pignous ho ʾIēsous tǭ pneumati autou hoti houtōs dialogizontai en heautois)*

Tǭ pneumati again intensifies the participle *pignous* (perceived): "Jesus perceived *to the very core. . .*" In other words, He totally sees.

John 11:33

> He was greatly disturbed in spirit (NRSV) (Greek: *enebrimēsato tǭ pneumati)*

NRSV rightly translates *tǭ pneumati*: "greatly disturbed" as the phrase intensifies the action of the verb *enebrimēsato* meaning to be angry or distressed.

Acts 6:10

> But they could not withstand the wisdom and *the Spirit* with which he spoke (NRSV) (Greek: *kai ouk ischuon antistēnai tē sophia kai tǭ pneumati hō elalei)*

NRSV translates *tǭ pneumati* "the Spirit." A more straightforward rendering is: "But they were neither able to respond to him *in wisdom* nor respond *in any way (tǭ pneumati)* to that which he spoke." *Tē sophia* emphasizes that they were unable to resist Stephen by their thinking. Therefore, *tǭ pneumati* indicates that they could not resist *in any way* Stephen's arguments against them. Overall, both prepositional phrases intensify the extent to which Stephen's accusers were unable to prevail over Stephen.

Acts 18:25

> And he spoke with burning enthusiasm and taught accurately the things concerning Jesus, though he knew only the baptism of John (NRSV) (Greek: *zeōn tǭ pneumati elalei kai edidasken akribōs ta peri tou ʾIēsou)*

Tǭ pneumati functions in the same ways as the adverb *akribōs* (accurately). The NRSV is a good translation of *zeōn tǭ pneumati elalei*: "he spoke with *searing* enthusiasm." *Tῷ pneumati* intensifies the verbal participle *zeōn* (burning) which I render: searing.

Acts 20:22

> As a captive to the Spirit *(dedemenos egō tῷ pneumati)* I am on my way to Jerusalem, not knowing what will happen to me there.

NRSV is syntactically possible, but it can also mean: "I am bound to the very core to go to Jerusalem" or less literally "compelled to go" which makes sense of the whole verse as it emphasizes that Paul is compelled to go to Jerusalem.

Ephesians 4:23

> And to be renewed in the spirit of your minds (NRSV) (Greek: *ananeousthai de tῷ pneumati tou noos hymōn*)

Some translations speak of the Spirit renewing your mind. However, a more straight forward translation is: "Let your thoughts be renewed *to the very core*." The Greek *tῷ pneumati* intensifies the verb *ananeousthai* (to renew) translated "to the very core." In other words, it refers to one whose thoughts are entirely renewed.

SEMITIC BACKGROUND

There is no occurrence of LXX translating the Hebrew *rûach* (spirit, breath, or wind) with *tῷ pneumati*. We cannot, therefore, be certain of the Semitic background to Matthew's *tῷ pneumati*. But it will be helpful to consider the use of *rûach*.

1 Samuel 1:15

> Deeply troubled (NRSV) (Hebrew: *qĕshat-rûach*)

Hannah when reproached by the priest Eli for being drunk tells him "I am a woman deeply troubled." The word *rûach* intensifies *qĕshat* which is how the NRSV has translates it.

Ecclesiastes 7:8

The patient in spirit (*ʾêrêk rûach*) are better than the proud in spirit (*migbah-rûach*).
Rûach (spirit) emphases the nature of having great patience or being very proud.

Psalm 51:17 (Hebrew v. 19)

> The sacrifice acceptable to God is a broken spirit. (Hebrew: *rûach nišbārāh*)

The verse refers to someone who has the means to offer a sacrifice in contrast to many who offer sacrifices to appear pious. The *broken spirit* describes those who know wholly that God is their Father and Creator in whom they trust to give to them according to their needs.

Proverbs 16:19

> It is better to be of a lowly spirit (*šĕphal-rûach*) among the poor
> than to divide the spoil with the proud. (NRSV)

"A lowly spirit" describes a truly poor person among the poor themselves. The word *šĕphal* translated "lowly" means a materially and physically poor person. The word appears thirty times meaning "to crouch" or "to bow down."[29] It is used with leprosy in Leviticus 13:20–21, 26 and in 14:37. *I suggest this is the closest Semitic parallel to Matthew 5:3*. I translate: "It is better to be the very poorest of the poor than be one who divides the spoils with the proud."

Proverbs 17:27

> One who spares words is knowledgeable; one who is cool in spirit (*qar-rûach*) has understanding.

Qar-rûach emphasizes the nature of being calm and collected: "very cool" or "very calm."

29. Harris, *Theological Wordbook*, vol. 2, 950.

Isaiah 54:6

NRSV translates the Hebrew *ʿātsabut rûach* as "grieved in spirit." The New Jerusalem Bible (NJB) translates "grief-stricken." NJB shows how *rûach* functions grammatically to intensify or deepen the grief.

Isaiah 57:15

> I dwell in the high and holy place, and also with those who are *contrite and humble in spirit* (*dakâh vûšphal-rûach*), to revive the spirit of the humble, and to revive the heart of the contrite.

Again the word *šĕphal* is found as in Proverbs 16:19 to refer to the economically and physically dispossessed *Dakâh vûšphal-rûach* refers to the deeply oppressed; *rûach* again heightens the nature of being powerless and voiceless (*dakâh vûšphal*).[30] The king cares for the poor in this verse. Brueggemann sees verse 15 to be "revolutionary" offering an alternative godly culture where the exalted God is present among the poorest of the poor.[31]

Isaiah 66:2

> But this is the one to whom I will look, to the humble and contrite in spirit (*ʿānī vûnkēh-rûach*), who trembles at my word.

The Hebrew for "humble" and "contrite" (*ʿānī vûnkēh*) refers commonly to the poorest of the poor. But in this verse it refers to those who are spiritually humble and contrite. The phrase: "who trembles at my word" suggests *ʿānī vûnkēh-rûach* are commended because they tremble at God's word. It is clear the groups are those who fear God. *Rûach* intensifies the humble and contrite nature of the people. The writer in adding "who trembles at my word" makes sure *ʿānī vûnkēh* are not confused with the economically and physically poor.

Qumran

Scholars seeking equivalents to Matthew's *hoi ptōchoi tǭ pneumati* to support a spiritualizing of the poor look to Qumran.

30. Brueggemann, *Isaiah 40–66*, 181–82.

31. Brueggemann, *Social Reading*, 229.

1QM 14:7 has *bʿnyy rûach*—"Among the poor in spirit [there is power] over the hard of heart . . .[32] However, there is a gap in the fragment; Martinez simply has: "By the poor in spirit [. . .] a hard heart."[33] Scholars tend to see this as referring to the spiritually humble.[34] Tilborg, however, suggests that "poor in spirit" connects with the line before it: "where there is talk of stumblers, a despondent heart, a mouth without sound, weak hands, knocking knees and a broken neck, it would seem better to understand 'poor in spirit' in a physical sense."[35] I am inclined to agree with Tilborg.

1QH 6:3 has *bʿnwy rûach*—poor in spirit. Again the fragment is not fully preserved. Martinez has: "those who love compassion, the poor in spirit . . ." There is little to conclude from this.

In 1QH 18:14–15 (in Martinenez 1 QH 23:15) we have: . . . *dk]ʿy ruach*—the broken of spirit.[36] It is generally accepted that this phrase relates to God's concern for the economically poor.

4Q521 (Fragment 2 column 2) line 6 is often used as a parallel for Matthew where it states that God considers the pious and He calls the righteous by name although *rûach* is the subject of the verb "to hover." Vermes translates: "For the LORD will consider the (*Hasidim*) and call the righteous by name. Over the poor His spirit will hover and will renew the faithful with His power."[37] The righteous and the pious do not refer to the poor. In line 12 we find (Martinez's translation):

> And the LORD will perform marvelous acts such as have not existed, just as He sa[id, for] He will heal the badly wounded and will make the dead live; He will proclaim good news to the poor and [. . .] He will lead the [. . .] and enrich the hungry. [. . .] and all [. . .].[38]

There is no mention of the poor in spirit. However, in 4Q521 the word translated "poor" is *ʿanvim* that often means the humble. But in this fragment the *ʿanvim* are the hungry and oppressed.

32. Vermes, *Dead Sea Scrolls*, 140.
33. Martínez and Tigchelaar, *Dead Sea Scrolls*, 137.
34. Davies and Allison, *Matthew 1–7*, 439.
35. Tilborg, *Sermon on the* Mount, 239, note 32.
36. Martínez and Tigchelaar, *Dead Sea Scrolls*, 199.
37. Vermes, *Dead Sea Scrolls*, 244.
38. http://www.textexcavation.com/qumran4q521.html.

OTHER FACTORS

Under this sub-heading I draw together more general observations that are relevant to my argument.

Why *ptōchoi* and not *tapeinos* or *praus*?

If Matthew intends to spiritualize *ptōchoi*, we might have expected him to have *tapeinos* or *praus* which *can* describe human piety rather than social class. Matthew uses these words elsewhere to describe characteristics of piety and non-violence (11:29 and 21:5 although not so in 5:5).

The way of life described as gentle and humble in heart (11:29) is specifically in contrast to a way of violence. I propose that Matthew presents Jesus as one who stands against violence and the suffering it causes, especially poverty and oppression.

In 21:5 Jesus is the true king whose kingship is defined by His humility and by His riding on a donkey. This is the king who is victorious because He relies and trusts in God for all His needs. Whose way is to free people from the slavery of self-aggrandizement and to redistribute the abundance of creation to all.

In short, if Matthew intends poor in spirit to refer to a pious group, surely he would have *tapeinoi tō̧ pneumati* (the meek in spirit).

Why does Luke not have *tō̧ pneumati*?

Most assume that Matthew has copied Luke 6:20 and added "in the spirit." My observations relating to *tō̧ pneumati* show that Matthew does not differ from Luke, but intensifies the poverty. I believe Luke abbreviated Matthew's *ptōchoi* by leaving out *tō̧ pneumati.*

Why not *en pneumati*?

We should also question why Matthew did not use a more appropriate prepositional phrase: *en pneumati* ("in the spirit;" see 3:11; 12:28; 22:43). In 3:11 we are told that Jesus will baptize in/with the Holy Spirit. Also note the following:

> But if it is by the Spirit (*en pneumati*) of God that I drive out demons, then the kingdom of God has come upon you. (12:28)

> How is it then that David by the Spirit (*en pneumati*) calls him LORD . . .? (22:43)

In 12:28 Jesus refers to the spirit of God that works through Him to cast out demons. In 22:43 Jesus states that David was inspired by the Spirit. This raises the question as to why Matthew 5:3 has a different phrase from *en pneumati* if he means poor endowed with the Spirit (i.e., spiritually poor).

In short, Matthew 5:3 uses *tō̜ pneumati* to intensify the poverty and not spiritualize it. If Matthew had wanted to spiritualize the poor he would have had: *ptōchoi en pneumati*, or better *tapeinoi en pneumati* or just *tapeinoi tē kardia*.

5:4–10

This study maintains that 5:3 is one of four beatitudes referring to the poorest of the poor in verses 3–6: *penthountes* (those who weep); *praus* (the meek or oppressed); *peinōntes kai dipsōntes* (those who hunger and thirst for basic food). Verses 7–10 describe the characteristics/fruits of the repentant that are necessary to create a poverty free creation so the people described in verses 3–6 need no longer exist: they are the merciful, the pure in heart, the peacemakers, and those who are persecuted on account of righteousness; they are people who seek God's goodness on earth.

It is more than coincidental that the two blocks of four beatitudes consist of thirty-six words. The beatitudes are carefully structured; "kingdom of heaven" provides the bookends in v. 3b and 10b. Further, the first four beatitudes are structured to emphasize the social group with "*p*" (Greek letter *pi*).

It should be noted that the tense of the verb in the clause introduced by "for" is future in verses 4–9. The future tense (shall be), rather than the present (is) in verses 3 and 10 points to the future completion of God's kingdom.

Penthountes (5:4)

Weeping or mourning is what the oppressed do (cf. Isaiah 61:2–3).[39] When God expected righteousness He heard a cry (Isaiah 5:7) suggesting that crying is the actions of those on the wrong side of injustice. The Old Syrian version has "*ʾabil*," which means mourning or sorrow. It also has the sense of being dried up (cf. Isaiah 24:7; Hosea 4:3 in Hebrew). In Isaiah 3:26 the ravaged mourn (*ʾabal*) and lament while in Isaiah 61:2–3, those who mourn (*ʾabal*; LXX: *penthousin*), are afflicted but will be comforted.

39. Brueggemann, *Social Reading*, 83–88.

Mourning is akin to "crying out" as Israel did when suffering under the burden of the yoke of oppression in Egypt. Brueggemann helpfully points out that weeping or grieving are "the most visceral announcement that things are not right."[40]

This beatitude is best interpreted as those crying out for deliverance from actual economic poverty (i.e., those who are utterly impoverished); it is undirected grieving, similarly found in Isaiah 14:31; 15:4; 61:3; Jeremiah 48:4, 34; 50:46; 51:54; Esther 4:1. Powell adds rightly:

> Commentators who think Matthew refers to people who are "sorry for their sins" or who "protest evil and injustice" or who "renounce earthly goods" are straining for applications that Matthew's readers would not be expected to deduce from this text . . . Most recent scholars recognize that "those who mourn" refers to people who are miserable and unhappy.[41]

Tilborg writes that "The whole of Jesus history is set against the background of Israel's liberation in which the exodus, the exile and the messianic liberation by David's son are used as 'leitmotiv' in order to overcome the evil of the experienced violence."[42] According to Exodus 3:7, 9, God does not hear the cry of the Israelites because they repent, God hears those who experience violence "on account of their taskmasters" who are described in Exodus 3:9 as oppressors. Deliverance to Israel means being released from oppression and being given their own land (Exodus 3:8).

Tilborg also interprets Matthew 5:4 in the context of the terror and dread of Herod slaying the innocent children in 2:16–18.[43] The mourners in 5:4, he argues, refer to the victims of violence who cry out in despair at the loss of their lands, children, husbands, and wives. Tilborg writes: "From the very first moment, Matthew starts his story from the point of view of violence, deceit and royal arbitrariness are matter-of-fact realities, as are the sufferings of people: the necessity to leave the country, the inconsolable mourning of Bethlehem's mothers, the impossibility to ever return to one's own city of birth."[44]

40. Brueggemann, *Prophetic Imagination*, 11.
41. Powell, *God with* Us, 124–25.
42. Tilborg, *Sermon on the Mount*, 22.
43. Ibid.
44. Ibid., 21.

The meek (praus) (5:5)

The meek here tend to be interpreted as a group of pious and non-violent people who patiently put up with their troubles; the word does not refer to a socially impoverished group of people. However, I argue that Jesus refers to the "humiliated" from whom all hope is taken. Their land is taken from them, they are mocked, exploited, and oppressed. They will be blessed by inheriting the earth. Tilborg points out that Matthew wrote in the context of land being confiscated.[45] Those without land are vulnerable to hunger and disease.

LXX mentions *praus* in Psalm 76:9 (Hebrew verse 10) as the oppressed. The Hebrew word it translates is *ʿanwyē -ʾeretz* (poor of the land). The *ʿānāw*, in contrast to *ʿānī*, denotes the spiritual state of humility. But in this Psalm it refers to the economically oppressed and *praus* can also refer to economically oppressed. There is sufficient evidence to show that *praus* can refer to economic poverty.[46]

Matthew uses *praus* elsewhere as referring to Jesus himself (11:29; 21:5). I argue elsewhere that in 11:29; 21:5, it refers to a person knowing his or her place before the Father Creator. However, this does not mitigate my argument about economic poverty vis-à-vis *praus* in 5:5.

Matthew 5:5 follows Psalm 37:11. Weiser in his commentary on the Psalms understands *praus* in 37:11 as referring to the oppressed: they are those who are vulnerable to the sword and bow of the wicked. He translates the word "humiliated."[47] The psalmist instructs them to refrain from anger and fretting (37:8), actions typical of the poor and oppressed. They are encouraged to trust in God to establish His reign in which there will be great abundance.

The *praus* in 5:5 are to be blessed with land, but not because they have been faithful to God: *for Matthew the aspect of being humiliated is central and not obedience.* In Psalm 37 the prominent aspect is the powerlessness of the humiliated. Jesus makes clear that a social group, *praus*, the humiliated, will be blessed with land and given *shalom*. However, in the Psalm, there is another group, the righteous, they too will inherit the land, not because they are impoverished, but because through their righteousness they forfeited their land through opposing the wicked because of their oppressive policies.

45. Ibid., 25. *Praus* in Hellenistic literature can describe people who have been made into beasts of burden, from whom all aggression is taken away; Wengst, *Humility*, 4–15.

46. See Wengst, *Humility*. Wengst does not mention Matthew 5:5.

47. Weiser, *The Psalms*, 312.

Those who hunger and thirst (5:6)

Jesus refers to the poor whose existence is not unlike hungry dogs searching among rubbish for the left-overs of others: "Blessed are those who hunger and thirst for (no preposition "for" in Greek) righteousness, for they will be filled. Their whole existence is dominated by the need to find something to keep them alive. In a previous chapter on "righteousness" I argue that righteousness is inseparable from food and basic items necessary for life when used of "justice in favor of the poor."

This group is in contrast to the closing beatitude of 5:10: "Blessed are those who are persecuted *for* (*heneken*) righteousness' sake, for theirs is the kingdom of heaven." In verse 6 Matthew has "who hunger and thirst [*for*] justice/righteousness" while verse 10 has "persecuted on account of justice/ righteousness." Verse 6 refers to those who seek justice which means basic necessities such as food, water, security, clothing, care, and friendship (cf. what the poor are offered in the parable of the goats and sheep). Powell writes well: "Elsewhere in Matthew, satisfaction of hunger and thirst serves not as a symbol for eschatological reward but as an image of God's overall concern for creation (6:25–26). Indeed, Matthew's Gospel affirms that provision of life's basic necessities reflects the goodness of God in a way that is not contingent on the *dikaiosynē* of humans (5:45)."[48]

MAKARIOI (BLESSED)

Makarioi occurs thirteen times in the First Gospel in the context of God's hospitable will for creation. Ringe argues that in the beatitudes "the accent is on the blessing as part of the liberation from the pain and oppression that marks God's eschatological reign."[49] I have previously emphasized that God creates abundance and joy and poverty is evil. Stassen's discussion is helpful:

> I translate *makarioi* as "joyful" because in its fifty occurrences in the New Testament it almost always means the joy of participation in God's action of deliverance. In the Old Testament, it usually promises future consolation to people in dire straits—meaning, whatever present situation is difficult will be reversed and justice, peace, and joy will break in. It is not simply "happy" in the sense of being in an upbeat mood. God is acting to deliver

48. Powell, *God With Us*, 128.

49. Ringe, *Jesus, Liberation*, 52.

> us, and we have the experience of being part of what the LORD of the universe is doing, who brings redemption and deliverance.[50]

Stassen emphasizes that *makarioi* means reversal when "justice, peace and joy break in;" these are material as well as spiritual needs. The two cannot be separated. The task of the disciple is to make *makarioi* those who are poor, oppressed, and in great suffering as a result of being deprived of the goodness of God in creation.

Makarioi is what God intended at the beginning of creation when He saw all that He had made was very good (Genesis 1:31); it is creation in a state of *shalom* where there is abundance and joy for all. The purpose of service is to do God's will bringing joy and abundance to the poor. *Makarioi* (blessed) therefore relates: (1) to the joy of knowing that life is service; (2) the joy of service that brings abundance.

The Syriac translation of *makarioi* in Matthew 5:3–12 is *ṭôbihon* and is related to the Hebrew *ṭôb* (good/ness) and which is used seven times by God to describe creation when He saw it in Genesis 1. The Syriac testifies that *ṭôb* was in some way related to joy and abundance. *Makarioi* occurs nine times in verses 3–12. In verse 5, blessed will be those who have no land in the sense that land will be given to them (first four beatitudes). The first four beatitudes refer to those who are in great material need while beatitudes 5–8 points to the non-poor.[51] For the poor to be *makarioi* they need land. Those who do have land are told by Jesus, in beatitudes 5–8, that to be *makarioi* they must give their lives on behalf of those who are weak and powerless.

In Matthew 11:1–5 John the Baptist's disciples ask Jesus if He is the expected messiah. He responds by telling them that He is the one who gives sight to the blind, makes the lame walk, cleanses the lepers, helps the deaf to hear, raises the dead, and proclaims good news to the poor. Directly following *kai ptōchoi euangelizontai* (and the poor have good news proclaimed to them) Jesus says: "blessed is anyone who takes no offence at me." *Makarioi* (blessed) is associated with good news being proclaimed to the poor. Jesus' ministry is linked to disciples who bring liberation to those who are marginalized (*ptōchoi*). 11:6 implies that as a result of Jesus' teaching and ministry some were offended and instead of being blessed were cursed.

In Matthew 24:46 *makarioi* is the consequence of one who does God's will. According to verse 45 what God desires is that a faithful servant cares for others particularly by giving food. These verses unambiguously show there is a link between *makarioi* and serving others. If a person lives according to the order of creation (i.e., living for others), such a person will

50. Stassen, *Living the Sermon on the Mount*, 39.

51. Powell, *God with Us*, 119–138.

experience *makarioi*. The link between service and joy is particularly evident in Tagore's poem: "I slept and dreamt that life was joy. I woke and I saw that life was service. I acted and behold, service was joy."

Therefore, the poor in spirit, those who grieve, the oppressed, and those who starve, can hope that their lack of *makarioi* will be changed and they will live abundantly on earth. They will truly see creation as good in the sense of experiencing it as abundant and joyful. However, verses 3 and 10 have the repeated structure: 'blessed are . . . for there is . . .' The tense of the clause beginning "for" (*hoti*) is present in verse 3 and 10 suggesting that they are blessed *now*. In the other beatitudes the verb in the clause beginning "for" is future. The sense of the present verb in these verses emphasizes that Jesus' healing ministry is at work *now*. The kingdom of heaven belongs to those who are sick and impoverished *now*.

Those in verses 7–10 refer to disciples. They are instructed to act with works of repentance showing mercy, acting in harmony with God's will; actively pursuing peace as an alternative to the false peace of the *status quo*; and being ready to suffer and die at the hands of those who wish to defend and maintain this false peace that encourages poverty. Matthew 11:7–8 has Jesus address the crowds who are described as those who went out to hear and live with John the Baptist. Such groups must relate to those in Matthew 3:5–6.

The disciples will be *makarioi* if they live in harmony with the way creation is inwardly ordered so that God's goodness is present. The disciples through their actions, which express limitless love, become channels of God's goodness and are consequently in a state of goodness (being blessed).

In short, a firm distinction should be drawn between the poorest of the poor who suffer through involuntary poverty (5:3–6) and those who suffer through solidarity with the poor (5:7–10: merciful, pure in heart, peacemakers, those suffering for fighting injustice). The key issue is that poverty is evil and that disciples must commit their whole being to address this evil in order to redistribute God's goodness in creation to those who are abused.

MATTHEW 5:3 AND 25:31–48

The parable about the hungry and thirsty, the naked, the stranger, the sick and the prisoner, who are the poorest of the poor (Matthew 25:31–46), is Jesus' final teaching. This list I believe recalls the poor in spirit in 5:3. The parable reveals the Last Judgment executed in favor of the poorest of the poor. In 5:3 Jesus emphasizes hope for the poorest of the poor; in the Last

Judgment the poorest of the poor are assumed to be God's special people and those who care for such are blessed.

The poorest of the poor provide thematic bookends through which Jesus' key concern for the poorest of the poor is reinforced. However, as in the case of Matthew 5:3, there is scholarly unity in disassociating the list of afflicted in Matthew 25:31–46 with the poor and suffering of the world.

Rowland, against the consensus, argues convincingly that the list refers to all the victims of injustice, all those who are excluded. The list does not refer to disciples who voluntarily take upon themselves poverty and humiliation. He argues his case observing that "throughout Matthew's narrative, the Son of man identifies himself with a much wider group than the disciples who are in need of succor, who are 'like sheep without a shepherd' (9:36; 4:23).[52]" Rowland remarks that: "the ideal of discipleship ceases to be embodied in the group of the disciples. This is seen most clearly in chapter 18, where the child is set over the twelve as the type of true greatness."[53] A child was generally considered a person of no importance in Jewish society . I reiterate: *a child does not refer to the virtue of humility. More likely it denotes the humiliated.*

Also in support of Rowland's argument is Miranda's discussion about Judgment Day. He argues that the biblical evidence firmly links such a day to the hope when justice is executed in favor of the poorest of the poor. He comments precisely on the Last Judgment in Matthew 25:31–46 as coinciding point by point with the Old Testament teachings about judgment being in favor of the poorest of the poor.[54] Miranda writes: "when the Bible speaks of Yahweh as 'judge' or of the Judgment whose subject is Yahweh, it has in mind precisely the means . . . to save the oppressed from injustice. This is the Last Judgment awaited down through all the centuries of expectation in the Old and New Testaments."[55]

Therefore, Jesus in instructing His disciples to be like children is challenging them to act in favor of the humiliated in bringing justice to those who are poor and vulnerable. The child represents prisoners with learning disabilities, those suffering from attachment disorders, those with mental health issues or any of the many vulnerable people unable to work and belong to society because they are excluded for whatever reason.[56]

52. Rowland, "Apocalyptic," 514.

53. Ibid., 515.

54. Miranda, *Marx*, 117.

55. Ibid., 114.

56. It is interesting that on the BBC News website http://www.bbc.co.uk/news/uk-36410539 prisoners with learning difficulties with indefinite sentences are the source of concern to politicians.

The list in verse 35 "covers the most basic needs of life in order to represent the meeting of human need of every kind."[57] Only in Matthew do we find this list. The list in verse 35 explicitly refers to the very poorest of the poor and refers back to the poor in spirit in 5:3. In this list there are three additions to those lists that appear elsewhere in Matthew of vulnerable and powerless people: the stranger, the naked, and the prisoner.

Stranger

"Stranger" (*xenos*) occurs also in Matthew 27:7. If those listed as the needy in the parable of the goats and sheep refers to those Christians who have voluntarily embraced hunger, it is not easy to explain how such disciples could be strangers.

The mention of "stranger" echoes the commandments to love the stranger (Deuteronomy 10:19: Hebrew *gēr*; LXX: *prosylētai*). In Deuteronomy 27:19 one of God's first commandments states: "Cursed be anyone who deprives the alien (*gēr; prosyloutou*), the orphan, and the widow of justice." Job describes himself as one who championed the cause of justice for the stranger (Job 29:16: Hebrew: *gēr;* LXX: *adounatōn*: incapable). A stranger is often listed alongside the widow and the orphan (Psalm 94:6; Deuteronomy 16; Psalm 146:9). Exodus commands: "You shall not wrong or oppress a resident alien, for you were aliens in the land of Egypt" (22:21; 23:9). Stranger (Hebrew: *gēr*) can represent one who is marginalized and poor or a person who is different.[58]

Xenos is not used to translate the Hebrew *gēr* but *nokry (*2 Samuel 5:19; Psalm 69:8; Ecclesiastes 6:2; Job 31:32*)* which occurs as a noun over forty times. In Proverbs the word is almost a technical word for a prostitute (2:16). In 3 Maccabees 6:3 the *xenos* is a synonym for one who perishes. The occurrence of *xenos* is found in Matthew 25:35, 43, 44 in terms of strange outsiders and in 27:7 vis-à-vis the burial ground of a stranger.

In short, at least one group in Matthew's list of the poorest of the poor (i.e., the strangers) are those particularly with learning disabilities, migrants, people who stand out as being distinct in a way that leads them to be excluded from the goodness of creation.[59]

57. Hagner, *Matthew 14–28*, 744.

58. However, *gēr* may also refer to one who has converted to the Jewish faith.

59. See work of Young, *Brokenness and Blessing*, 88–92. Yong, *Theology and Down* Syndrome, 21 observes that "The Bible does not say anything about what we today call intellectual disability."

Naked

Being naked often refers to one who is poor and helpless: truly at the bottom of the social pile. In Job 22:6 (cf. verses 7 and 10) naked is synonymous with being poor (cf. Isaiah 58:7; Ezekiel 18:7, 16; 23:29). In Matthew 5:40, following Wink's interpretation, Jesus says how those being sued for their outer garment should be ready to give the oppressor their undergarment. Augustine understood Jesus to be talking about nakedness: "give to him *whatever clothing thou hast*."[60] Wink writes: "Clothing signifies one's social location, gender, and status . . . Therefore to strip naked voluntarily before the creditor and magistrate in a context intended to shame the poor into repayment, is to defy the hierarchical system of classification in its entirety."[61]

Prisoners

Only in Matthew 25:31–46 are prisoners named as victims in need of care.[62] To visit the prisoners brings to mind Jesus' teaching about loving your enemy: there were many thieves and petty criminals in prison. I imagine those in prison in the ancient world were vulnerable and easily misled and seen as a threat to so-called "decent folk." It is assumed that such feared people will be visited by the disciples. Jesus speaks of prisoners alongside the sick. They were to be visited because they were excluded and deprived of many basic human needs.

In short, Matthew's Jesus mentions the visiting of prisoners as an act of compassion for those whose basic needs are denied. It is likely that visiting would also entail taking food and drink to such people.

SUMMARY

- To romanticize poverty and the poor is patronizing whilst emptying Jesus' teaching of its revolutionary and subversive intent.
- The *poor in spirit* (5:3) refers to *the very poorest of the poor*; those who have no reason to hope.

60. Augustine, *Sermon on the Mount* 1:19.60; Wink, *Engaging the Powers*, 370.

61. Wink, *Engaging the Powers*, 371.

62. Ignatius of Antioch also has a similar list in which prisoners, the widow, the hungry, and thirsty appear (*Smyrnaeans* 6). To care for such people is service in imitation of God's service.

- The phrase *tō̜ pneumati* should be translated "to the core" suggesting *that those who are poor in spirit* are those *poor to their very core* or *the very poorest of the poor*.
- Jesus distinguishes Himself and His disciples from the poorest of the poor.
- Jesus in His Sermon on the Mount addresses the non-poor instructing them to repent and live a life worthy of repentance through bringing blessings to the poorest of the poor.
- *Makarioi* (blessed) relates: (1) to the joy of knowing that life is service; (2) to the joy of service that brings abundance.
- Poor in spirit in 5:3 and the list of the poor in 25:35, 42 emphasize the centrality of the poorest of the poor in Matthew. Moreover, the list in Matthew 25 reinforces my argument that the poor in spirit are the poorest of the poor.

FOOD FOR THOUGHT

I am drawn to Ezekiel's lament that whilst Israel has an "excess of food, and prosperous ease" she does "not aid the poor and the needy" (Ezekiel 16:49). Such grieving of prophetic figures over the suffering of the poorest of the poor because of the wealth of respectable society is well known. Jesus, from my work on this chapter, leaves me in no doubt that His message is truly in the tradition of subversive prophetic anger and lament over the suffering of creation.

Matthew particularly depicts Jesus teaching the non-poor who had the means to address the gap between the poorest of the poor and themselves. We must bring to mind that neither Jesus nor His disciples understood themselves to be the poorest of the poor, those who mourned, those who were oppressed, or those who hungered and thirsted for basic items needed for survival. They may have experienced hunger, oppression, and sadness, but they chose that way of life (cf. Matthew 8:20). They embraced a way of life that sought to embrace the excluded. They had left the relative security of fishing, farming, tax-collecting, the trades, and perhaps soldiering. This suggests that they were sufficiently intellectually and physically able to work in a way that helped contribute to the needs of their household. However, I have suggested that many were not so intellectually and physically able. These are the poor in spirit.

We know from studies of those in prison today, that many are the victims of abuse and humiliation from a very young age. Jesus knew too well from walking through the villages, sitting by the well, worshipping on the Sabbath, that the population consisted of many with learning difficulties and mental health issues.

I have rooted my discussion in the assumption that Jesus accepted that the goodness of God is the abundance and joy God desired for all creation. This has reinforced the extent to which Jesus was outraged at the existence of the poorest of the poor. My understanding of *hoi ptōchoitǭ pneumati* as the poorest of the poor makes perfect sense of Jesus' final teaching section that illustrates that if someone does not care for the poor, they will be condemned. Therefore, those in the last four beatitudes are called to be in solidarity with the poorest of the poor.

However, this perspective may permit a patronizing attitude from the non-poor to the poor. The poorest of the poor are reduced to the indignity of being passive receivers. They feel themselves incomplete human beings. This sometimes unwitting attitude of superiority has two very negative consequences.[63] First, such an attitude undermines and devalues the poor. Secondly, those who give are in danger of inflated egos seeing themselves as "deliverers of the poor."[64]

Liberation theologians have made similar arguments and most have the ring of truth. However, the fact remains that many who are poor, in the sense I argue, are often in no position to speak out for themselves or help themselves. The poorest of the poor whom Jesus speaks of are poor to their core: a woman abandoned by her family perhaps with a child with severe learning disabilities is in no position to help herself or her child; someone in prison, lost to society, is in no position to help him or herself.

PRAYER

Lord Father Creator, may I know myself so that I may know Your will; take away my heart of stone and give me a heart of flesh, so that I may learn how to love my brothers and sisters because in them, in their meanest guise, I am encountering Your only begotten son, Jesus Christ, the Lord. Amen

63. Myers, *Walking with the Poor*, 114.

64. Ibid., 114–15.

9

Matthew 8:1–4 and 21:14

Subversive Messiah: Inclusion and Priesthood

Christians must commit themselves to the new communities of welcome, to live with people who have no family, and to show them that they are loved and can grow to great freedom and that they, in turn, can love and give to others.[1] *—Jean Vanier*

They that offered in the Jews' temple were to wear the holy garments. So are you to do that are the true Christians, and are called a royal priesthood. What! are all true Christians priests? Yes. What! are women priests? Yes, women priests. And can men and women offer sacrifices without they wear the holy garments? No. What are the holy garments men and women must wear? The fine linen and they must go in white. What! is this the priest's surplice? Nay . . . it is the righteousness of Christ, which is the righteousness of the saints, this is the royal garment of the royal priesthood, which everyone must put on, men and women.[2]
—George Fox, 1667

George Fox (1624–1691), Quaker founder, understood priesthood in the context of righteousness and mercy seeing humans as bearers of God's image to the extent to which they are channels of His goodness in

1. Vanier, *Community*, 283.

2. *QF&P* 19.31.

creation. Fox understood Jesus to be one who taught that priesthood is not for an exclusive group of elite men but for the whole of humankind. God is within everyone making them priests.[3] For that divine seed to grow permitting people to reach their priestly potential, human beings must be striving to heal the world of poverty. Joseph Pickvance writes of Fox's understanding of priesthood: "The Jewish priesthood is paralleled by the members of the Church, who thus become 'the priesthood of all believers.' In Fox's understanding of the role of the new priesthood of believers and disciples, obedience and self-giving are as necessary from them as they were in Christ himself."[4] These Quaker insights are relevant in my consideration of Matthew in this chapter.

I pay particular attention in this chapter to Matthew's first (8:1–4) and last healings (21:14). The first recounts Jesus' encounter with and healing of a leper while mention is made of the priests in the temple in Jerusalem. The last healing of the lame and the blind occurs in the Jerusalem temple. The leper, the lame and blind are of the poorest of the poor. It is more than coincidental that the first and the last healing stories involve the temple. I believe they cast Jesus in the role of the high priest subverting the priestly elitism that thought only the high priest could stand in the place of God in forgiving sins (9:1–8).

I consider, also, 8:17 and 9:1–8 in order to help understand 8:1–4 and 21:14. I examine Matthew 8:17 particularly in the light of Jesus' quote of the Hebrew of Isaiah 53:4. In 8:17, Matthew angles Jesus' actions in the light of the high priest bearing the sins of others.[5] According to 9:1–8, Jesus upsets the authorities by doing what was only lawful for the high priest: forgiving the sins of the paralytic man (9:3).

In short, Jesus is the high priest who is the son of man who is True Human. He exemplifies in His self-giving what all humans should do to be True Human.

CREATION, PRIEST, AND TEMPLE

Central to any understanding of a priest is the Temple. The Temple represents how creation should be. The priest in the Temple is an example of how a person should be True Human in creation. This is about self-sacrifice.

3. There are close parallels with Wink's *The Human Being* regarding his understanding of the son of man to be a term applied to human beings who are fulfilled Human Beings through their lives being committed to service of others.

4. Pickvance, *Christ in Quaker Thought*, 54–55.

5. Barker, *The Revelation of Jesus Christ*, 7, 47, 136.

Norman Wirzba observes: "In ancient Israelite tradition the priest was associated with the temple understood as the place where heaven and earth meet. By drawing people's attention to the altar, and then encouraging them in the work of self-offering sacrifice, relationships that had been defiled by sin could be repaired and made whole. To live in the context of the temple is thus to commit to relationships governed by justice, peace, and thanksgiving."[6] Further he comments: "As priests we begin to see creation as an altar of God's offering. This altar becomes the inspiration for our offering of the world and ourselves."[7] The altar as a metaphor highlights that "the incomprehensible, self-offering of God is daily made manifest."[8]

Margaret Barker similarly states: "The temple was a microcosm of the creation . . ."[9] These words set Jesus' healings and forgiving of sins in the context of the Temple as representative of God's intentions for creation wherein each is ready to give all that the other may flourish.

However, the Temple in the time of Jesus had long been seen as the domain of the elite and privileged as well as being thought to be the place where God dwelt. N. T. Wright comments: "The poorer classes evidently regarded the Temple as symbolizing the oppression they suffered at the hands of the rich elite."[10] Indeed, within the Bible itself a few texts can be found to be elitist. The high priest, for example, must have no physical defect (Leviticus 21:16–24 and 22:1–13).[11] Melcher discusses several Dead Sea Scroll texts that appear to have been influenced by Old Testament elitist texts such as these.

The Temple Scroll, for example, prohibits certain persons from entering the Temple city (11Q19 XLV, 7–18). It further bans the blind person from entering the Temple. In the Rule of the Congregation (1QSam): "the crippled in the legs or hands, the lame, blind, deaf, or mute, anyone with a visible defect is not able to enter."[12] Melcher, however, considers Leviticus itself, particularly 19:14 and verse 18b, where love of neighbour, as well as the deaf and blind, is emphasized. She concludes: "One way we can avoid reviling the deaf and putting stumbling blocks before the blind is to allow both full access to the altar, to the worshipping community, and to God."[13]

6. Wirzba, *Food and Faith*, 206.

7. Ibid., 207.

8. Ibid., 126.

9. Barker, *The Revelation of Jesus Christ*, 48; Alison, *Undergoing God*, 53.

10. Wright, *Jesus and the Victory of God*, 412.

11. Melcher, "Visualizing the Perfect Cult," 55–87.

12. Ibid., 68.

13. Ibid., 69.

MATTHEW AND THE TEMPLE

Jesus believed the Temple was a good thing and rooted in the goodness of God when it functioned to emphasize generous self-giving. However, Jesus saw that the Temple was more like a battlefield evident in the huge gaps that existed between the powerful and the powerless. In 23:35 we read of those murdered between the sanctuary and the altar: "so that upon you may come all the *righteous* blood shed on earth, from the blood of righteous Abel to the blood of Zechariah son of Barachiah, whom you *murdered* (*ephoneuesate*)[14] between the sanctuary and the altar" (parallel Luke 11:51). 23:35 suggests that sacrifices in the Temple were no longer rooted in *ḥesed* but were murderous. Matthew is distinguished from Luke in reinforcing the killings of both Abel and Zechariah. Matthew, in short, emphasizes that the Temple sacrifice is an act of murder.

Matthew 27:51 states that the Temple veil was torn from top to bottom when Jesus died. There is, because of Jesus' death, no separation between where God dwells and where creation begins. Creation is now the place where God's goodness fully dwells through human beings harmoniously living out God's intentions of mercy, such as in Jesus' readiness to die for humankind. Only in Matthew Jesus' death suggests that His act of self-giving results in His emergence from the Holy of Holies as God: "The earth shook, and the rocks were split. The tombs also were opened, and many bodies of the saints who had fallen asleep were raised. After his resurrection they came out of the tombs and entered the holy city and appeared to many" (27:51–53).

The earth quake and the rocks splitting are signs of God's presence. The quaking earth and splitting rocks signify cosmic order registering Jesus' death; but also the appearance of God as the veil separating the *outer-temple* from the *Holy of Holies* where God dwells is torn down. God is revealed in the cosmic tremors. There is no special place in creation, all creation is good. All humans are priests when they are faithful to God's Torah.

BEARING SIN AND HEALING (MATTHEW 8:17 AND 9:1–8)

I consider Jesus' healing ministry and bearing of sin as actions of True Priest and True Human. One who exemplifies and models self-giving.[15]

14. Matthew's *ephoneuesate* is a much stronger word than Luke's *apolomenou*.

15. See Bredin, "Being human and priest," 10–11.

Jesus demonstrates in His healings that all humans are authorized to heal and forgive sins. Healing and bearing the lot of another are central to restoring God's goodness in creation. Swartley argues that healing is to bring *shalom* particularly through "new supportive relationships."[16] Jesus' actions are truly Human and relational. I consider first 8:17 and 9:1–8 as preparatory to examining the first and last healings in Matthew.

8:17

Sin and illness go together. Human sin has a deeply negative effect upon all creatures (Genesis 3:17–19; 9:2–3), including also the degradation of the earth (Isaiah 24:5).[17] Matthew 8:17 alone of the Gospels has Jesus quote Isaiah 53:4: "He took our infirmities and bore our diseases." Matthew prefers the Hebrew: "He bears our sins, and suffered for us" (my translation).[18] These are the actions of the priest (cf. Exodus 28:38). Margaret Barker writes: "Jesus' miracles are the high-priestly work of taking away sickness or disability or uncleanness which were believed to cut people off from the community."[19] Jesus, as the high priest, bears the sins of the world; this is another way of saying Jesus lives His life so that others can flourish.

Barker further notes that: "The high priest was . . . the visible presence of the Lord with his people . . ."[20] If we assume that living with mercy is God's intention for humanity, and that the high priest represented God, then Jesus is representing true Humanity in showing mercy.[21] In accepting Barker's view we must see Jesus' actions of healing as recreating creation in the tradition of the Temple, the whole creation is the Temple, and fulfilled Human Beings are all priests caring and serving creation.[22]

Likewise James Alison sees the Temple to be a microcosm of creation, and in the Holy of Holies, it was believed by Jews that the Creator dwelt. He observes: "creation started from the Temple Veil outwards, while the Holy of Holies was beyond time, matter and space. The rite of atonement was about the Lord himself, the Creator, emerging from the Holy of Holies so as to set the people free from their impurities and sins and transgressions."[23]

16. Swartley, *Health, Healing*, 52.
17. Fretheim, *God and World*, 69–89.
18. Greek: *houtos tas hamartias hē mōn pherei kai peri hē mōn odunati.*
19. Barker, *The Revelation of Jesus Christ*, 7.
20. Ibid., 8, 34–40.
21. Wink, *The Human Being.*
22. Barker, *The Gate of Heaven.*
23. Alison, *Undergoing God*, 53.

Crucially for Alison this Jewish priestly rite was understood differently from pagans' sacrifices; he writes: "They understood . . . that it was pagan rites that sacrificed victims in order to keep creation going." Alison comments that according to the Jewish rite: "it was actually *God* who was doing the work, it was *God* who was coming out wanting to restore creation, out of love for his people. And so it is YHWH who emerges from the Holy of Holies dressed in white in order to forgive the people their sins and, more importantly, in order to *allow creation to flow*."[24] Jesus, therefore, is the authentic High Priest emerging from the Holy of Holies to offer Himself "as a concrete living out and demonstration of God's love for us."[25] Crucially this is evident in His work of liberation, His proclamation of the good news to the poorest of the poor.

In short, 8:17 underlies the subversive message of the Bible and Jesus in which the idea of sacrifice is inverted (i.e., sacrifice is showing mercy). In other words, creation is not a battlefield but an abundant expression of God's goodness. Jesus uncovers the human structures of killing and violence that are based on "convincing ourselves of our right and duty to do it, and therefore building ourselves up over and against our victims."[26]

9:1–8

In looking at 9:1–8, I believe Jesus is alluding to the High Priest. However all creation is now the Holy of Holies, where God's presence is depicted throughout. Further, all human beings are authorized to forgive sins by taking the sufferings of others upon themselves.

Jesus' healing of the paralyzed man echoes the High Priest when saying "your sins are forgiven." This is why Jesus is accused of blasphemy by the scribes (9:3). It appeared that Jesus was claiming to be acting as God, a claim that is permitted only to the High Priest on the Day of Atonement.[27] Jesus teaches that the role of the priest and the Temple is not to offer sacrifices but to show mercy (12: quoting Hosea 6:6). Jesus further declares that He is greater than the Temple (12:5) emphasizing that the Temple foundations are mercy (*ḥesed*). Jesus indeed elsewhere castigates the Jerusalem cult for its sacrifices because they were not true sacrifices since the priest did not offer himself for others (in 23:23 Jesus repudiates the elite for not showing

24. Ibid.
25. Ibid., 55.
26. Ibid., 59.
27. Ibid., 52.

mercy to the poor). Jesus acts as a priest showing mercy through living for others. Only in Matthew Jesus teaches that all people are able to forgive sins:

> "But so that you may know that the Son of Man (*ho hyios tou anthrōpou*) has authority on earth to forgive sins"—he then said to the paralytic—"Stand up, take your bed and go to your home." (9:6)

Following Walter Wink, I interpret *ho hyios tou anthrōpou* (the son of the human being) as Human Being; he is to be a priest (i.e., fulfilled Human Being). Wink observes: "According to Matthew, then, 'the son of the man' in this narrative is not limited to Jesus, but indicates any person who 'knows' God's will regarding forgiveness, indeed, who knows God's very nature, that God is, at the core, forgiving."[28] His understanding is reinforced by 9:8: "they glorified God, who had given such authority to human beings (*anthrōpois*)" (9:8). Wink claims that *ho hyios tou anthrōpou* is "an ideal figure and stands for the manifestation of the Kingdom of God on earth in a people wholly devoted to the heavenly king."[29] He further adds: "Jesus' mission was to create the kingdom of the saints of the Most High—a fully human community that honored the integrity and uniqueness of all people. Jesus and His disciples *together* 'should be the Son of Man, the remnant that saves by service and self-sacrifice, the organ of God's redemptive purpose in the world.'"[30]

In short, Jesus' role as the son of man is to serve others and that demands working towards the removal of poverty and oppression (20:28). One example of this is to challenge others to embrace those who are being excluded (see especially 18:10–14; 24:45; 25:31–46). In forgiving the man's sins Jesus removes the sick man's pain of being excluded from society.

THE FIRST AND LAST HEALINGS (8:1–4 AND 21:14)

I believe that Matthew's first and last healings are intentionally placed to be first and last to emphasize Jesus commands to reject exclusion and embrace all.

28. Wink, *The Human Being*, 78.
29. Ibid., 79.
30. Ibid.

8:1–4

Davies and Allison comment that "No disease was more dreaded in the ancient world than 'leprosy.'"[31] So abhorrent was the leper that he was commanded to warn others to avoid contact by shouting out "unclean" (Leviticus 13:45–46). The man of 8:1–4 does not warn Jesus shouting "unclean." The leper says: "LORD, if you wish, you can cleanse me." It is incorrect to argue that the leper is cleansed because of his faith and trust in Jesus. Nothing in this verse suggests this. The man has heard rumors about Jesus and has nothing to lose but approach him. The sick man acts in the hope that his material existence will be improved.[32]

The language of these verses is that of the Temple cult. Jesus is approached as though He were a High Priest although in the eyes of the Temple authorities He is not. But we must also take into account that Jesus says He is greater than the Temple thus claiming to be greater than the High Priest (12:6). Further, the man seems to put the ball in Jesus' court; Jesus could have said: "no, I can't cleanse you because I am not a priest, and you know this." Instead, Jesus touches the man (contrary to Leviticus 5:3) and then cleanses him; through touch He takes the sin upon himself (cf. 8:17). The leper's kneeling and addressing of Jesus as "LORD" however should not be interpreted as depicting the sick man's actions as anything other than opportunistic as one would expect of a seriously ill person who hears about a healer. But the action does suggest the man's actions are of one who acts as if Jesus is the High Priest.[33]

How does this relate to Jesus' command to the man to show himself to the priests and offer the gift commanded by Moses? The reason for doing so depends on how the Greek *eis marturion autois* ("for a witness to them" in v. 4) is understood. It should be read as Jesus instructing the former leper to show himself to the Temple authorities so that he can be included into society. The man is to bear witness before the Temple authorities about Jesus' actions: Jesus is the High Priest.

31. Davies and Allison, *Matthew 1–7*, 198.

32. It is evident in exegesis of Luke's parable of the prodigal son that it is easy to miss the point that the act of healing and forgiving is the key point. The parable of the prodigal son is not about the son's repentance, but about the Father's mercy. So also in Matthew 8:1–4.

33. Grundmann, *Das Evangelium nach Matthäus*, argues that the leper in kneeling before Jesus implies worship, thus Jesus represents a new cultic center taking the place of the temple; see also Barker, *The Revelation of Jesus Christ*, 8, argues the kneeling implies the action of worship of the High Priest who is the visible presence of God.

In short, Jesus acts and thinks in the tradition of the Temple cult; He takes upon Himself the diseases of the man, and through this action cleanses him and restores him into the bosom of society.

21:14

After Jesus' demonstration in the Temple only Matthew states: "The blind and the lame came to him in the Temple, and he cured them." Schweizer rightly comments: "Since this is also the only passage in the first three gospels to mention a healing in Jerusalem, it must be especially important to Matthew."[34] Many argue that 21:14 should be read in the context of 2 Samuel 5:8 suggesting that Jesus subverts the Temple hierarchy,[35] as well as showing Jesus violating a Davidic prohibition of 2 Samuel 5:8. According to 2 Samuel 5:8 (cf. Leviticus 21:16–24; Josephus *JW* 5.227; 1QSam 2.5–7; 1QM 7:4–5), the lame and the blind are those David hates. David says: "The blind and the lame shall not come into the house" (2 Samuel 5:8). However, if Matthew has David's prohibition in mind, how do we explain the blind men in 20:29–34 calling Jesus "son of David" suggesting that David was understood as one who might heal the blind? Further, if the blind and lame were forbidden from entering the city, how did they get into the city or outer court in the first place? Matthew makes it clear that they entered with no assistance. According to Acts 3:1–2, the lame could be carried to the Temple gate, but it makes clear the lame would lay daily at the gate of the Temple. So, according to Acts, they did not enter the Temple.

It is hard to imagine how lame and blind people unaided could gain access to the Temple. I suggest, therefore, that Matthew has interpolated this tradition to highlight Jesus as one whose work was to heal and restore the excluded in society. Their presence and Jesus' cleansing of them depict Jesus as bearing their suffering and poverty. The Temple now exists through Jesus' compassion and when others show it.

I agree that Matthew alludes to 2 Samuel 5:8 in order to subvert the idea of the Davidic Messiah being one who excluded others. Matthew makes clear that the blind believed Jesus to be King David depicting David not as one who hated the blind, but in the light of the hope that David would heal the blind and there would be none who are excluded.

Further, Matthew may have in mind the hope found in Jeremiah 31:8–9 (cf. Isaiah 25:6–9: note "for all peoples). Verse 8 particularly emphasizes

34. Schweizer, *Matthew*, 407. In spite of this commentators tend not to give this verse much attention. Beare has one line (417).

35. Keener, *Matthew*, 502.

the "blind and the lame." The hope of the remnant returning from exile to Zion includes the blind and the lame and it is this that Matthew has Jesus alluding to. Jesus' message is one of good news to the poor. He will heal the afflicted, give sight to the blind, release the oppressed and the prisoner.

However, perhaps crucial to understanding the healing of the lame and blind is Matthew's quote from Hosea 6:6 about mercy not sacrifice. Swartley observes well: "Jesus is a minister of mercy."[36] Jesus' healing of the lame and blind is an alternative to the "commerce of robbery." His healing of the lame and blind "defines the proper cultic activity of the temple."[37] It anticipates the time when the scattered and vulnerable will have a shepherd (cf. Ezekiel 34:4–6; cf. also Matthew 18:10–14 and 25:31ff). Perhaps central is Isaiah 35:5–6 that speaks of the eschatological hope when the blind will see and the lame will walk.

In conclusion, Matthew's "lame and the blind" underline Jesus as one who is in solidarity with the helpless and not because they were seen as faithful. It is likely that their presence in the Temple after Jesus' actions of symbolic protest and cleansing alluded to the hope of healing and *shalom* in Isaiah 35.

SUMMARY

- Jesus addresses those who are culpable of excluding others.
- 8:17 underlies the subversive message of the Bible and Jesus in which the idea of sacrifice is inverted (i.e., sacrifice is showing mercy).
- 9:1–8 depicts Jesus as the Son of Man who saves by service and self-sacrifice.
- Jesus is the model of a high priest that all human beings should aspire to.
- Matthew 21:14 has Jesus challenging prejudice and social and economic marginalization.
- Jesus lives in the environment where the Temple is understood to be a microcosm of creation signifying it as God intended ordered according to Torah, based on righteousness, mercy and love.[38]

36. Swartley, *Israel's Scripture Traditions*, 173.

37. Ibid.

38. Swartley, *Health, Healing*, 53 picks up on words such as righteousness, justice, mercy, law and love, as motifs semantically linked to healing.

- Jesus, through self-sacrifice, lives as God intended for creation. He is the new Temple, but greater (cf. 12:5).
- Jesus' healing actions are initially about inclusion back into society and the household (see Matthew 25:31–46).

FOOD FOR THOUGHT

Against the tendencies of society to put the blame on the sick person for his or her sickness, Jesus shows to society that sickness is rooted in universal human sin. Those working towards peaceable communities must recognize in themselves their tendencies to exclude others. He invites them to repent and thereby develop cultures of inclusion and peace.[39]

I have previously written: "It is vital that we create possibilities to be with the despised and rejected."[40] I further comment in the same publication that we see the poorest of the poor "as someone to fear" and that such fear "prevents true revolution."[41] The poorest of the poor are those who are sick and perceived as sinners and evil whereas the non-poor are good.[42] Yet these poorest of the poor: the hungry, thirsty, naked, migrant, sick, and prisoner (Matthew 25:35) are in Matthew none other than Jesus' own (25:40). To reject them is to deny Jesus and refuse all that He reveals, through these poorest, to the non-poor (25:43).

Jesus is the True Priest in the sense that He is at the same time True Human marked by His life rooted in mercy and self-sacrifice. 8:1–4 and 21:14 refer to excluded groups. Jesus acts to reinstate them to society. He exemplifies the full Human Being who is a priest in the sense that God intended all to be priests. He is one who always acts to bring about a restored society in the midst of division and exclusion. Mercy and self-sacrifice are at the heart of how Jesus restores them.

The Temple in these texts is deliberately set in the context of people who are excluded by it. Matthew places Jesus in the midst of the excluded. In the first healing He acts to enable the leper to enter the Temple from which he had previously been excluded. The final healing, begins with the first healing. Now Jesus heals openly and explicitly in the midst of the Temple. This suggests the extent to which healing in the way Jesus did it was threatening to the Temple and dangerous to Jesus. Matthew highlights

39. Ibid., 64.

40. Bredin, *True Beauty*, 23.

41. Ibid., 20.

42. Volf, *Exclusion*, 83.

emphatically in the obvious redactional account how upset the authorities were by the challenge to their policies regarding the poor and the excluded.

In short, all human beings are priests when they are channels of God's goodness that leads to the transformation of society from one of exclusion to one of embrace.

PRAYER

Dear Lord Goodness, the whole earth is Yours, You have called us to be a priestly kingdom, transforming us from within to form a creation of abundance. Help us to be Your priests, Just Humans embracing all so they too can be channels of Your goodness. Amen

10

Matthew 18:1–14

The Greatest in the Kingdom of Heaven

Contact with people who are weak and crying out for communion, is one of the most important nourishments in our lives. When we let ourselves be really touched by the gift of their presence, they leave something precious in our hearts.[1] *—Jean Vanier*

Vanier has in mind particularly people with learning difficulties. I quote him because he sets out what will be the main point of this chapter: the greatest in the kingdom of heaven are the poorest of the poor, the excluded, and the ignored. Unless the non-poor repent and treat all as brothers and sisters they exclude themselves from God's love.

In 18:1–14 we hear of the strange message about the kingdom of heaven belonging to a "child," and "one of the least of these" (vv. 5, 10). They are further known as the despised, those led astray, and led to destruction. Jesus has in mind powerless people who are both feared, perceived strange, other, sinful, immoral, and deranged.

The phrase "those who believe in me" in 18:6 will be examined in terms of my claim against the scholarly consensus that "the child," and "one of the least of these," are non-disciples experiencing extreme exclusion. *I propose they are those who are led astray because they are vulnerable and*

1. Vanier, *Community*, 186.

exploitable (cf. 18:6). Ultimately, they are the most powerless people of Jesus' society and that makes them defenseless to mistreatment.

18:1–14 confronts the reader with the message: the kingdom of heaven is the domain of the vulnerable (the child and one of the least of these). I propose that Jesus' message is that the greatest in the kingdom are those perceived to be the least on earth. In Matthew 10:8 Jesus states that the arrival of the kingdom is directly linked to the sick, the dead, the lepers, those possessed by demons. In 11:5 Jesus states that His message is to the poorest of the poor. Important to my reflections on these verses are Richard Rohr's words: "*The experience of 'powerlessness' is where we all must begin.*"[2] I suggest that this radical idea expressed in the context of the first step of Alcoholics Anonymous elucidates the original setting of Jesus in 18:1–14. Jesus by teaching about being like the child is not teaching His disciples to become powerless and impoverished. Jesus addresses the arrogance of the disciples challenging them to acknowledge their own powerlessness before God by taking the log out of their own eye (7:3). *However, we must not confuse this with the erroneous idea that the child is a metaphor for piety.* The child means one who is powerless and excluded. We must not push the metaphor beyond this.

I will raise one final point before launching into my argument in detail. Vanier's words at the beginning of this chapter are helpful in understanding 18:1–14: in becoming like the child we are to be open to the powerless and excluded for they are channels of God's grace to the non-poor opening their eyes to how God wants them to be by showing them also the horror and pain the non-poor cause the poor. God shows to the non-poor their sin of exclusion through contact with the poorest of the poor. Who are these people today where Jesus dwells? I imagine Jesus is black and beaten, He is the drug addict serving an indefinite prison sentence (IPP)[3] who falls off His prison cell toilet seat, marks on His arms, dead from taking spice;[4] He is one who sits on the park bench wine soaked; He is twenty people living in a one room tenement. He is all this and much more.

In short, Jesus understood the will of God to be acting in preference to those in situations of extreme material and physical poverty.

2. Rohr, *Breathing Underwater*, xvii.

3. For the meaning and injustice of those serving IPP (Imprisonment for Public Protection) see https://www.justice.gov.uk/downloads/legislation/bills-acts/legal-aid-sentencing/ipp-factsheet.pdf.

4. Those not familiar with the drug called spice, see https://www.theguardian.com/society/2014/may/15/synthetic-cannabis-serious-health-problems-english-prisons.

MY BIASES

My reading of 18:1–14 is influenced by having spent many years among people with learning disabilities, working as a Quaker Prison Chaplain, also as one who has lived in rural Zimbabwe and Tanzania, and with people whose poverty has been induced by addiction, particularly alcohol and drugs. My proposed interpretation envisages the child, and the least of these, and the lost sheep, as characterizing helpless victims including both children and adults—the reviled and marginalized. They are those whose most basic needs are withheld or offered grudgingly and conditionally. They are susceptible and vulnerable to believing anything anyone says to them if what is said gives hope of some basic kindness even if it is given with an ulterior motive.

As I consider these verses I am struck by how every society is marked by its need to look down on others. In the prison setting prisoners loathe those convicted of sex offenses against children. Among sex-offenders there is a lowest layer of those held in contempt. In care homes people with less complex disabilities look down on those with more profound and complex disabilities. In night shelters those who are not addicted to alcohol or drugs consider the addicts who they share the shelter with contemptible crack heads.

Human existence and survival are rooted in finding others to deride and metaphorically and literally sacrifice. It seems that people feel better about themselves when they blame and pour scorn on others. Jesus opens up an understanding in which all are brothers and sisters; no one is better than another in God's eyes. Through looking at the other we must first be open to what God is saying to us through the other (7:3). Those pejoratively known as junkies or crack heads are in fact Christ.

18:1–5

These verses depict Jesus and His disciples together most probably in the midst of other people in a busy agrarian village or town. It is important to pause to imagine the crowds of people milling around Jesus in the villages, towns, and countryside. My time in rural Tanzania and Zimbabwe has proven to be an antidote to my own European Post-Enlightenment urban existence in reading Matthew. In rural Africa I became aware particularly of children with twisted emaciated bodies, with wild haunting eyes making sounds without coherent words. I was made acutely conscious of children with snotty noses, loose jaws, and unfocused eyes. I encountered so many children with learning disabilities in villages. They are far more visible in parts of Africa than in the UK or US, mainly because there are more in economically underdeveloped and undernourished nations, but also, because they can't be hidden away in care homes such as I have worked in the UK. Jesus and His disciples knew more of this world than we do in our world. The gospel provides a window into this world with children throwing themselves in fire and water due to their disabilities (Matthew 17:15). Children were not pampered and were seen as second class (Matthew 19:13–15). It was a world where a mother would be excluded from society because she had a badly disabled daughter (cf. 15:21–28).[5]

Against this backdrop, the disciples ask: "who is the greatest in the kingdom of heaven?" The twelve disciples were not above squabbling over who was the best among themselves. In Matthew 20:20–28, Jesus teaches that the humble child is the greatest in the kingdom of heaven (Matthew 18 and 19:13–15), but still, two of the twelve, James and John act selfishly to get ahead of the other disciples by gaining a special place with Jesus in heaven. This results in conflict with the other ten disciples (20:24) leading Jesus to teach against ruling oppressively over others (20:25–26). They are suitably put in their place by Jesus with His message that being great means being a servant (see 20:26).

The disciples' question about who is the greatest depicts them as slow in understanding Jesus' message. They struggle to comprehend that the kingdom of heaven is not about domination and exclusion. This should not surprise the reader; the disciples themselves were not of the poorest of the poor, they inherited values rooted in competition, battle, and blame (cf. how Jesus compares such ways with the rulers and elites in 20:25).[6]

"Who is the greatest in the kingdom of heaven?" It is an interesting question particularly in the light of the dominance of patriarchy, the priestly classes, the Jewish rulers in Jerusalem with its expensive Temple for which they (disciples) were paying taxes, and of course the brutal Roman regime (cf. Matthew 2 and 20:25).[7] From what we know of Jesus in the previous chapters of Matthew, He would be disappointed with the disciples' question. In response Jesus more than likely makes eye contact with a child beckoning

5. I would add however that I have in the UK met many parents with children with learning difficulties who feel isolated and marginalized.

6. Volf, *Exclusion*, 87 states that he uses "exclusion" as a substitute for "domination" as outlined by Wink. He writes: "as a rule the purpose of domination is to exclude others from scarce goods, whether they are economic, social, or psychological."

7. It is interesting that the disciples in Matthew 24:1–2 are impressed at the Temple buildings. They appear to invite Jesus to also praise them. Jesus instead states that all these impressive buildings will be destroyed.

him to come to Him. From my own experience of adults, they tend to avoid contact with people with learning disabilities. The child comes to Him as Jesus knew he would. *I reiterate: this child may have physical, mental and/or learning disabilities.* This child would not expect a teacher to notice him or her; rather, such a child would expect to be rebuffed (cf. 19:13–15). Suddenly, Jesus turns to His disciples and says to them: "he is the greatest in the kingdom of heaven" (18:4b). This is a staggering statement. The child Jesus points to is valueless, despised and easily corrupted.

Jesus' teaching is totally against the grain of society where the educated and landowners are the empowered ones. They are the greatest and they rule oppressively (20:25). They see themselves as favored by God evident in their ownership of land and possessions. We know the disciples are scandalized when He says that it is hard for the rich and powerful to enter the kingdom of heaven (19:23–25). 20:25 and 19:23–25, are best understood in the light of 18:1–14 as well as the teaching that the last will be first and the first will be last (cf. 19:30 and 20:16).

Jesus challenges the mentality that led the disciples to ask the question about who is the greatest. *Jesus is not commending being poor and oppressed.* He teaches against thinking that leads society to despise the poor and powerless. Matthew emphasizes this by saying that these vulnerable people (children) are so special to God that their angel sees the face of the Creator Father (18:10). When Jesus says "become like this child" (18:3) He does not mean to become literally powerless and humiliated. Instead He exposes the wrong attitude that led the disciples to ask "who is the greatest in the kingdom of heaven?" Jesus warns that we must stop striving to improve our place in society.

In short Jesus impresses upon His disciples that greatness in the kingdom of heaven is not measured in terms of worldly success. What is great in a world that encourages competition and self-striving has nothing to do with God's will. The attitude and economic policies that lead people to see others as commercial commodities has nothing to do with Jesus' teachings.

18:6–9

In verses 6–9 Jesus challenges the sin of looking down on the least of God's creatures (cf. Mark 9:42–8). Verse 7 is distinctly from Matthew's pen: "Woe to the world because of stumbling blocks! Occasions for stumbling are bound to come, but woe to the one by whom the stumbling block comes." Verses 6–9 are intended to be read in the light of vv. 1–5. The child of vv. 1–5 is susceptible to stumbling, one who is led astray and ultimately to destruction (cf. vv. 12 and 14). The world exploits people who are vulnerable and causes them to stumble from doing God's will. People whose basic needs are withheld are those whose lives are impoverished and miserable. People who have wealth also stumble because they are too concerned with protecting and hoarding what they have (cf. 6:25–34). In short, the woe against the world is a cry of anguish against its ethos of blame, domination, and exclusion. However, the "least of these" find a special place with God even though they stumble and err. They are the poorest of the poor whom God embraces unconditionally: *tōn pisteuontōn eis eme* (those who believe in me) (v. 6). Jesus' words "those who believe in me" refers to people who are vulnerable and accept everything on face value. Hagner suggests it has associations with "their humble demeanor."[8] There is no need to see the phrase referring to a disciple. It means one who is vulnerable, and easily corruptible.

The idea that a pious disciple is led astray is not easy to comprehend in verse 6. Those led astray are not ones who are faithful to God's Torah, in Psalm 119:165 we read: "Great peace have those who love your Torah; nothing can make them stumble" (my translation).

Jesus refers not to a disciple that is about to stray in matters of faith, but a defenseless person easily conditioned and corrupted. According to 15:12, the Pharisees stumble on account of Jesus' teaching (*ton logon eskandalisthē -san*) in the sense of not doing the will of God. Jesus admonishes Peter for being a stumbling block (*skandalon*) to Himself (16:23) meaning that Peter was seeking to prevent Jesus from doing the will of God. My suggestion is that those rejected from society are at risk of being deployed for evil on account of their marginalized status. They are prevented from keeping Torah—doing God's will because they are inclined inevitably to do anything in order that their suffering may be relieved. The powerless, however, are not admonished by Jesus unlike the Pharisees and Peter. They are favored by God. But those who cause them to stumble and err, will be severely punished. A disciple, however, who loves Torah will not stumble even if poor and enduring persecution. Jesus suffers greatly but He does not stumble. In short, the description "those who believe in me" refers to the susceptible and defenseless nature of being excluded.

In sum, "those who believe in me" refers to those who suffer from extreme material poverty and are easily led astray. They are exploited and are unable to experience the peace that comes with keeping God's Torah (cf. Psalm 119:165).

8. Hagner, *Matthew 14–28*, 522.

The vulnerable person who is easily led astray may be maimed, lame and blind. Jesus chastises those who cause others to stumble and suffer through their policies of exclusion and blame. Jesus warns that it is preferable to be disabled in the kingdom of heaven than to be thrown into the fires of hell whole bodied (vv. 8–9). Jesus' hyperbole is informed by His observations that the least of creation who are despised are the lame, maimed, and blind. Better to be despised than to despise would appear to be Jesus' key message.

18:10–14

Verses 10–14 give an account of the parable of the lost sheep (also Luke 15:3–7). Verses 10 and 14 are distinct to Matthew:

> Take care that you do not despise one of these little ones; for, I tell you, in heaven their angels continually see the face of my Father in heaven. (v. 10)

> So it is not the will of your Father in heaven that one of the least of these should be led to ruin (*hina apolētai hen tōn mikrōn toutōn*). (18:14; my translation)

Verse 10

Jesus warns against looking down on the poor (little ones), the disabled, the unemployed and so on. Jesus teaches that these "little ones" each have an angel that sees the face of the heavenly Father (verse 10). In spite of them appearing useless and unworthy, far from God and indeed cursed by God (cf. Isaiah 53:4), in fact the child is close to God. In short, Matthew's Jesus emphasizes God's special care of the vulnerable and easily exploited.

Verse 11

This verse is omitted in some key manuscripts such as Sinaiticus and Vaticanus and it is likely that the verse is a later addition. However, brief observation may be helpful.

> for the son of man came to save those who have and are being destroyed (Greek: *ēlthen gar hyios tou anthrōpou sōsai to apolōlos*).

The Greek *apolōlos* is in the perfect tense suggesting one who is truly destroyed. The verse provides an interpretation of those who err, they are those who have been lost to society by being corrupted. I have seen many such people in prison.

Verses 12–14

This is the parable of the lost sheep although it does not have the phrase "lost sheep." "Lost" fails to do justice to the Greek *planōmenon* (to be led astray). The one sheep goes missing because he is excluded or is corrupted from the ninety-nine sheep that did not go astray (*planōmenon*) (18:12). The verb *planaō* has the sense of being deceived elsewhere in Matthew (24:4, 5, 11, 24). In verse 14 Jesus teaches that "your Father in heaven does not wish one of the least of these to perish." The Greek "to perish" is *apolētai* which is also the word used in 18:11.

Observing Ezekiel 34 also helps in understanding Matthew 18:12. According to Ezekiel 34, the prophet attacks the shepherds of Israel for not feeding the sheep (v. 3). They have not strengthened the weak, healed the sick, bound up the injured, but have ruled harshly (vv. 4–6). In particular the prophet condemns them because the shepherds fed themselves and not the sheep (v. 8). Ezekiel states that God will rescue them from their darkness (v. 12) and feed them in good pasture (v. 14). In LXX 34:16 the Greek verb *planaō* refers to the sheep that suffer. Those that err in verse 16 are the injured and the weak.

Therefore, the sheep in Matthew 18:12 that are led astray correspond to the simple and vulnerable child which also refers to the weak and injured. Perhaps the sheep represents the one who has been abused, misled or neglected through lack of care. The main point of the parable is that what is of value, what is successful, what is productive, in worldly terms, has nothing to do with the kingdom of heaven. The quintessential idea for the disciples who hear Jesus is that they care for that lone sheep that has been led astray and will perish unless they act.

SUMMARY

- "The child," and "one of the least of these," are non-disciples experiencing extreme exclusion.

- "Those who believe in me" (v. 6) refers to those vulnerable people who are led astray because they are defenseless, easily led astray, and exploitable.
- Jesus by teaching about being like the child addresses the arrogance of the disciples challenging them to acknowledge their own powerlessness before God by taking the log out of their own eye (7:3).
- The disciples' question about who is the greatest depicts them as slow in understanding Jesus' message.
- The vulnerable person who is easily led astray may be maimed, lame and blind.
- Jesus warns against looking down on others, particularly the poor, the disabled, the unemployed and so on.

The main point of the parable of the straying sheep is that what is of value, what is successful, what is productive, in worldly terms, has nothing to do with the kingdom of heaven.

FOOD FOR THOUGHT

QF&P 1.02.22 states: "Remember that each one of us is unique, precious, a child of God." A Quaker prisoner writing for *Insidetime* wrote an apology to those he had offended called "I'm so sorry." He wrote, "We are one world, made up of many different people, each one of us has a unique gift and offering to give. If I do not let you do that by being you, I rob the world of that gift. With love."[9]

Jesus emphasizes the need for the disciples to rethink the way they see others and how they perceive the kingdom of heaven. They are not to think of themselves as having a special place with God in contrast to others, but to see others as being special to God, in spite of their poverty and suffering. The very question the disciples ask belies arrogance and slowness to turn from their supercilious attitudes.

All are God's children and we must all treat others as brothers and sisters. The kingdom of heaven is, therefore, a place where the least have a place in God's bosom. It is neither a place where one looks down on another nor is it one where people squabble over who is the greatest. The task of the disciple is to work for the benefit of the least in society incorporating them into the community and seeking a place where they are valued and not looked down upon.

9. See *Insidetime: the National Newspaper for Prisoners & Detainees*, October 2016.

In the midst of our prisons today are lost sheep. Many prisoners are people with learning difficulties or serious mental health issues perhaps resulting from fighting for their country in war zones. Many of them are young and unprotected in the prison system having committed crimes because they were trusting and easily led astray. Society is structured to allow the wealthy to manipulate its population to want more, to consume, to be addicted to what is dangerous; many are vulnerable and incapable of discerning between the complex choices of what is right and wrong.

I began this chapter with a quote from Jean Vanier emphasizing that each, even those who are far from God, are special to God. Vanier in his writings based on his experiences of living with people with learning difficulties for over fifty years has learnt that such people are channels of God's goodness, and woe to those who look down upon them.

PRAYER

Lord, help us to commit our whole being to the labor of making peace. That we may overcome inequality through love. Give us vision to see a world liberated from violence, where no one is despised. Amen

11

Matthew 11:28–30

Jesus as Wisdom

I slept and dreamt that life was joy. I woke and I saw that life was service. I acted and behold, service was joy. —Tagore

In 11:28–30 Jesus exhorts the non-poor who are weary from the burden of competing and battling in a war zone to be as Jesus: gentle and humble in heart (v. 29). This is the way of Sabbath rest (finding rest; see v. 28) through trusting God as their Creator. The yoke God intends human beings to bear is one of being expressions of mercy and love in alignment with God. This is what Jesus means by teaching "my yoke is easy, and my burden is light" (v. 30).

Rabindranath Tagore's words stress that service and mercy are the essence of the order of creation; in other words, creation is hard-wired so that human beings serve the Creator through caring and preserving His creation. Only through serving others can God's true joy be experienced. Only through service will the yoke a person bears be light; only through service can a person be gentle and humble in heart and find rest/peace.

In this chapter I argue that Jesus is depicted as Wisdom who teaches "my yoke is easy, and my burden is light" (Matthew 11:30). My argument is influenced by the biblical idea that Wisdom is imaged as a human being in the context of a benevolent environment.[1] Wisdom utterings such as "do not wear yourself out to get rich; be wise enough to desist" (Proverbs 23:4) are helpful as background to Jesus' words in verses 28–30.

In short, Jesus teaches in these verses that through living by mercy, love, and care, can human beings feel joy that God intends for them.

WISDOM, CREATION, AND THE OLD TESTAMENT

Biblically "Wisdom promotes virtues such as prudence and justice and avoidance of vices such as contentiousness, indolence, and disregard for the poor and needy; all are grounded in a creational perspective."[2] Fretheim writes of Wisdom in Proverbs:

> Wisdom, therefore, has to do with both moral order and cosmic order and is related to every dimension of each. The "house" built by Woman Wisdom (9:1; cf. 14:1; 24:3–4) may be a reference to both orders, into which she invites everyone to 'walk in the way of insight' (9:6). Woman Wisdom, in effect, is the "glue" that holds everything together in a stable and harmonious whole. The text thus speaks of a highly interrelated world—a spiderweb, if you will—in which all things are woven together and each creature affects every other, positively or negatively.[3]

For Fretheim, "wisdom is so built into the infrastructure of the creation that God's character and purposes for the world can be reasonably, if not fully discernible to human probing and reflection."[4] Walther Zimmerli also writes: "Wisdom thinks resolutely within the framework of a theology of creation."[5] Crenshaw similarly observes that the wise person is "one who both *creates* order and brings his life into harmony with the *established* order of the universe."[6] It is no surprise then that Brueggemann commenting on Wisdom writes: "Wisdom is the critical, reflective, discerning reception of Yahweh's gift of generosity. That gift is not for self-indulgence, exploitation, acquisitiveness, or satiation. It is for careful husbanding, so that

1. Fretheim, *God and World*, 209.
2. Ibid., 204.
3. Ibid., 207.
4. Ibid., 219.
5. Zimmerli, "The Place and Limit of the Wisdom," 148.
6. Crenshaw, *Ancient Israelite Wisdom*, 23.

resources should be used for the protection, enhancement, and nurture of all creatures."[7]

Woman Wisdom is depicted as instructing and inviting people to be wise which is to live in harmony with the order of creation. Fretheim extends his study of Wisdom to the book of Job. There he finds similarities with Genesis 1:28. Job is to "gird up" his loins (38:1; 40:6) and "be the man" he was created to be.[8] He is made to be like God. When God addresses Job He challenges him to act likewise.[9] God especially, Fretheim argues, makes Job aware of the range of God's parenting work in all creation (note parental images in 38:8–11, 28–29). He does so to encourage Job and his descendants to live in harmony with Wisdom that teaches the order of creation. Wisdom therefore functions as an intermediary between God and human beings and the rest of creation. At the heart of what Wisdom teaches is generosity, restraint and care of others. Human beings are created to flourish when they care and nurture.[10]

MATTHEW 11:28–30

These verses I argue should be understood in the context of Matthew depicting Jesus as a manifestation of Wisdom calling human beings to a life of nurture, care, restraint, and generosity.

> Come to me, all you that are weary and are carrying heavy burdens (*hoi koiōntes kai pephortismenoi*) and I will give you rest. Take my yoke upon you, and learn from me; for I am gentle and humble in heart, and you will find rest for your souls. For my yoke is easy, and my burden is light.

Jesus' invitation is spoken of as personified Wisdom. The very essence of these verses is generosity.

In what way is 11:28–30 relevant to my argument that Jesus' teachings must be understood in the context of the poorest of the poor? The obvious point would be to argue that those who are weary and carry heavy burdens refer to the poorest of the poor. However, this not my position. Wengst discusses the yoke that is a burden in terms of the violence the poorest of the poor experienced through the oppressor.[11] Wengst, however,

7. Brueggemann, *Old Testament Theology*, 532.
8. Fretheim, *God and World*, 242.
9. Ibid., 240.
10. Ibid., 239.
11. Wengst, *Humility*, 38.

also writes: "The original context of this call seems most likely to have been discipleship of Jesus. Here Jesus calls people out of oppressed and oppressive circumstances to his discipleship, the new community of his disciples which escapes the conditions of exploitation and domination and in which these conditions are no longer to hold."[12]

In contrast to Wengst, I don't see Jesus inviting the poorest of the poor to discipleship in 11:28–30. Weary and heavy laden (*hoi koiōntes kai pephortismenoi*) are not terms used to refer to the poorest of the poor. They describe the lot of the non-poor who do battle every day oppressing others in order to hold on to what they have in terms of position and possessions. I propose the yoke Jesus invites the non-poor to bear is one of service and care, sharing creation's abundance especially with the poorest of the poor who have experienced the injustices of a way of life rooted in battle.

In short, 11:28–30 must be understood in the context of creation being an expression of God's goodness. When people live to serve, people experience joy.

WISDOM AS TEACHER OF MERCY

Jesus' words of exhortation echo personified Wisdom's call (Proverbs 8:1–7; 9:4–5; Sirach 24:19; 51:23–27) inviting her children to abandon the worldly yoke rooted in obsession with earthly treasures and self-seeking. Instead, they are to bear the yoke of humility (not humiliation) as exemplified in Jesus through trusting in God who is Father of an abundant creation. It follows from this that to live by showing mercy is the basis of Wisdom's call.

WISDOM, KINGSHIP, AND HUMILITY

Wirzba's definition of humility from a creation perspective is particularly relevant when considering Matthew 11:28–30: "It is . . . the realization that for our living we depend on others, even sacrifices of others."[13] He warns: "When we turn away from the creation that God has made, preferring the worlds of our own making, and when we refuse the humble life of service and care, preferring instead a life of conveniences and self-glorification, we at the same time separate ourselves from the world and the God of life at work in it."[14] For this reason Sirach claims that "the greater you are, the more

12. Ibid., 39.

13. Wirzba, *Food and Faith*, 52.

14. Ibid., 78.

you humble yourself . . ." (3:18). In other words, to trust God and not to rely on one's own limited understanding is a key message of Wisdom (cf. Proverbs 3:5–7). In other words "humility" describes one who is in unity with God; it is not about self-debasement or self-loathing or being impoverished. The psalmist tells us a lot about humility in describing the proud as those who do not trust in God (Psalm 40:4). The humble trusts God for all their needs; in other words, they know "everyone is a mere breath" (Psalm 39:11). According to the book of Deuteronomy, the Godly King is humble unlike the kings of other nations:

> When he has taken the throne of his kingdom, he shall have a copy of this law written for him in the presence of the levitical priests. It shall remain with him and he shall read in it all the days of his life, so that he may learn to fear the LORD his God, diligently observing all the words of this law and these statutes, neither exalting himself above other members of the community nor turning aside from the commandment, either to the right or to the left, so that he and his descendants may reign long over his kingdom in Israel. (17:18–20)[15]

The King according to the law is to keep Torah; it is to be his way of life. The King was entrusted to create an order in society that permitted justice, righteousness, mercy, and *shalom* which underlie created principles. Zechariah 9:9 also knows of this tradition:

> Rejoice greatly, O daughter Zion! Shout aloud, O daughter Jerusalem! Lo, your king comes to you; triumphant and victorious is he, humble and riding on a donkey, on a colt, the foal of a donkey.[16]

JESUS AS HUMBLE WISDOM

Luke 7:35 refers to children vindicating Wisdom; yet for Matthew Jesus is Wisdom who is vindicated through His actions and words (11:19). Jesus is shown as Wisdom who is known through His healing work. Further, Luke 11:49 states that "Wisdom of God" sends prophets and apostles whereas

15. There are a number of Old Testament texts that develop the themes of Deuteronomy 17. For example, Psalm 72 verses 1, 4, 13–14; also Proverbs 8:15–16, 20; 11:11; 28:15–16; 29:2, 4, 14.

16. Of the gospels it is cited only in Matthew 21:5.

Matthew has Jesus saying: "I send you prophets, sages, and scribes," (23:34). In short, Jesus is Wisdom personified in Matthew.[17]

It is argued nevertheless that humility and gentleness (*praus* and *tapeinos*) used of Jesus do not refer to religious characteristics but to Jesus' poverty and economic status. However, while Jesus was neither rich nor privileged, He nowhere describes himself as poor in Matthew.[18] On the contrary, He speaks of the poor as a separate group on several occasions (19:21; 26:11). I suggest instead that we interpret *praus* and *tapeinos* as synonyms referring to Jesus' trust and knowledge of God as hospitable Creator.[19]

HUMBLE KING (21:5)

21:5 depicts Jesus as the humble King of Zechariah 9:9. Jesus is the wise King greater than Solomon (12:42). In order to fully appreciate this verse we must consider Matthew's use of arrogant kings and leaders as a foil for Jesus' humility.

Solomon is mentioned three times in Matthew (1:7; 6:29 and 12:42). The first occurrence in 1:7 shows Jesus to be a descendent of Solomon. In 6:29 he is portrayed as being rather fond of his clothes. This is noteworthy because Matthew appears to comment on the clothes a person wears four times vis-à-vis John the Baptist (3:4),[20] Herod Antipas (11:8), Solomon (6:29) and Jesus (27:28–31). Explicitly clothing is used to mock Jesus in 27:28–31 where the soldiers dress Jesus as a King (cf. Mark 15:16–20). John the Baptist is held up as the greatest of all men (11:11) and therefore his way of life in the desert, including his clothing and food, are held up as exemplary. Jesus mocks Herod Antipas regarding his clothing in 11:8. *Therefore I think that Solomon too is being mocked.*

The first mention of Solomon is in 1:6; here we find the unusual mention of a woman in the genealogy. What is even more striking is that the woman is unnamed and is referred to as "the wife of Uriah." It is likely that Matthew refers to Uriah to remind his readers of David's cowardly murder of Bathsheba's righteous husband, Uriah (2 Samuel 11:14–21).[21] Solomon is thus shown even in conception to be tainted.

17. D. A. Carson "Christological Ambiguities in the Gospel of Matthew" argues against this view.

18. In contrast to the helpful work of Myles, *The Homeless Jesus in the Gospel of Matthew,* although he does not discuss 11:28–30.

19. This however this is not so for Matthew 5:5.

20. Luke makes no mention of John's clothing, Matthew follows Mark 1:6.

21. Bredin, "Gentiles and the Davidic Tradition," 97.

Jesus says of Solomon: "yet I tell you, *even* Solomon in all his glory was *not* clothed like one of these (Matthew 6:29). Matthew's emphatic "not even" suggests mockery: *not even* Solomon is as glorious as the grass of the field. Jesus would know that Solomon is criticized (see 1 Kings 11:1–43). Solomon is unlikely to be held up as an exemplary figure by Jesus or Matthew given their praise of John the Baptist in his rudimentary clothes. Solomon is seen as one who is set against God in Matthew 6:29; he is considered vain and one who worried about his clothing yet in spite of this worry, even the grass which is here today and thrown into the fire tomorrow is better arrayed than Solomon.[22] The phrase, referring to Solomon being in his fine clothes,"in all his glory" observes Carter, is something that only belongs to God (4:8: 5:16; 6:2); again mockery of Solomon.

In 21:5 Jesus is the true king whose kingship is defined by His humility and riding on a donkey. This is the king who is victorious because He relies and trusts in God for all His needs. Jesus' mission is to free people from the slavery of self-aggrandizement and to redistribute the abundance of creation to all.

THE WEARY AND HEAVY LADEN

Jesus addresses potential or actual disciples when referring to them as "the weary and heavy laden." It is possible to imagine in view of the rest of the Gospel that they would have been ordinary peasants, tax-collectors, women, children, gentiles, Jews, those in power, educated and non-educated.

Matthew's description of them being weary and heavy laden does not mean they are the poorest of the poor, but rather they are the non-poor who are worn down by living according to a way of life that encourages them to strive only for themselves struggling to keep their heads above water. It is the yoke the elite placed on households. It is a yoke in the sense of an order or path which taught the opposite of being *praus* and *tapeinous* which I suggest are attributes that follow from knowing and fearing God as Father Creator. The Pharisees, however, described in Matthew, are proud and arrogant, evident in their lack of faith, justice and mercy (23:23). They thought themselves wise in their own eyes and proud of their being held in high honor (cf. Proverbs 3:5–7).

22. So also Carter, *Matthew and the Margins,* 178.

THE YOKE

Some scholars argue that the yoke refers to Torah as perceived by the Pharisees evident in their minute attention to rules and regulations in contrast to Jesus' understanding of Torah as something that enabled people to live according to love and mercy. Craig S. Keener writes: "Jesus speaks of a figurative bondage of unprofitable labor under an inadequate understanding of God's law."[23] Matthew's Jesus deplores the Pharisees for placing heavy loads on the people and preventing people from worshipping God (23:4). The yoke refers to the oral traditions developed by the Pharisees (cf. 15:1–9). Such laws were developed for the purpose of excluding people and separating Jews from the rest of creation and humanity. Instead Jesus speaks of the Torah as loving one's neighbor and supporting one's parents (5:43–48; 15:4–6).

In what way is Jesus' yoke lighter? It is lighter because it is to be in alignment with God's order for creation. This means to bear God's yoke is to trust God. When a person lives not for his or her own interests, a person lives with the blessing of the Creator Father.

However, the yoke is often associated with being a burden. In Exodus, Israel is accustomed to slavery in Egypt. When Israel is released, the new yoke of trusting in God does not obviously seem easier. This is no surprise. Israel was accustomed to living in oppressed and constrained conditions struggling and fighting to eke out an existence from an inhospitable creation. Therefore to comprehend life dependent on God's mercy was hard to adjust to: to trust in God rather than one's own strength goes contrary to the fallen nature of human beings.[24]

But to trust in God is the yoke Jesus invites His audience to bear. This means a new way of life rooted in repentance and bearing the generous acts of repentance; for tax-collectors this might mean returning money they have taken (cf. Zacchaeus in Luke 19:8).; it might mean giving up wealth; it could mean giving up privileges, homes, fields, family (see Matthew 19:29). This yoke is easier in the sense of carrying it *is to live in harmony with God's will* which is to trust in God who has formed a creation that is abundant.

The "rest/Sabbath" the disciples are promised is one of living in harmony with God by learning *praus and tapeinos*. Pride and arrogance will ultimately lead to destruction because they set a person against God (cf. Psalm 2:2). The way of Jesus is easier because it is in harmony with the way

23. Keener, *Matthew*, 348.

24. People serving long sentences in prison become institutionalized and fear the day of their release. They are accustomed to living in a cell with massive restrictions placed on them.

God intended for humans. But what does this mean in practice? It must have had its attractive sides! In practical terms Jesus envisioned a lightening of the yoke of life because it meant that people would live not in competition with each other, but in sharing and working together. It would bring the joy of new qualities of relationships based on friendships and cooperation that cross all divides. This would ultimately lead to an equable distribution of wealth (cf. Acts 4:32–35).

SUMMARY

- Life is joy to the extent that life is service.
- Biblically Wisdom is to be equated with goodness and generosity.
- In 11:28–30, *the weary and heavy laden* describes a way of life rooted in a worldly understanding that creation is scarce, and life is a battlefield with relationships rooted in competition and not care.
- Wisdom in 11:28–30 is Jesus inviting the non-poor to bear His yoke, which is to trust God, and cease from the existence of everyday battle that results in their exhaustion and the existence of poverty.

FOOD FOR THOUGHT

Mercy, Torah, and Wisdom are related. They each express aspects of God's righteousness and goodness which are the foundation of creation. God's creation is ordered to encourage and direct each of its parts to be merciful. This is God's will, when *shalom* is established. Torah is one aspect that emerges from creation teaching that the way of righteousness is to live for others. Jesus as Wisdom is presented as one who is in harmony with God; this harmony is expressed in Jesus being described as humble and gentle in heart. "Humble" and "gentle" do not describe a submissive figure, but one whose will is that of God. "Humble" and "gentle" are attributes of one who is God's child, one who lives for others. To live for others is to live according to the way of mercy in line with the law. To live in harmony with God is to live at odds with the competitive world that encourages greed and selfishness. When Jesus describes His way as easy, He refers to the way that God intended for His creation. God's creation is made for *shalom* and established through the teaching about living according to God's love.

PRAYER

O gracious and holy Father, give us wisdom to know you, intelligence to understand you, diligence to seek you, patience to wait for you, eyes to behold you, a heart to meditate upon you, and life to proclaim you; through the power of the Spirit of Jesus Christ our Lord. —Attributed to St Benedict

12

Matthew 19:30—20:16

The Unemployed: The Last Will be First

The fear of unemployment causes more unhappiness and does more to lower self-confidence than any other element in life. —QF&P 23.67

Poverty caused by enforced idleness, and in the presence of plenty, is so glaring an injustice that no man should accept it tamely. —QF&P 23:69

The famished millions are famishing not because there is not enough food produced in India but because they have no work to do.[1] *—Gandhi*

One of the most deadly sins is to deprive the laborer of his hire.[2] *—Dorothy Day*

I am startled as I read the parable of the workers in the vineyard in Matthew 19:30—20:16 because I see its message is about the goodness of God in creation expressed in generous but inefficient actions counter to the way of the world. This parable in many ways reiterates the keys themes that have dominated the previous chapters of this book.

1. Ellsberg, *Gandhi on Christianity*, 38.
2. Day, *Selected Writings*, 111.

I argue this parable is about Jesus' expectations that non-poor disciples be willing to shed blood, sweat and tears for the weak and excluded, being as the Lord of Creation intended for them making them in His image. I think this parable has strong claims to preserve the most radical of Jesus' message and teaching. I find it impossible to imagine in any way spiritualizing or depoliticizing the alternative message this parable communicates. I am left amazed by it and astounded at how Jesus has somehow become the property of the elite classes, and tamed to fit into comfortable affluent lives.

Gerald West writes: "Africa is able to illuminate the biblical message in a way that Western biblical scholarship has not been able to do."[3] Having spent some time in Zimbabwe and Tanzania, I have found such sojourns helpful to my interpretative lens. I recall, for example, two different reactions to this parable when teaching: (1) comfortably off white males training for ordination in the UK; (2) Theological students and Church leaders in Tanzania. The first group felt the whole message made no sense and had no meaning for our world. Many of these students had previously been especially successful and important businessmen. My students in Tanzania thought it made perfect sense. Many of them had experienced life predominantly working in their fields (*shambas*), and caring for the community around them; some were ex-prisoners. In Tanzania my students were much more comfortable with the idea that each person is dependent upon another person. The idea of one person benefitting over and against another would be viewed with suspicion. In contrast, I have discovered that many in Western society find this parable's message problematic. I recall preaching on this text one day and afterwards being confronted by an angry hard-working man who said Jesus could not possibly have taught this parable as its message was utter nonsense. There is no surprise in this attitude. Throughout my life I have been encouraged to elevate greed from being shameful to honorable and by the saying: "you get what you earn."

The focus of this chapter is the parable of the workers in the vineyard that is found only in Matthew 20:1–6. The parable narrates how the owner of a vineyard rises at dawn to hire workers while agreeing the normal day's wage of one denarius (vv. 1–2). The owner goes out later in the day hiring laborers at an acceptable rate of pay. Finally, the owner hires more workers with only one hour's light remaining. At the end of the day the foreman begins paying those who only toiled one hour, while paying last those who had worked the whole day. Those who worked all day, when seeing that those who worked one hour were paid a full day's salary, expected that they would be paid more than they had agreed at the beginning of the day. When they

3. West, "Biblical Hermeneutics in Africa," 24.

received the same amount as those who labored one hour, they grumbled to the owner that they had been mistreated by him.

INTERPRETING THE PARABLE

I will examine the parable by taking into account both its social and literary contexts. I consider the parable also within its immediate literary context within Matthew 19–20. The original setting, key themes, and *dramatis personae* of the parable, are taken into account before drawing out the parable's key message and its application for today.

Social Setting of the Parable

The work of archaeologists in Galilee provides some helpful background to understanding the Galilee of Jesus' time. Household buildings uncovered by archaeologists in Galilee reveal the extent to which families were linked together. The very design of the houses in Galilee according to Marianne Sawicki, involved construction to facilitate community for in so doing humans found blessing. In today's technological societies houses are designed to emphasize individualism and separation so it is hard for us to imagine the close proximity in which people and families lived in Galilee in the time of Jesus. From archaeological work done in Galilee "we can infer that people lived near their domestic animals, and that sleeping, and eating all occurred within the same enclosure."[4] Houses were built in a way that reinforced the sense of kinship and, according to Sawicki, "The closeness of the quarters may also encourage non-kin workers in the house to join its lineage through marriage where possible."[5]

Matthew 19:30—20:16 is set in the midst of a culture of exclusionary unemployment and abusive labor practices. This occurs in the context of colonization where the agrarian societies were being overrun by Hellenization. Archaeological evidence suggests that the Galilean agrarian household was challenged in Hellenistic times where grand mansions began to appear in Galilee.[6] Sawicki offers the following insight: "These grand villas offered or imposed an alternative choreography to that of the village house, thereby challenging indigenous relationships and destabilizing their perceived

4. Sawicki, *Crossing Galilee*, 20.

5. Ibid., 20.

6. Ibid., 21.

inevitability."[7] Such evidence suggests that an underlying clash of cultures was present in Galilee around the time of Jesus based not only on literary evidence but also on the basis of these mansion houses found in Galilee. Sawicki also observes that this society was being disturbed: "In the case of Galilee, that means the advent of Hasmonean administration, which diverted labor and land out of the traditional kinship arrangements while leaving them otherwise intact, followed by the advent of Herodian and Roman administrations, which escalated that diversion in order to support large-scale urbanization and the expansion of international commerce."[8] Scholars are united in observing that under Roman occupation, the laws regarding land were reformulated and implemented to serve the interests of the Romans and their local agents. Legal protection of the land was abolished or just ignored. Instead the land became "an object of trade."[9] This context provides something of the social setting for Jesus' parable in 19:30—20:16.

Schottroff indeed detects that the parable has its context in the midst of the devastation of Galilee's kinship cultures; she writes that the parable "illuminates economic misery and its causes at the time of the Gospel of Matthew."[10] In the midst of a colonized society, many of its people had experienced violence and plunder. It is not the time to discuss this, but taking into account what we today call post traumatic or attachment disorders may help the modern reader to empathize with the conditions of many living in ancient Galilee and this may yield some exegetical fruit. In such a harsh society those who were not among the physically and mentally strongest were at risk of exclusion evident through lack of access to food, work, and generally the resources of creation.[11] Ultimately such people struggled to work while the strong did not wish to give them a chance to work.

Wilson observes well the parable in this social setting noting that "Bailiffs and landowners would have passed them [i.e., the worthless] over and chosen workers that were able-bodied. Consequently, they . . . would go hungry, get weaker, and be susceptible to disease due to malnutrition."[12] In short, the parable would be familiar to Jesus' audience.

7. Ibid., 22.

8. Ibid., 91.

9. Tilborg, *Sermon on the Mount*, 24.

10. Schottroff, *Parables of Jesus*, 217.

11. Wilson, *For I was Hungry*, 220 interestingly and plausibly states "the interpretation of this parable should be set in the Gospel context of food shortage scenario."

12. Ibid., 223. I imagine that those who are hired last are also the victims of trauma that is common in a colonized area.

Immediate Literary Context

This parable is set within the context of Jesus moving south towards Jerusalem (19:1). Many crowds followed him (19:2a). In the midst of these crowds are those who are healed (19:2b) suggesting that the crowds brought to Jesus the poorest of the poor. We know also that a child was brought to him, one I have argued represents one of the poorest of the poor (19:13–15). This surely leads the reader to draw from this that the crowds are being portrayed positively. Jesus' disciples, however, admonish the crowds for bringing the child to him suggesting that they are deliberately depicted badly in contrast to the crowds who bring the sick.

I believe, therefore, that Matthew depicts the disciples in a negative way. In line with this is his presentation of the disciples questioning Jesus. I suggest the question be read as an unwise one (19:10–12, 27). Interestingly they question Jesus as do the Pharisees (19:3–9); further, the rich man also asks Jesus what he must do to have eternal life (19:16–22; cf. also Luke 10:25) again not a wise question. The flaw, claims Bailey, is that "inheritance is not payment for services rendered."[13] The disciples, Pharisees, and the rich man are deliberately contrasted with the crowds who bring the sick to Jesus.

Matthew has Jesus address only the twelve disciples (see 19:23). Consequently, the parable is addressed only to the disciples as it follows "Jesus said to his disciples . . ." It is significant, therefore, that 19:23–26 records Jesus teaching about wealth. In 19:27 Peter, who is representative of all the disciples, questions Jesus in respect of His instructions on rewards the disciples may receive for their obedience. Peter's question is interested only in the rewards they will gain for following Jesus.[14] This question in verse 27 is central to understanding the literary context of the parable in 19:30—20:16.

To recap, the parable is aimed at only the disciples and the question they unwisely ask in 19:27. It helps to recall also that the disciples have admonished the crowds for bringing a child to Jesus, they are then depicted as wanting to know what their rewards will be for obedience (19:27). They are self-interested not unlike the Pharisees and the rich man. We know that the disciples have not given up everything to follow Jesus, as the references to Peter's mother-in-law in 8:14, to the mother of James and John in 20:20–21, and to "the house" in 9:10, 28; 13:1, 36; and 17:25 demonstrate. Davies and Allison are right to note that the question in 19:27 is full of self-interest

13. Bailey, *Jesus Through Middle Eastern Eyes*, 286.

14. It is also not dissimilar to the rich man's question about what he must do to have his reward of eternal life (19:16).

arguing that Jesus in His response in His parable is warning the disciples to beware "lest they likewise become examples of the first becoming last."[15]

The parable is significantly sandwiched between "the first will be last" and "the last will be first" (19:30 and 20:16). We must assume that Matthew intentionally frames the parable within these verses to show that in God's reign those who are considered the least (last) in society will be great (first). Shillington rightly sees the parable being a promise for the unemployed.[16]

The disciples who hear this parable are not unlike the grumblers who are resentful of the workers employed for only one hour. Peter's question in 19:27 echoes the grumblings in 20:11–12. The allusion is significant and fits with Davies and Allison who also detect in Jesus' teaching a warning to the disciples. *The parable is told to the disciples as a challenge and warning to repent lest they who are first become last.*

19:30—20:16

This parable harks back to the first beatitude in Matthew 5:3: "Joyful and abundant are the poorest of the poor, for to them belongs the kingdom of heaven."[17] The disciples are privy to Jesus' teaching on the Mount and to His teaching in this parable. They are the non-poor who are challenged to see that the last will be first.

The Kingdom of Heaven is Like . . . (v. 1a)

The parable begins: "the kingdom of heaven is like . . ." It is a way of saying "imagine if God's goodness was present in creation it would be like . . ." The reader is drawn to see things from the divine perspective. In other words, the parable is like a window looking out upon creation presenting a perspective dominated not by selfish reward and self-interest, but one in which generosity and self-giving are paramount.

We need to jump ahead to 20:15–16 to perceive this divine perspective. The parable points to a way of life rooted in the goodness of God that is specifically that of showing mercy. In 20:15 the owner is described as being good; but society, in direct contrast, is evil. NRSV is correct to translate "good" as "generous." Those who are considered worthless (the last and least) in the world (Greek: *argous* in 20:3) will be first when God's will is

15. Davies and Allison, *Matthew 19–28*, 53.
16. Shillington, "Saving Life and Keeping Sabbath," 91.
17. My translation based on chapter 8 of this book.

done on earth (v. 16). The kingdom of heaven is a place of generosity where no one will be in need.

The disciples are challenged by this message. They have asked what their reward will be for following Jesus at the same time as admonishing the crowds for bringing the child to him. The question reveals self-interest and their actions in rebuking the crowds also show jealousy and selfishness. I believe the disciples are called to see themselves as the grumblers who resent the owner's generosity and goodness, in order that they may repent.

Vineyard (vv. 1b, 8)

In this parable, the vineyard is central. The vineyard is amply attested in the Old Testament as representing re-creation (Isaiah 5; 27; Jeremiah 12:10; Psalm 80).[18]

- In Psalm 80 Israel is described as a vine created from the chaos and darkness of life in Egypt (80:4a). Perhaps echoes of creation from chaos in Genesis 1:2.
- According to Isaiah 5, the vineyard is the house of Israel (5:7) that is representative of God in restoring creation. God expected Israel to give fruit in bringing justice (5:7). Alas this is the vineyard that yields injustice and violence through disobeying God (5:6).
- In Isaiah 27 the vineyard is Israel who will "fill the whole world with fruit" (see especially verse 6). The vineyard is a vision of hope.
- According to Jeremiah 12:10, Israel is the vineyard who disobeys God and becomes a desolate land. This perhaps echoes, like Psalm 80:4a, the desolation from which God formed life described in Genesis 1:2.

The vineyard represents Israel as renewed creation that is to bear fruit and be a blessing to all. The vineyard metaphor draws the readers' attention to the familiar image of vineyard in the Old Testament. The vineyard is also creation alluding back to Genesis 1–2. The vineyard is not a battlefield but a place where all can be involved in the production of its fruits. There is no need for jealousy or greed. It is a place that is rooted in the characteristics of its owner who is good (generous in NRSV). Consequently, all are to be like and have the perspective of the owner who is God.

18. Davies and Allison, *Matthew 19–28*, 71.

Those Considered Worthless/Unemployed

Matthew has a liking for lists of disabled people (4:23–25; 10:7–8; 11:5; 15:3). Similarly from the Dead Sea Scrolls there is a catalogue of disabled people made visible by being in the list: maimed, paralyzed, lame, blind, deaf, dumb, and aged (1QSa 2 lines 5–6). The list makes noticeable distinct groups of the poor. I suggest it functions to emphasize well-known groups that were understood to represent the poorest of the poor and the powerless. When the Old Testament lists: orphan, widow, and refugee, it does not make them invisible but visible. I propose that the groups mentioned in these lists were considered worthless and unable to work in the fields effectively.[19]

When the landowner sees people standing around waiting for work with only an hour left he may have assumed that they were indeed being lazy. He asks them why they have been standing around all day being worthless (*argous*) (20:6).[20] The question intimates that the Lord of the Vineyard sees the men as worthless. I think it is likely that the master's reproach echoes general views held by employers and the non-poor against an underclass:[21] ex-prisoners, migrants, people with learning difficulties, and those suffering from mental and physical disabilities. They are seen as unprofitable and therefore unemployable, and consequently, are excluded because they are seen to be substandard and worthless.

But their reply to his question challenges the master; they say that they have waited all day and no one hired them. Their reply reveals that they cannot find work—in other words, they are the marginalized. Who are they? They are the widows, orphans, migrants, the naked, hungry, thirsty, lame, deaf, leper, sick, perhaps women who are marginalized, and ex-prisoners.

The Grumblers (vv. 2, 10–12)

These grumblers are strikingly similar to those who did not heed commands about giving to the poor (Deuteronomy 15:11–17). I think it is possible that they represent Israel who had experienced God's generosity when He brought them out of Egypt yet showed no compassion to others. I also offer the suggestion that underlying Matthew's depiction of the grumblers is the Cain and Abel story found in Genesis 4.

19. See Wilson, *For I Was Hungry*, 206, note 232.

20. In 12:36 *argos* suggests worthless. Wilson, *For I Was Hungry*, 223 note 50 suggests *argos* is best translated "unemployed."

21. Hagner, *Matthew 14–28*, 571.

It is well attested in Jewish and New Testament sources that Cain was seen as the *type* of an unrighteous person who exploited the poor and weak. Gutiérrez follows Alonso Schökel's analysis of Genesis 4:4–5:[22]

> and Abel for his part brought of the firstlings of his flock, their fat portions. And the LORD had regard for Abel and his offering, but for Cain and his offering he had no regard. So Cain was very angry, and his countenance fell.

Schökel argues that these verses show God has a preference for Abel because he is the youngest and most vulnerable. However, the text is not deliberately set against Cain for being stronger, but to warn Cain to think about his younger brother and protect him.[23] Von Rad helpfully recalls that the Hebrew for Abel is *hebel* arguing that the original hearer would know this as meaning futile.[24] Consequently, Abel's sacrifice is not about its acceptability to God but is best understood within the context of God's unconditional mercy. Von Rad further adds that crucial to Genesis 4:4–5 is Exodus 33:19: "I will be gracious to whom I will be gracious, and will show mercy on whom I will show mercy."[25] Therefore, Genesis 4:4–5 is best read as describing God's unmerited gift to the poorest of the poor.

Volf takes a similar approach to his reading of Cain and Abel seeing that every human being is potentially Cain and Abel;[26] "Cain's envy and murder . . . prefigure . . . how *all human beings* tend to behave towards others."[27] He further observes: "Cain, [was] the name of honor which means 'to produce,' 'to bring forth;' the birth of the second was a matter of course and he received a name whose meaning marked him as inferior: Abel, 'breath,' 'vapor,' 'sheer transience,' 'worthlessness,' 'nothingness.'"[28] For Volf, Cain has failed to be his brother's keeper. He points out that "By his own act of exclusion he excluded himself from all relationships."[29]

Now I return to the parable properly. It is noticeable that the parable states that the grumblers' (the type of Cain) eyes are evil (20:15) whereas the owner's are good. Cain is not acceptable to God because Cain is envious of God's preference to Abel in showing him unmerited love. The last workers

22. Gutiérrez, *The God of Life*, 115–16.

23. Ibid.

24. Von Rad, *Genesis*, 100.

25. Ibid., 101.

26. Volf, *Exclusion*, 92–98.

27. Ibid., 93.

28. Ibid., 94.

29. Ibid., 97.

are *types* of Abel (Hebrew: *hebel*) which means "futility." Cain is jealous thinking that Abel gets a better deal out of God when he is worthless. In his jealousy he murders Abel and Cain's reaction to God about not being his brother's keeper reveals the world-view of not caring for others, particularly having no concern for those perceived as useless.

Genesis 4:9 proves helpful in this discussion of the parable. In this verse Cain replies to God's question as to Abel's whereabouts: "Am I my brother's keeper" (4:9). God had indeed designed Cain to be his brother's keeper. Gutiérrez sums up that Cain through his actions is portrayed as rejecting "the free and unmerited love of God, who prefers the poor, and thus turns into the attitude of a Cain.[30] Cain rejects the inner order of creation, the covenant. Instead he embraces a covenant of death.

To restate: Cain is like the grumblers who act against the master out of jealousy for the master's unmerited love to others. Like Cain, this attitude is rooted in not caring for others. Shillington rightly observes that the grumblers "were concerned only for themselves, not for their Jewish comrades who were not so fortunate."[31] So perhaps also Cain. If the first workers had a worldview that was rooted in care for others they would not have grumbled to the owner of the vineyard. If they understood that creation is God's and is the expression of His goodness they would have known why the owner ordered those who had worked only for an hour to receive the same largesse as those who had toiled all day.

The Owner

The owner of the vineyard is *oikodespotēs*—housemaster in 20:1 and *ho kurios tou ampelōnos*—LORD of the Vineyard (20:8) which "encourages the reader to identify the figure with God."[32] The owner is the dominant figure receiving more attention than the other characters. He is the hero of the parable and his message is: "be your brother and sister's keeper."

The parable gives a very precise characterization of the owner which is rooted in the goodness of God. The owner says: *ego agathos eimi*—I am good. As we know from the creation narratives God is depicted as generous and His creation and household can only flourish when generosity is embedded in creation. God is said to be good because of the abundance of

30. Gutiérrez, *The God of* Life, 116.

31. Shillington, "Saving Life and Keeping Sabbath," 97; he is also critical of Herzog for not paying enough attention to the subjects in the narrative who did not have a full-day's wage.

32. Davies and Allison, *Matthew 19–28*, 73.

His limitless love. The following words of the parable in verse 15 reinforce the characterization of the owner as being generous by comparison with the grumblers: "or is your eye evil because I am good?"

Elsewhere in Matthew the eye is said to be the lamp of the body (6:22–23). These verses help us in understanding the eye (*ophthalmos*) in 20:15. In 6:22–23 Jesus teaches:

> The eye is the lamp of the body. So, if your eye is healthy (*haplous*), your whole body will be full of light; but if your eye is unhealthy/evil, your whole body will be full of darkness. If then the light in you is darkness, how great is the darkness! (6:22–23)

The phrase "your eye is evil" in 6:23 occurs at the end of the parable in 20:15. If the eye is healthy the whole body is in the light; *haplous* can mean "generous."[33] If the eye is generous then the whole body is in harmony with God (i.e., being full of light). Further, given the context of Matthew 6 relating to wealth (vv. 19–21 and v. 24) such generosity relates to mammon; in fact, Jesus is challenging a worldview that makes worldly goods its master. In short, the master asks them if they are grumbling because their eyes look without generosity (goodness) upon their fellow brothers and sisters while the master sees and acts generously.

In sum, the householder is "good" because he subverts the *status quo*; he reverses the expected order of things, while challenging the mind-set dominated by reward in terms of selfish gain. Reward, on the contrary, is the joy of doing God's will. The parable grants us a glimpse at God's kingdom as the equalizing of life in the Jewish marketplace.[34]

Response to the Grumblers

We, in the West, perhaps find the message of this parable unpalatable because we empathize with those who feel resentful at being treated unfairly; that is unless my reader is from the poorest of the poor and therefore different from my assumed reader who is educated and comfortably off. The parable's depiction of those grumbling because they are paid the same as those who work and achieve less is seen as unfair. I have heard people complaining at being paid the same as those with learning disabilities. In 2014 the then UK government Welfare Minister commented that people with learning difficulties should be prepared to work for less than those without

33. Bauer, Arndt, and Gingrich, *A Greek-English Lexicon*, 85.
34. Compare also Shillington, "Saving Life and Keeping Sabbath," 101.

such disabilities stating that they were "not worth the full wage."[35] With no doubt Jesus attacks such grumbling yet some may have sympathies with the 2014 Welfare Minister.

In short, this parable specifically relates to people who were thought useless and a drain on others. Moreover, society resented any compassion that was shown to them. Those depicted as grumbling are representatives of society. Consequently, this parable is a shocking counter-cultural indictment against resentment and lack of generosity.

The Last Will be First (19:30 and 20:16)

The parable begins in 19:30: "first will be last, and the last will be first," and concludes in 20:16: "the last will be first and the first will be last." I suggest that the parable is framed in terms of the weak and impoverished; God favors the most vulnerable. The first are the non-poor who will find in the end that they are not at the top but at the bottom (i.e., last). The impoverished who are last will be blessed, joyful and abundant.

Those who worked all day were weak and reliant on others for the most rudimentary necessities of life. This depiction of those who moan about the good fortune of those who were more at risk than them reveals in overstated tones the extent to which humans are ungenerous, resentful and godless. The grumblers knew what poverty is, and they should have shown generosity to those who were in poverty. The fact that the owner pays them the same as the others reveals the extent to which God shows His favor to them.

Unable to Keep Torah if Poor

One central, but neglected, aspect of being poor and oppressed is that a person is not able to keep Torah. The psalmist makes this clear: "Redeem me from human oppression, that I may keep your precepts" (119:134). Shillington has particularly made an argument for this regarding this parable.[36]

Shillington comments that the poor and unemployed "cannot truly observe Sabbath as they ought because they have little or no product of work to celebrate come Friday at sundown."[37] He picks up significantly on the

35. http://www.bbc.co.uk/news/uk-politics-29628557. For the policies of President Trump on disabilities see http://www.slate.com/articles/health_and_science/medical_examiner/2017/01/as_a_disabled_person_i_m_terrified_of_the_trump_administration.html.

36. Shillington, "Saving Life and Keeping Sabbath," 87–102.

37. Ibid., 100.

relationship between the law regarding Sabbath and being poor. He writes: "Every Israelite has a right to life from the land . . . How can a destitute Israelite honor his religious heritage in the Holy Land given to sustain life? How can he observe the law of Sabbath if he has neither work nor livelihood to celebrate on the seven days of the week?"[38] Shillington points out that "Sabbath keeping in the command of Exodus 20 is motivated by the celebration of the Creator God who gave the earth to humans who reflect the divine image, who sustain their lives from the gift of the land."[39] He argues that those in the parable who were not hired cannot celebrate the Sabbath for they experience creation as hostile and godless. They are prevented by society from being able to worship God because they are excluded from God's goodness and mercy.

It is clear from this that being vulnerable and being the poorest of the poor meant obedience to Torah was not possible (cf. Psalm 119:134 above). A person who is unable to fulfill their potential cannot do God's will. However, such a person is still favored by God because he or she is prevented from doing so because of the actions of others. Matthew 19:30—20:16 also is about the owner acting instead to allow the excluded to do as God intended, but is also a call to excluders to practice inclusion.

Torah's Critique of Inequality

Shillington writes regarding being unemployed and keeping the Sabbath: "the intent of the Sabbath command to equalize the human family is violated by gross inequality of human life in the stratified social situation in agrarian Palestine."[40] The Sabbath laws bring to mind that God is the Creator who has ordered creation in such a way that all are equal, and its goodness is self-giving love. Shillington makes links to Matthew 20:1–16: "The unemployed and undernourished of God's human household could scarcely enter God's rest one day in seven, and be at one with their fellows. The parable implicitly puts a provocative question to the Sabbath regulators: What are you doing to provide work-and-life for the community you call to rest on the Sabbath of the LORD your God?"[41] The Sabbath command is a call to equalize the human family that has been violated by gross inequality in the stratified social situation in agrarian Palestine.[42] Israel was ordered to keep the Sabbath to

38. Ibid., 98.
39. Ibid., 99.
40. Ibid.
41. Ibid.
42. Ibid.

recall God's goodness shown to it, to remember that it was once a slave in Egypt and was now to liberate the oppressed and the landless. Israel is not to do what Egypt did to it. The existence of poverty revealed the extent to which creation fell far short of God's goodness/will. Recalling Sabbath was a call to work towards executing justice in favor of the poorest of the poor.

In brief, the parable is a warning to those who are fit and fortunate to be able to benefit and flourish through their labor. They are to imagine themselves as the grumblers and must repent of their lack of goodness by working towards establishing justice on earth.

SUMMARY

- 19:30—20:16 is set in the midst of a culture of exclusionary unemployment and abusive labor practices.
- Matthew intentionally frames the parable around the least (last) in society who will be great (first).
- The reader of the parable is drawn to see things from the divine perspective.
- The parable points to a way of life rooted in the goodness of God that is specifically one of showing mercy.
- The vineyard represents creation not as a battlefield but a place where all can be involved in the production of its fruits.
- The group who work one hour are the poorest of the poor who are shown the distinctive acceptance and mercy of the Lord of the Vineyard.
- The first workers represent Cain whose grumbling is best understood as rooted in their attitude of not caring for others.
- The owner represents the God of creation who is good, echoing Genesis 1.
- The owner's act of generosity was surprising and shocking. It is a counter-cultural indictment against resentment and lack of generosity.
- Unemployment prevents a person keeping the Sabbath.

FOOD FOR THOUGHT

Through work human beings are to glorify God's name. Through work human beings bring dignity to others. God and His goodness are evident in His creation when people live for others and not for themselves. Working in the vineyard is a crucial aspect of being human. To prevent any from noble work according to ability is to prevent them from having a relationship with God. In the parable the worldview dominated by efficiency and good economic competitive sense is subverted. Creation is about love and not efficiency. The parable is a call to the non-poor not to grumble about the poorest of the poor, but to take joy in working to care for their brothers and sisters. Only in this work can creation be a place where God's goodness dwells.

I recall in my work as prison chaplain a prisoner who was prevented from working in the prison because he was disabled. He was an elderly man who had worked hard his whole life. The man was distraught at not being able to do something of use. Thankfully the prison compassionately enabled the man to work appropriately to his abilities. The man was given dignity. The man's depression left and he was able to participate in the daily life of the prison community.

The master gives the men the one thing they desperately wanted—a job which gave them dignity and value. There is no promise to pay them, but they accompany him to the vineyard. The master represents God who acts to show love to the rejected. The parable focuses on the gift of limitless love God has for those who are in desperate material need. Only in the realm of God's kingdom are the least seen as wanted and worthy. This parable is truly good news to the poorest.

The parable reveals Jesus' profound critique of the principle of pay and reward that still today many Christians find difficult to handle. This parable, I propose, turns upside down the worldview of competition and battle in which creation is seen as a place of scarcity. Through this parable we glimpse at the values that God intends for human beings in order to make His goodness fully and dynamically present in all creation.

PRAYER

O Father of Creation, may we through Your gift of mercy, be Your light shining in the darkness. Make us to live dynamically, hovering skillfully over the chaos, bringing order out of darkness, serving You Lord Creator by serving others limitlessly as You care for us unconditionally. Amen.

Epilogue

Caring for my Brothers and Sisters

One of the Psalms of ascent that Jesus most likely sang after the last supper is Psalm 121 (Matthew 26:30). In vv. 3–8 the verb "keep/care" (*šāmar*) occurs six times with God as its subject. God is one who cares vigilantly for creation as opposed to slumbering (v. 3b). In being a care-giver God is one who keeps people from the piercing sun and moon (vv. 5–6). He cares so much that He stops evil from coming upon those who live by His will (v. 7). God is one who keeps constant watch over His creation (v. 8). In being made in God's image human beings are to be care-givers of their brothers and sisters.

In the earliest chapters of the Bible God asks Cain, the first murderer: "Where is your brother?" to which he replies: "Am I my brother's care-giver (*hăšōmēr*)" (Genesis 4:9). Cain's retort represents the extent to which human beings fall short of living as God designed them to live: God ordered human beings to care for and preserve each other. They are to be living sacrifices. In other words, we are not to live for ourselves, but for others (cf. Matthew 20:28; cf. Philippians 2:4). The Bible makes clear that God formed human beings to preserve and give care (*lĕšomrâ*) to all creation (Genesis 2:15). The same Hebrew verb "to keep" (*šāmar*) is also the word used to keep God's Torah (Deuteronomy 4:40). To give careful and vigilant attention to Torah is to live in harmony with the inward-order of creation: goodness, righteousness, mercy, and *shalom*.

As I bring this book to its conclusion, I stress that God made us to care for and nurture our sisters and brothers. These sisters and brothers are not restricted to the same family blood, color of skin, or same economic status. The poorest of the poor have the same heavenly Father as the non-poor and it is task of the non-poor to treat the poorest of the poor as children of their heavenly Father.

It should be clear to my reader that I have sought to show that Jesus expected and taught the non-poor to care and nurture for all creation. Such teaching I believe occurred in the context of Jesus' preference for the poorest of the poor. I have argued that this is so because God has given, and so those made in His image must also give, for what they have is not their own, but God's. Quaker poet John Greenleaf Whittier puts it well in his poem *The Eternal Goodness*:

> No offering of my own I have,
> Nor works my faith to prove,
> I can but give the gifts He gave,
> And plead His love for love.

In the Sermon on the Mount, Jesus makes clear the importance of disciples being care-givers. He urges disciples neither to grumble, mock nor accuse the poorest of the poor of being sinners (7:1–5). Instead, disciples are to examine their lives asking to what extent they live according to how God ordered them. Such is implied in 7:9 where Jesus emphasizes the importance of showing generosity. Even the wicked know this (cf. Matthew 5:46b, 47b). Jesus teaches in Matthew 7:12 that doing to others as you would have them do to you is Torah and the prophets. This way of life is imagined as entering a narrow gate and following a path that is not so much difficult as restricted: life is to be lived with restraint and care for others (7:13–14). Matthew 7:16 fits within Jesus' teaching against false prophets who are visible through not producing fruits (7:15–20). This is followed by Jesus' warnings to His disciples against self-deception (vv. 21–23) observing that those who claim to prophesy in God's name as well as casting out demons and performing mighty works are rejected by God. These are the people who seek the approbation of others by performing their works of righteousness. However, they are deemed as actions that bring no rewards from the Father in heaven (6:1–21). In 7:24–27 we find a parable about those who build their houses upon firm foundations and who overcome the chaos of flooding and storms. The rain, flood and winds mentioned in 7:25 echo the pre-creation vision of a non-place described as a formless void and darkness (Genesis 1:2), a place without *shalom*. To do God's will is to obey God's commandments which Jesus lays out in the Sermon on the Mount.

Peter Maurin and Dorothy Day tried to live the Gospel about Jesus, working to remove poverty through solidarity with the poor. They both made a sharp distinction between voluntary poverty and imposed poverty; one that I emphasize in this book. Robert Ellsberg writes:

> By "voluntary poverty" Dorothy did not mean idealization of misery and squalor. She was careful to distinguish between the dignity and freedom of voluntary poverty—the freedom that comes when there is nothing one fears to lose—and the bondage of destitution. The latter was the fruit of injustice . . . The poverty she espoused meant reducing the area given to self-interest, learning to locate the ultimate source of security elsewhere than in material values. To become poor was to become dependent on God and available to others, and to withdraw from the spoils of exploitations, for, as the Church Fathers frequently taught, all that we owned beyond our needs was stolen from those who were hungry.[1]

I believe their vision and understanding of Christian mission is well suited to what Matthew's Jesus would reinforce. In today's society, especially among Western Christians, Ellsberg's words are hard to take. I find them hard to accept with my secure home and comforts. We may even wish to disagree with these teachings. But I believe these words as well as my opening quote from Henri Nouwen in the main Introduction to this book give us a picture of a Jesus who had a preference for the poorest of the poor, and called the non-poor to repent through bearing good fruits. Jesus calls the non-poor to be downwardly mobile. This does not mean for example not earning money, but working for the redistribution of creation's abundance.

I leave the reader with the words of Robert Ellsberg commenting on the faith of Dorothy Day, words that seems appropriate for concluding this book:

> Put simply, God wished us to be our brother's keeper. The failure to realize this . . . was what lay behind most of what were called economic and political problems. Hunger and unemployment, properly speaking, were spiritual problems. They arose because modern society had made the bank account, rather than the Sermon on the Mount, the ultimate values. The dollar was worshipped instead of Christ, and Christians were thus unable to recognize Christ in their neighbors. The antidote was to be found in the Works of Mercy: feeding the hungry, clothing the naked, sheltering the homeless—not through the impersonal agency of the State, but as Christ had commanded, "at a personal sacrifice."[2]

1. Day, *Selected Writings*, xxxvii.
2. Ibid., xxviii–xxix.

PRAYER

Make us worthy, Lord, to serve our brothers and sisters throughout the world who live and die in poverty and hunger. Give them through our hands this day their daily bread, and by our understanding love, give peace and joy. —Mother Teresa of Calcutta

Bibliography

Abbott-Smith, G. *Manual Greek Lexicon of the New Testament*. Edinburgh: T. & T. Clark, 1923.

Alison, J. *Living in the End Times: The Last Things Re-imagined*. London: SPCK, 1997.

———. *Undergoing God*. London: Darton, Longman & Todd, 2006.

Allison, Dale C. *The New Moses: A Matthean Typology*. Minneapolis: Fortress, 1993.

Argyle, A. W. "Evidence for the View That St. Luke Used St. Matthew's Gospel." *Journal of Biblical Literature* 83 (1964) 390–396.

Bailey, K. E. *Jesus Through Middle Eastern Eyes: Cultural Studies in the Gospels*. London: SPCK, 2008.

Barker, M. *The Gate of Heaven: A History and Symbolism of the Temple in Jerusalem*. London: SPCK, 1991.

———. *The Revelation of Jesus Christ*. Edinburgh: T. & T. Clark, 2000.

Barth, K. *Church Dogmatics*. Vol III. Pt. 1. Edinburgh: T. & T. Clark, 1958.

Battle, M. *Ubuntu*. New York: Seabury, 2009.

Bauckham, R. "For Whom Were the Gospels Written?" In *The Gospels for All Christians: Rethinking the Gospel Audiences*. Edited by R. Bauckham, 9–48. Grand Rapids: Eerdmans, 1998.

———. *James*. New Testament Readings. London: Routledge, 1999.

———. *Jesus and the Eyewitness: The Gospels as Eyewitness Testimony*. Grand Rapids: Eerdmans, 2006.

Bauer, Walter, W. F. Arndt, and F. W. Gingrich. *A Greek-English Lexicon of the New Testament and Other Early Christian Literature*. Chicago: The University of Chicago Press, 1952.

Beare, F. W. *The Gospel According to St. Matthew*. Oxford: Blackwell, 1981.

Berry, T. *The Great Work: Our Way into the Future*. New York: Three Rivers, 1999.

Bouma-Prediger, S. *For the Beauty of the Earth: A Christian Vision for Creation Care*. Grand Rapids: Baker Academic, 2001.

Bredin, M. "Being human and priest," *The Friend*, 13 (January 2017) 10–11.

———. *The Ecology of the New Testament: Creation, Re-creation, and the Environment*. Colorado Springs: Biblica, 2010.

———. "Gentiles and the Davidic Tradition." In *A Feminist Companion to the Hebrew Bible in the New Testament*, edited by A. Brenner, 95–111. Sheffield: Sheffield University Press, 1996.

———. *Jesus, Revolutionary of Peace: A Nonviolent Christology in the Book of Revelation*. Paternoster Biblical Monographs. Carlisle, UK: Paternoster, 2003.

———. *True Beauty*. Grove Spirituality Series. Cambridge: Grove, 2007.

Brueggemann, W. *Isaiah 40–66*. Westminster Bible Companion. London: Westminster John Knox, 1998.

———. *Peace*. St Louis: Chalice, 2001.

———. *The Prophetic Imagination*. Second Edition. Minneapolis: Fortress, 2001.

———. *A Social Reading of the Old Testament: Prophetic Approaches to Israel's Communal Life*. Edited by P. D. Miller. Minneapolis: Fortress, 1994.

———. *Theology of the Old Testament*. Minneapolis: Fortress, 1997.

Bryant, C. *Jung and the Christian Way*. London: Darton, Longman & Todd, 1983.

Carson, D. A. "Christological Ambiguities in the Gospel of Matthew." In *Christ the Lord: Studies in Christology Presented to Donald Guthrie*, edited by H. H. Rowdon, 97–114. Leicester: InterVarsity, 1982.

Carter, W. "Construction of Violence and Identities in Matthew's Gospel." In *Violence in the New Testament*, edited by S. Matthew and E. L. Gibson, 81–108. London: T. & T. Clark, 2005.

———. *Matthew and Empire: Initial Exploration*. Harrisburg, IL: Trinity, 2001.

———. *Matthew and the Margins: A socio-political and religious reading*. Sheffield: Sheffield Academic, 2000.

Crenshaw, J. L. *Studies in Israelite Wisdom*. New York: Ktav, 1976.

Crosby, M. H. *Finding Francis, Following Christ*. Maryknoll, NY: Orbis, 2007.

———. *House of Disciples: Church, Economics & Justice in Matthew*. Maryknoll, NY: Orbis, 1988.

Davies, W. D., and D. C. Allison. *The Gospel According to Saint Matthew*. Vol. 1: *Matthew 1–7*. International Critical Commentary. London: T. & T. Clark, 1988.

———. *The Gospel According to Saint Matthew*. Vol. 3: *Matthew 19–28*. International Critical Commentary. London: T. & T. Clark, 1997.

Davis, E. F. *Scripture, Culture and Agriculture: An Agrarian Reading of the Bible*. Cambridge: Cambridge University Press, 2009.

Douglass, J. *The Nonviolent Coming of God*. Eugene, OR: Wipf & Stock, 2006.

———. *The Non-Violent Cross: A Theology of Revolution and Peace*. 2nd printing. New York: Macmillan, 1970.

Day, D. D. *Dorothy Day: Selected Writings*. Edited and with an Introduction by R. Ellsberg. Maryknoll, NY: Orbis, 1983.

Dunn, J. D. G. *The Theology of Paul the Apostle*. London: T. & T. Clark, 1998.

Ellsberg, R., ed. *Blessed Among All Women: Women Saints, Prophets and Witnesses for Our Time*. London: Darton, Longman & Todd, 2006.

———. *Gandhi on Christianity*. Maryknoll, NY: Orbis, 1991.

France, R. T. *The Gospel According to Matthew*. IVP Commentaries. Leicester: InterVarsity, 1985.

———. *Matthew: Evangelist and Teacher*. Grand Rapids: Academie, 1989.

Fretheim, T. E. *God and World in the Old Testament: A Relational Theology of Creation*. Nashville: Abington, 2005.

Gardner, R. B. *Matthew*. Believers Church Bible Commentary. Scottdale, PA: Herald, 1991.

Gillet, L. *The Burning Bush*. Springfield, IL: Templegate, 1976.

———. *In Thy Presence*. New York: St. Vladimir's Seminary, 1977.

Girard, R. *Things Hidden Since the Foundation of the World*. Stanford: Stanford University Press. 1987.

Gnuse, R. *You Shall not Steal: Community and Prosperity in the Biblical Tradition*. Eugene, OR: Wipf & Stock, 1985.

Gorman, M. J. *The Death of the Messiah and the Birth of the New Covenant*. Cambridge: James Clarke, 2014.

Grassi, J. A. *Informing the Future: Social Justice in the New Testament*. New York: Paulist, 2003.

Grimsrud, T. "Healing Justice." In *Peace and Justice Shall Embrace: Power and Theopolitics in the Bible*, edited by Ted Grimsrud and Loren Johns, 64–85. Telford, PA: Pandora, 1999.

Grundmann, W. *Das Evangelium nach Matthäus*. Theologischer Handkommentar zum Neuen Testament. Berlin: Evangelische Verlagsanstalt, 1968.

Gutiérrez, G. *A Theology of Liberation: History, Politics, and Salvation*. London: SCM, 2001.

———. *The God of Life*. London: SCM, 1991.

Gwyn, D. *The Covenant Crucified: Quakers and the Rise of Capitalism*. London: Quaker Books, 2006.

Hagner, D. A. *Matthew 1–13*. Word Biblical Commentary 33A. Dallas, TX: Word Books, 1993.

———. *Matthew 14–28*. Word Biblical Commentary 33B. Dallas, TX: Word Books, 1995.

Häring, B. *The Healing Power of Peace and Nonviolence*. Slough, UK: St. Paul, 1986.

Harris, R. L., ed. *Theological Wordbook of the Old Testament*. 2 vols. Chicago: Moody, 1980.

Held, S. *Abraham Joshua Heschel: The Call of Transcendence*. Bloomington: Indiana University Press, 2013.

Herzog, W. R. *Parables as Subversive Speech: Jesus as Pedagogue of the Oppressed*. Louisville, KY: Westminster John Knox, 1994.

Heschel, A. J. *The Prophets: An Introduction*. 2 vols. New York: Harper, 1962.

Hill, D. *The Gospel of Matthew*. New Century Bible Commentary. Grand Rapids: Eerdmans, 1972.

Horsley, R. *Jesus and the Spiral of Violence: Popular Jewish Resistance in Roman Palestine*. San Francisco: Harper, 1987.

Howatch, S. *The High Flyer*, New York: Ballentine, 1999.

Jesudasan, I. *A Gandhian Theology of Liberation*. Maryknoll, NY: Orbis, 1984.

Julian of Norwich, *Enfolded in Love: Daily Readings with Julian of Norwich*. London: Darton, Longman & Todd, 1989.

Keener, C. S. *The Gospel of Matthew: A Socio-Rhetorical Commentary*. Grand Rapids: Eerdmans, 2009.

Kloppenborg, J. S. "Poverty and Piety in Matthew, James, and the Didache." In *Matthew, James, and Didache*, edited by H. van de Sandt and J. K. Zangenberg, 201–232. Society of Biblical Literature Symposium Series, 45. Atlanta: Society of Biblical Literature, 2008.

Larkin, K. *The Eschatology* of *Second Zechariah*. Kampen, Netherlands: Kok Pharos, 1994.

Leech, K. *True Prayer: An Introduction to Christian Spirituality*. London: Sheldon, 1980.

Lester, A. D. *The Angry Christian: A Theology for Care and Counseling*. Louisville, KY: Westminster John Knox, 2007.

Lohfink, N. F. "The Appeasement of the Messiah: Thoughts on Ps 37 and the Third Beatitude." *Theology Digest* 44 (1997) 234–41.

———. *Option for the Poor: The Basic Principle of Liberation Theology in the Light of the Bible*. 2nd ed. Berkley Lectures Series 1. N. Richland Hills, TX: Bibal, 1996.

Lowery, R. H. *Sabbath and Jubilee*. Understanding Biblical Themes. St Louis: Chalice, 2000.

Malchow, B. V. *Social Justice in the Hebrew Bible*. Collegeville, MN: Glazier, 1996.

Martínez, F. G., and E. J. C. Tigchelaar. *The Dead Sea* Scrolls. *Volume One 1Q1–4Q273: A Study Edition*. Leiden: Brill, 1997.

McConville, G. "The Old Testament and the Enjoyment of Wealth." In *Christ and Consumerism*, edited by C. Bartholomew and T. Moritz, 34–53. Carlisle, UK: Paternoster, 2001.

McFague, S. *Blessed are the Consumers: Climate Change and the Practice of Restraint*. Minneapolis: Fortress, 2013.

McNamara, M. *The New Testament and Palestinian Targum to the Pentateuch*. Rome: Pontifical Biblical Institute, 1966.

Melcher, S. "Visualizing the Perfect Cult: The Priestly Rationale for Exclusion." In *Human Disability and the Service of God, Reassessing Religious Practice*, edited by N. L. Eiesland and D. E. Saliers, 55–87. Nashville: Abington, 1998.

Merton, T. *Gandhi on Non-Violence*. New York: New Directions, 1965.

Miranda, J. *Marx and the Bible: A Critique of the Philosophy of Oppression*. Eugene, OR: Wipf & Stock, 1974.

Myers, B. L. *Walking with The Poor: Principles and Practices of Transformational Development*. Revised and Expanded Edition. Maryknoll, NY: Orbis, 2011.

Myles, R. J. *The Homeless Jesus in the Gospel of Matthew*. The Social World of Biblical Antiquites, Second Series, 10. Sheffield: Sheffield Phoenix, 2014.

Nouwen, H. J. M. *The Return of the Prodigal Son: A Story of Homecoming*. London: Darton, Longman & Todd, 1994.

Pallares, J. C. *A Poor Man Called Jesus: Reflections on the Gospel of Mark*. Maryknoll, NY: Orbis, 1985.

Pickvance, J. *Christ in Quaker Thought and Practice*, New Foundation 6. Gloucester, UK: George Fox Fund, 1993.

Powell, M. A. *God with Us: A Pastoral Theology of Matthew's Gospel*. Minneapolis: Fortress, 1995.

Preus, J. A. O. "Righteousness in Matthew: Does Matthew's Gospel Teach Justification by Grace Through Faith Alone?" Unpublished MDV thesis., Concordia Lutheran Theological Seminary, 2015.

Rad, G. von. *Genesis*. Old Testament Library. London: SCM, 1956.

———. *Old Testament Theology*, vol. 1. London: SCM, 1975.

Ringe, S. *Jesus, Liberation, and the Biblical Jubilee: Images for Ethics and Christology*. Eugene, OR: Wipf & Stock, 1985.

Rohr, R. *Breathing Underwater: Spirituality and the Twelve Steps*. Cincinanati, OH: Franciscan Media, 2011.

Rothschild, F. A., ed. *Between God and Man: An Interpretation of Judaism; From the Writings of Abraham J. Heschel*. New York: Free Press, 1959.

Rowland, C. C. "Apocalyptic, the Poor, and the Gospel of Matthew." *Journal of Theological Studies* 45 (1994) 504–18.

Rukundwa, L. S., and Van Aarde, A. G. "Revisiting Justice in the First Four Beatitudes in Matthew (5:3–6) and the Story of the Canaanite Woman (Matt 15:21–28): A Postcolonial Reading." *Harvard Theological Studies* 61 (2005) 927–51.

Ryne, T. J. *Gandhi & Jesus: The Saving Power of Nonviolence.* Maryknoll, NY: Orbis, 2008.

Sakwa, M. M. *Bible and Poverty in Kenya: An Empirical Exploration.* Leiden: Brill, 2008.

Sawicki, M. *Crossing Galilee: Architectures of Contact in the Occupied Land of Jesus.* Harrisburg, PA: Trinity, 2000.

Scheidel, W., and S. Friesen "The Size of the Economy and the Distribution of Income in the Roman Empire." *Journal of Roman Studies* 99 (2009) 61–91.

Schmid, H. H. "Creation, Righteousness, and Salvation: 'Creation Theology' as the Broad Horizon of Biblical Theology." In *Creation in the Old Testament*, edited by B. W. Anderson, 102–17. Philadelphia: Fortress, 1984.

Schnackenburg, R. *The Gospel of Matthew.* Grand Rapid: Eerdmans, 2002.

Schottroff, L. *The Parables of Jesus.* Minneapolis: Fortress, 2006.

Schweizer, E. *The Good News according to Matthew.* London: SPCK, 1976.

Shillington, V. G. "Saving Life and Keeping Sabbath." In *Jesus and His Parables: Interpreting the Parables for Jesus Today*, edited by V. G. Shillington, 87–102. Edinburgh: T. & T. Clark, 1997.

Sim, D. C. *The Gospel of Matthew and Christian Judaism. The History and Social Setting of the Matthean Community.* Studies of the New Testament and Its World. Edinburgh: T. & T. Clark, 1998.

Sophrony, Archimandrite. *The Monk of Mount Athos.* Crestwood, NY: St Vladimir's Seminary, 1989.

Stassen, G. H. *Living the Sermon on the Mount: A practical Hope for Grace and Deliverance.* San Francisco: Jossey-Bass, 2006.

Swartley, W. M. *Covenant of Peace: The Missing Peace in New Testament Theology and Ethics.* Grand Rapids: Eerdmans, 2006.

———. *Health, Healing and the Church's Mission: Biblical Perspectives and Moral Priorities.* Downers Grove, IL: InterVarsity, 2012.

———. *Israel's Scripture Traditions and the Synoptic Gospels: Story Shaping Story.* Peabody, MA: Hendrickson, 1994.

———. *Slavery, Sabbath, War & Women: Case Issues in Biblical Interpretation.* Scottdale, PA: Herald, 1983.

Tamez, E. *Bible of the Oppressed.* Eugene, OR: Wipf & Stock, 2006.

———. *The Scandalous Message of James: Faith Without Works Is Dead.* New York: Crossroad, 2002.

Tilborg, S. van. *The Sermon on the Mount as an Ideological Intervention.* Assen, Netherlands: Van Gorcum, 1986.

Tomkins, S. *John Wesley: A Biography.* Oxford: Lion, 2003.

Vanier, J. *Community and Growth.* Revised Edition. London: Darton, Longman, & Todd, 1979.

———. *Drawn into Mystery of Jesus through the Gospel of John.* New York: Paulist, 2004.

Vermes, G. *The Dead Sea Scrolls in English.* 4th ed. London: Penguin, 1995.

Volf, M. *Exclusion & Embrace.* Nashville: Abingdon, 1996.

———. *Free of Charge.* Grand Rapids: Zondervan, 2005.

Ware, K. *The Power of the Name: The Jesus Prayer in Orthodox Spirituality*. London: Pickering, 1989.

Weaver, D. J. "'Thus You will Know them by their Fruits': The Roman Characters of the Gospel of Matthew." In *The Gospel of Matthew in its Roman Imperial Context*, edited by J. Riches and D. Sim, 107–27. New York: T. & T. Clark, 2005.

Weiser, A. *The Psalms: A Commentary*. The Old Testament Library. London: SCM, 1962.

Wengst, K. *Humility: Solidarity of the Humiliated; The Transformation of an Attitude and Its Social Relevance in Graeco-Roman, Old Testament-Jewish and Early Christian Tradition*. Philadelphia: Fortress, 1988.

West, G. "Biblical Hermeneutics in Africa." In *African Theology on the Way: Current Conversations*, edited by D. S. Stinton, 21–31. London: SPCK, 2010.

Wilson, C. *For I was Hungry and You Gave me Food: Pragmatics of Food Access in the Gospel of Matthew*. Eugene, OR: Pickwick, 2014.

Wink, W. *Engaging the Powers: Discernment and Resistance in a World of Domination*. Minneapolis: Fortress, 1992.

———. *The Human Being: Jesus and the Enigma of the Son of the Man*. Minneapolis: Fortress, 2002.

Wirzba, N. *Food and Faith: A Theology of Eating*. Cambridge: Cambridge University Press, 2011.

———. *The Paradise of God: Renewing Religion in an Ecological Age*. Oxford: Oxford University Press, 2003.

Woodley, R. S. *Shalom and the Community of Creation: An Indigenous Vision*. Grand Rapids: Eerdmans, 2012.

Woolman, J. *The Journal and Major Essays of John Woolman*. A Library of Protestant Thought. Edited by P. P. Moulton. Richmond, IN: Friends United Press, 1989.

Wright, C. J. *Old Testament Ethics For the People of God*. Leicester: InterVarsity, 2004.

Wright, N. T. *Jesus and the Victory of God*. London: SPCK, 1996,

Yoder, J. H. *The Politics of Jesus: vicit Agnus noster*. 2nd revised edition. Grand Rapids: Eerdmans, 1994.

Yoder, P. B. *Shalom: The Bible's Word for Salvation, Justice, & Peace*. Nappanee, IN: Evangel, 1987.

———. "Shalom Revisited." In *The Meaning of Peace: Biblical Studies*, edited by P. B. Yoder and W. M. Swartley, 1–13. Elkhart, IN: Institute of Mennonite Studies, 2001.

Yoder Neufeld, T. "'Righteousness and Peace Will Kiss': The Peaceableness of the 'Super-righteous.'" In *Struggles for Shalom: Peace and Violence across the Testaments*, edited by L. L. Brenneman and B. D. Schantz, 155–67. Eugene, OR: Pickwick, 2014.

Yong, A. *Theology and Down Syndrome: Reimagining Disability in Later Modernity*. Waco, TX: Baylor University Press, 2007.

Young, F. *Brokenness and Blessing: Towards a Biblical Spirituality*. Sarum Theological Lectures. London: Darton, Longman & Todd, 2007.

Zehr, H. *Changing Lenses: A New Focus for Crime and Justice*. Scottdale: Herald, 2005.

Zerwick, M. *A Grammatical Analysis of the Greek New Testament*. Translated by Mary Grosvenor. Unabridged 5th revised edition. Rome: Biblical Institute Press, 1996.

Zimmerli, W. "The Place and Limit of the Wisdom in the Framework of the Old Testament Theology." *Scottish Journal of Theology* 17 (1964) 146–58.

Scripture Index

OLD TESTAMENT

Genesis

Exodus

Leviticus

Psalms

Proverbs

Proverbs *(continued)*

Ecclesiastes

Isaiah

Jeremiah

Sirach *(continued)*

Baruch

4 Ezra (2 Esdras)

5 Ezra

3 Maccabees

NEW TESTAMENT

Matthew

Matthew *(continued)*

Colossians

James

2 Peter

1 John

Revelation

Qumran

JEWISH AND CHRISTIAN APOCRYPHAL LITERATURE

2 Baruch

Jubilees

4 Maccabees

1 Enoch

TARGUMS AND RABBINIC LITERATURE

Sipra on Numbers

OTHER ANCIENT LITERATURE

Author Index

Quaker Faith and Practice (QF&P) Index